The Search for
the Winning Horse

The Search for the Winning Horse

WITH A REALISTIC GUIDE TO HANDICAPPING

Richard Sasuly

HOLT, RINEHART AND WINSTON
New York

*Published by Holt, Rinehart and Winston,
383 Madison Avenue, New York, New York 10017.*

*Published simultaneously in Canada by Holt, Rinehart and
Winston of Canada, Limited.*

Library of Congress Cataloging in Publication Data

Sasuly, Richard, 1913.
    The search for the winning horse.
    1. Horse race betting.   I. Title.
SF331.S27   798'.401   78-14189
ISBN 0-03-047441-8

First Edition

Designer: Betty Binns
Printed in the United States of America
10 9 8 7 6 5 4 3 2 1

CONTENTS

when applied to another handicapping basic—a
horse's condition today

APPENDIX

A Guide for Handicappers

ACKNOWLEDGMENTS

It seems unlikely to me that anyone cited in a horseplayer's book would be blamed for the book's errors. Still, out of respect for tradition, I hereby absolve all those named below (and thank them collectively for keeping me from stubbing a toe more often).

Since I cannot meaningfully thank the hundreds with whom I have exchanged opinions while watching horses run, I will content myself with singling out the few to whom my debt is greatest: Martin Ritt, Joshua Shelley, Joe Reggiardo, Stan Isaacs, Jule Fink, Barry Silverman, and Thomas N. Saunders.

The book contains a number of statistical notions; in connection with these, several statisticians helped generously. I am grateful to E. Myles Cooper and Mark W. Eudey for ideas and the shaping of ideas. I thank Judith B. Cohen, Paul Gottlieb, and Beth Berkov for having kindly reviewed sections of the book.

I had the benefit of the wisdom of one of the best of trainers, C. B. Hixon, and one of the most senior of stewards, Russell F. Brown. Among many others who helped me far beyond their official duties at racetracks were: Darryl Hove, Kermit Henderson, Gordon Hall, Ralph Barnes, Harry Krovitz, William J. Ward, H. W. Brundage, Howard Freeman, Robert S. Wuerth, Blaine Johnson, Ron Supinski, and Harry Fillion.

Finally, I acknowledge that singular debt which feels lighter as it grows larger: L.D.S., among many other graces, celebrated the winners but forgot the losers before I did.

The Background of Thoroughbred Racing

THEY DON'T ALL DIE BROKE

Toss a pebble into a crowd and nine times out of ten you will hit someone who accepts the proposition: Smart investors can make money in the stock market.

Nearly as often, the same person will flatly *disagree* with a corresponding statement: Some horseplayers win consistently, betting at racetracks, year after year.

Actually, both statements are true—I think. I say "I think," which introduces a faint note of uncertainty. But the uncertainty concerns the stock market. I have to take it on faith and general principles that master players consistently beat the market averages. The proof is hard to come by. As for the track, I am sure I have found winners there. And this should not be surprising. I know more about racing and have spent far more time at racetracks than I have dabbling in stocks.

I have offered these observations in various places to many doubting people. The doubters generally hold to their positions with a commendable steadfastness. It is comfort-

3

ing to know that, sooner or later, they will fetch out the bromide: All horseplayers die broke. Because I do not like to cause confusion and unhappiness, I have ceased to reply: J. P. Morgan and John D. Rockefeller, Pittsburgh Phil and Chicago O'Brien, in their graves, all had the same net worth.

But two kinds of people do listen with interest and sometimes seem convinced by what I have to tell them about the track. They are: scientists and others with respect for probabilities, and—most curious—perfectly sound and sober experts in finance who realize that investment, speculation, and gambling are all connected on a spectrum of risk.

Nothing in my own upbringing helped me understand any of the great games of gambling. At home I sometimes heard hushed mention of one uncle, presumed the smartest of the lot, who drank too much and was a gambler. People clucked when they spoke of him and shook their heads sadly.

The first person I myself knew to be a horseplayer was my immediate boss when I was seventeen and a copyboy on the *Washington Post*. I received my pay weekly, in cash, in a small envelope. It was a matter of some pride to stand in line with composing room men waiting to be paid. But I rarely made off with more than half my wages. My boss regularly borrowed the other half to pay his bookie. He was a North Carolinian, saturnine and gentlemanly, and he often repaid me.

A few years later, on another job, in California this time, I met a young man who was already a committed horseplayer. He assured me that it was possible to beat the game.

I found his argument reasonable. My friend was a responsible fellow and an excellent statistician. Furthermore, I had recently done some calculating that convinced me there might be more to games of chance than chance itself. Favorable (and perfectly honest) gambling situations did exist. I had had a couple of losing evenings shooting craps. I sat down to try to understand the odds in the game. The odds for or against shooting a natural, or "crapping out," or making any specific point seemed clear enough, though the information was not particularly useful against players of any experience. But was it more favorable to hold the dice or to bet against the shooter? I sweated over that question. Clearly, it was basic, and it was not well understood. I concluded that betting against the dice gave a small but distinct advantage (in a private game, of course; in a casino, the rules guarantee the house an edge).

How I reached this conclusion I do not recall. I may well have been right by chance. Nevertheless I was right, as I later learned from more solid sources. From then on, I held to the notion that judgment as well as chance entered into some gambling games, including betting on horse races.

For a number of years I went no further with this idea. I went to the races, when I could, simply because I enjoyed them. In the back of my head the thought remained: This game can be beaten. But I went racing only for a day off from the sometimes grim business of making a living. I knew I could count on a light and pleasantly mounting sense of excitement from the moment I entered a grandstand and passed rows of cashiers' and ticket sellers' windows, and caught my first glimpse of a totalizator board with its flashing, changing numbers, recording every bet made at the track. I could count on the pleasure of watching the horses come onto the track, in ambling procession, riders in bright silks perched on tiny saddles. I might try to divine the condition of the horses as they passed and in the end simply admire the swaying of the most graceful and muscular of all rumps. A few minutes more and the gambler's cloudy view of the future would close in tight, and I would face the decision: to bet or not to bet. A final wait, in silence now, and the starting gates would clang open and the horses would spring forward to settle the issue on the track.

To be sure, with the passage of time I did learn something about handicapping, about trying to forecast the running of a race. I read what there was to read. I listened to my neighbors at the track, heard wisdom and nonsense, and tried to sift wheat from chaff. It seemed quite clear I suffered no great financial damage through betting on horses, but still I kept no records. I did not feel I had anything to prove.

A change came during a business trip to Los Angeles. I ducked out of a meeting early—my colleagues did not miss me and the world did not slow in its turning—and went to Hollywood Park. There I met a friend named Edward, and sat next to him through most of the day's races. I had long suspected that Edward was a winner at the track, if ever I had known one. But how do you settle a point like that? Ask him outright? Embarrassing, and ridiculous. If he said no, that might merely signify fear of the Internal Revenue Service. If he said yes, how to prove it? Ask for a record of all the mutuel tickets he had bought, say, in the last two years? Out of the question.

But, in the course of conversation about handicapping and handicappers, late in the afternoon, I did ask Edward another question:

"Who was the best horseplayer you've ever known?"

Rather to my surprise, he answered without hesitation. "No doubt about that. It was a man we called the Brain."

He went on to tell me what he knew about the Brain, a man who had recently died, whose name actually was Al Winderman, and how the Brain did his work. For the rest of that day I continued to think about our conversation. I slept on it and awoke with a decision made. I determined finally to prove for myself whether or not there were consistent winners at the racetrack.

I did. And there were. It took much more time than the telling suggests, and more visits to tracks—from grandstand to backstretch—than I can count. But in the end I was convinced that Thoroughbred racing is less the sport of kings than the king of gambling games. It is, in fact, one large-scale, publicly organized form of gambling in which a small number of master players can win, without recourse to fixes or thievery or anything else illegal.

I began my investigation at a time when I was doing science writing. One day I interviewed a gifted young neuroanatomist at the University of California Medical Center in San Francisco. We talked at length, and in answer to a question of his I mentioned where I had been the day before—which was Golden Gate Fields. Scientists, like reporters, can be led along, far from their normal paths, by their own curiosity. The neuroanatomist wanted to know how often I went to the races, and why. And then he quizzed me closely on my reasons for thinking that some horseplayers actually are winners.

The scientist was a fellow in the Cardio-Vascular Research Institute. The fellows as a group were senior research people, busy all week with their own projects. Saturday mornings they met to discuss more informally any topic, outside their own work, that engaged their fancy. Several weeks after the interview I was surprised by an invitation to meet with the Institute fellows at a Saturday session to talk—not about public policy, or relations between scientists and writers, but about Thoroughbred racing.

I boned up on the life of Cardano to show that gamblers invented probability math. That was a waste of time. The distinguished fellows had their own ideas about probability. They wanted to know about racing itself. They kept me an extra hour discussing how things worked at the track, and how it was possible to win there, and, their ultimate question, how appearances could so differ from reality.

Word spreads in curious ways. Another several months passed, and, again surprisingly, I received another invitation, this time from Stanford University. I was asked to meet with a seminar of some twenty graduate students in the Graduate School of Business, to talk to them about racing.

At Stanford I had an experience, well known I suppose to teachers, but new enough to me to be remarkable. I learned more from the students than they could have learned from me.

To start with, I learned that the students were sharp, not at all stuffy, not inclined to curry favor, but ready to examine unfamiliar ideas. Perhaps it startled me that they were not put off by my suggestion that some horseplayers, over the long haul, might be winners.

Next I attempted to describe individual winning players I had found at the track. I listed qualities they had in common. They worked hard. They had discipline, and they stayed sober. They had keen powers of observation and clearly recalled the action they saw on the track. They could pick out patterns in a mass of information. Above all, as we say at the track, they had an opinion.

I pointed out that the description did not match the fictitious figure of the dashing riverboat gambler. But no explanation was needed. The plan of the seminar permitted comparison of a serious and successful gambler with his counterparts in the respectable businesses of speculation and investment. Apparently, the whole group recognized what I was trying to describe. It seemed to be a reasonable model for any master player in a game based on predicting futures.

Finally, and for me most important of all, I took away with me the notion that the case for demonstrating winners was just about as good at the racetrack as in the stock market. I repeated the same seminar with the succeeding class a year later, and the idea was reinforced.

And at that point this book took its final shape.

A word is needed about what constitutes a winner.

At the racetrack the answer is clear enough. A winner is someone who comes out ahead. He may lose any single bet. In fact, he is likely to. The winners I know lose a majority of their individual bets. Some players claim, without proof, to have won more than 50 percent of all their bets. I suspect that they are as rare as the Great Auk. In my experience, winners have many losing days, some losing weeks, a few losing months, and even an occasional losing meeting. But over the whole year, and especially over a span of years, they finish ahead. They win enough on the winning bets to more than make up for the ones lost. The winners are few in number, but none of them in the long run wins by chance.

The matter of the stock market is far more complex. Pick a long enough time span and it may be that anyone can win. The averages, followed far enough back, give that impression. Here, one problem, among many, is that not everyone can buy a stack of chips and stay in the game for forty or fifty years. By my definition, the winner, over a reasonable length of time—like five or ten years—is one who consistently beats the market averages. And those are the winners who are hard to find.

The scholarly literature about the stock market contains many references to random walk theory. This is the well-known theory that holds, in effect, that the market so efficiently reflects the sum of everyone's knowledge you might as well pick stocks at random (confining your choices to the kinds of stocks that best serve your needs—dividend producers, growth stocks, and the like). Throwing darts against a financial page is the system most often mentioned. If everyone did it, no one could, on the average, finish ahead.

The beginner is often urged to get "professional" market advice. No evidence is offered that the bulk of this advice gets the beginner further ahead than the dartboard technique. This is not to say that professional advice is useless. If, as I believe, it is possible to beat the averages, it is also possible to do consistently worse. Professional advice—which follows the rule of the prudent man and says play safe—can prevent that.

In my search for the stock market winner, the one who consistently beats the averages, I went to a broker I know. He works for a major brokerage, in an office with a dozen or more other brokers, each with perhaps two to three hundred customers. My broker friend agreed to ask his associates a question for me. It seemed self-evident that most of the customers were doing well enough, or felt they had enough grounds for hope, to remain in the market. But did any customers stand out? Did any do sufficiently better than the averages to be called winners? With full guarantee of privacy, no names to be used, this was the question we put to each of the other brokers. None of them came up with clear-cut winners. A few thought they had a couple of possibilities. One in particular seemed about to come up with a special case, but then he veered off, perhaps alarmed by the threat to privacy.

A last point about the difficulty of proving that anyone consistently wins in the stock market: The action is too slow. Horseplayers are easier to study—for somewhat the same reasons the geneticist studies mice rather than elephants. At the track each bet is a separate and complete transaction. A horseplayer can find action on as many days of the year as he wishes or the state of his health and nerves permits. He can easily be at a racetrack two hundred times a year. The average card has nine races. Suppose the player averages only three bets a day (the winner is a highly selective player; part of his discipline is to pass a majority of races, all of those about which he has no firm opinion). Still, he will have made at least six hundred bets, or complete win-or-lose transactions, in the year. It must be a rare investor in the stock market who turns over as many as a few score stocks in a year.

What has been said here about the stock market applies to many other fields. Touts and hucksters, always ready to show the way to instant wealth in the stock market and at the racetrack, make the same claims about commodity markets, for example, or real estate. The claims are equally outrageous, and ungrounded scientifically, whatever the field. None stands up to the simplest question: If beating the game is that easy, why betray so miraculous a secret, whether in a book or a supposedly private formula?

A special case can be made for the casino game of blackjack. Devotees of the game (and salesmen of blackjack systems) can rightly claim that their turnover is far more rapid than the horseplayer's. They can make tens of thousands of bets while the horseplayer is making hundreds. Furthermore, some of their other claims are justified.

Blackjack has simple rules, but correct strategy for playing the game is far from simple. In the 1960s a mathematician, Edward O. Thorpe, with computer assistance, calculated a nearly perfect blackjack strategy (and launched a minor industry for system salesmen). Thorpe's basic method can be learned in a week or two. With it, the player can walk into any casino, play as long as he wishes, and come close to breaking even.

For anyone who likes the inside of a casino, it may be enough of an ego reward to break even while others go steadily about the work of making the house rich. Of course, Thorpe and the system promoters trying to profit from his work went a step further. Thorpe showed that the deck sometimes favors the player over the house. The player can establish when this happens by following, and mentally recording, the fall of cards in the course of play. If at the right moment the player increases the size of his bets, Thorpe showed, he can actually beat the house—to the extent of perhaps 1.5 percent of the total he bets. These figures are also incontestable. But unfortunately they are not a formula for sudden wealth.

First, the ordinary swings of luck are so much greater than his edge that the player must be prepared to sweat out weeks of concentrated labor at the blackjack table. Second, card counting, despite claims to the contrary, is not for everyone. And finally, card counting, and thereby winning, is a public act. The house can protect itself at any moment by shuffling the deck. I find myself wondering how any successful blackjack player can render himself invisible to the casinos year in and year out.

The horseplayer can bet what he wants, when he wants, on any horse of his choice. No one behind the ticket sellers' windows cares. The basic point is that the horseplayer is pitting his judgment against that of other players, not against the house. Betting on Thoroughbred racing remains a game in a class by itself.

This book, then, is the result of a search for winners at the racetrack. It goes step by step through the knowledge that all horseplayers should acquire and that the shrewd ones can turn to their own advantage.

It does not offer a quick and easy course to riches. Rather, it demonstrates that no such thing exists.

Necessarily, the book covers topics known to all experienced players. No one can avoid the basics: class, speed, pace, recent and past form, conditions of a race, track variants and post positions, racing strategy. All have been written about many times. What is different here is the method of treatment. The book looks for history and reasons behind old rules. It offers only a basic minimum of cookbook rules. It assumes that, given intelligent understanding, a good player will settle on his own rules. In the technical Appendix a player can find all the help he needs to make charts and tables of his own.

The hunt for winners and their methods also leads onto new ground. The book contains chapters on matters generally ducked, or treated evasively, or altogether overlooked.

Do touts and books of systems have anything to offer?

Is the game straight enough to be taken seriously?

What can be learned from the remarkable information network, running through channels as complicated as computer wiring, among a racetrack crowd?

What kinds of self-mastery do all the winning players share in their different ways? And how can they go about making the single most important calculation for a player—the minimum odds that justify a bet?

Finally, the book offers its own evidence that the pursuit of winners is a sport for all seasons, through good times and bad.

A STOCK EXCHANGE FOR POOR PEOPLE

In the early 1950s, in New York, I went to the Jamaica track with a friend on a cold, raw, overcast day in October. In the course of that day I suddenly thought I understood what brings most people to the races.

The sky threatened a dismal rain. A North Atlantic storm wind blew across the track, undiluted, from Jamaica Bay. As sensible men would, we took shelter in the cavernous depths within the grandstand and drank hot bouillon to keep the bone marrow from congealing.

The Jamaica track is gone; the other New York tracks long ago absorbed its racing dates. In the years since I have seen the same inner depths of grandstands more times than I wish to count. Details vary from place to place, but always the same crowds of horseplayers slowly shuffle about in their massed thousands. They move around, and look about, but always their heads keep turning back in one direction, toward a totalizator board. The tote board registers all bets. Every ninety seconds or so it recomputes the odds on each horse in the race coming up. The board is an oracle, cold, nervous, and impersonal, with numbers blinking on and off at intervals. It knows nothing about the running of a race. Rather, it reflects a mass state of mind. It sucks up a thousand opinions, and whims and hunches, and reduces them to numbers.

My friend that day waved his hand toward a tote board and said: "Our ticker tape."

I thought he was right. And the realization that struck me on that gray October day at Jamaica still strikes me, whenever I return to a track: A racetrack is a stock exchange for poor people.

Of course, not everyone at a racetrack is poor. Some are downright rich. But the price of the smallest odd-lot transaction on this exchange—the cheapest mutuel ticket—is $2. Nearly anyone can get into the game. A racetrack is one big, solid, American institution run absolutely without class or racial discrimination. Black man or white, rich man or poor, recent immigrant or old settler—each has exactly the same right to pick a horse, and bet on it, and sometimes win the bet.

To be sure, it is very unlikely that anyone could start with a ten-dollar bill and run it up to a fortune at a racetrack. Even a first-rate handicapper would most likely hit a streak bad enough to wipe him out before he had built a workable bankroll. A beginner at the track would be wise to budget a set amount for betting, and count it all as a cost of entertainment. Any winnings will come as an unexpected bonus.

What, then, is the minimum roll that might launch an already accomplished horseplayer? No one number can be set as a flat limit, but it seems to me that a $500 roll, and a betting limit of no more than 5 percent of the roll on a single wager, would carry him over nearly all the ups and downs of pure chance. He would then be left to demonstrate his own skill. A merely good player, one who can hold his own, could stay afloat indefinitely with a $500 roll. A first-rate player—a genuine, certifiable winner—could go on to build the roll to the point where it would yield a hard-won living. As will be demonstrated later, not many players can do this. Still, scarcely any business offers a fair start with so little capital.

At this point, the hackneyed and pseudo-psychiatric questions have to be faced: Don't gamblers, at bottom, really want to lose? Aren't they in fact punishing themselves?

And doesn't this compulsion make mockery of any talk of winners at the track?

It would, if true. But it is not true.

As for compulsive gamblers, the ones who have to lose, I know some. I do not know how many there are, nor do I want to attempt a catalog of other compulsions. I am reasonably sure that if all compulsive losers were somehow herded away from the track, they would find other places equally handy for self-destruction.

More to the point, I can make one unconditional guarantee about a crowd at any racetrack. I can lead anyone sufficiently interested to a number of gamblers who most earnestly seek to win and who rejoice when they succeed.

The matter of investment, speculation, and gambling recurs. How many people are competent to judge the distinctions among them? In the decade of the 1970s a fair number of morally righteous, hard-working, provident, middle-class people entrusted their savings to brokers for investment in the stock market. In a certain percentage of cases, money thus invested was lost. I doubt that anyone, of any psychiatric persuasion, would say the unfortunate investors wanted to lose.

A more serious question can be raised concerning the odds against a horseplayer's winning. In the stock market, at least, it appears that over the very long run random bets, or transactions, do win. At the racetrack the player faces an iron law: Random betting in the long run will lose about 17 percent of the total bet—the amount of the state's takeout from the parimutuel system. Why try to win against such a handicap?

The first part of an answer has already been offered. For people with little capital, no better or fairer market is open. A second answer is the assertion, also made here, that some master players can overcome the handicap by the exercise of superior judgment. Many others cling to the hope of joining the winners.

But still another answer must be given. For many of us, racing offers rewards which sometimes make dollars gained seem trivial.

The Thoroughbred horse is a handsome sight at rest. He is

exciting to watch in a stretch battle, nostrils flared, every muscle strained, as his rider flails his whip to gain the lead. But that is a surface part of the matter.

The horseplayer who takes only a few steps toward becoming expert necessarily realizes the value of self-mastery. Above all, he learns the meaning of having an opinion. He learns that without a real opinion, one of his own, he must lose. Having an opinion, he may also lose, but he has a chance of winning.

As the player progresses and enters the high ground where mists conceal the future, he gets a keener sense of the probabilities that govern all affairs. He confronts the humbling notion that very nearly anything can happen. Sometimes what happens is merely the unpredictable: the player sees an odds-on favorite, obviously the class of the field, backed by more than half the crowd, pull up lame and finish last. Sometimes it is the unimaginable. A few years ago I had a bet on a filly named Why More Worry running in a race on the turf course at Hollywood Park. She led by many lengths through the stretch and was still running smoothly, with nothing else in the field even remotely threatening, when a few yards from the finish she spooked at a shadow and jumped the inner rail of the course. Her rider managed to stay on, and she went past the finish—still far in the lead, but off the course. She never crossed the actual finish line and was automatically placed last in the race.

Such hardships only increase the greatest of rewards, at least for some of us. Sometimes we really can peer ahead through the murk. Sometimes we do see clearly what has not yet happened.

Every player of any skill remembers such cases. For myself, I remember a cool fall afternoon at Bay Meadows, near San Francisco. I arrived in time for a six-furlong race for $5,000 claimers. The obvious choices were a couple of horses named With Destiny and Spanish Mod. It occurred to me that they both had early speed. What if they fought it out in the backstretch? They might finish each other by the turn. In the entries I saw a horse, Old Frank S., of at least equal class, that had been running well at a mile. It seemed to me he might catch the leaders in the homestretch. The odds were attractive, and I bet on him to win.

At the start, Spanish Mod and With Destiny broke on top.

Beside them was a third speed horse, Tommy Kid. The three raced the length of the backstretch like a matched team, straining for the lead. Meanwhile, Old Frank S. lay back, running smoothly, a little off the pace. At the far turn the leaders began to falter. Old Frank S. moved around them on the turn, as if fate were pushing him. He showed in front at the head of the stretch and lengthened his lead all the way to the wire.

I had an astonished sense of having seen the race before it was run. It felt almost as if one held the universe like a ball. And opened a trap door on the side, and looked in, and there was the axle of the universe, turning around in its oil bath, just the way it had to be.

THE NOBLE BEAST

The Greeks thoroughly despised the Trojans.
The one favorable term they used for their
Trojan enemy was "tamers of the horse." To the whole of Troy,
they attached the epithet "having excellent foals." If the Trojans
had managed to enter a horse in the memorial races for Patro-
clus, how much weight would the Greeks have put on him?

Thus, man's friendly, often admiring, and sometimes pain-
ful association with horses goes back to antiquity. And, over
that span of thousands of years, man has done what he can to
improve the breed, citing, at various times, the urgent needs of
national defense, agriculture, and the welfare of the $2 bettor.

Curiously, among long-range human designs, this one has
succeeded better than most. Horses almost certainly do run
faster. Horse racing in particular has succeeded so well that it
has established a separate breed of horse, with the proper
name of "Thoroughbred."

The Thoroughbred traces his lineage in the same genealogy,
no matter where he stands or races. "Thoroughbred" in this
sense is not a general term applying to pure specimens of a

breed. It is itself the name of the breed. Racehorses, anywhere in the world, are Thoroughbreds, unless specifically described as "quarter horses," "standard breds," "Appaloosas," or something else.

In the literature of the racetrack a little history goes a long way. Accordingly, all sources, to save trouble and confusion, have agreed that establishment of the Thoroughbred line dates from the late seventeenth century in England when a number of outstanding stallions were imported from the Middle East. The names of three stallions are invariably recited: the Darley Arabian, the Byerly Turk, and the Godolphin Barb.

Captain Byerly's Turk apparently saw duty as a cavalry charger in Ireland. The Barb, according to romantic history, through some mischance wandered into ordinary trade and was found pulling a cart in Paris before being retrieved for England's royal stud. Without doubt, all specimens of what became Thoroughbred racehorses trace to one of these three founding fathers. But history rarely yields pleasingly neat answers to questions. It is a clear fact that when Mr. Darley's Arabian came to the royal stables, and pricked his ears and looked over the field, much Arab blood had already intermingled in the king's brood mares.

The true beginning of the Thoroughbred might reasonably be sketched on a grander historic canvas. Before gunpowder the wars between European Christianity and Middle Eastern Mohammedanism had been in part a contest between two kinds of horses. European armies, loosely organized around the heavily armored knight on horseback, used a big-boned, ponderous horse who carried weight and endured. Such horses must have resembled, on a somewhat smaller scale, the dray horses who, around 1900, pulled wagons heaped with beer kegs. The Arabs, or Saracens, based their more mobile tactics on light cavalry. Lightly equipped, they rode agile, speedy, short-coupled horses.

It is fair to suppose that the Crusades, along with all else, produced, as inevitably as mating in springtime, a cross between horses which did not share men's lust for battle. Some of the get from these crosses must have blended the elements of durability and speed. British writers have noted that horse breeders tend toward conservatism. Nevertheless, after some centuries for contemplation and debate, stud masters began to pursue such crosses intentionally. From the time of Charles II the English royal stables led the way. Royal breeding efforts received their ultimate endorsement, half a century later, from the gamblers of England.

An outburst of all forms of gambling took place in England during the 1700s. Betting on horse races became a serious matter. Since some gamblers truly do wish to win, it is not surprising that betting on horses had an immediate effect on horse breeding. Horseplayers of the day could not avoid noting that three horses successively dominated the turf for some twenty years in the middle of the eighteenth century. Their names were Eclipse, Herod, and Matchem. Eclipse never lost a race; the others lost rarely. Among a people who had produced Newton, it was no feat to observe that the three unbeatable racers were descended from—the Darley Arabian, the Byerly Turk, and the Godolphin Barb. Breeders as a matter of course bred to these three lines of descent. The first studbook was begun in 1791. To it we owe our sketchy knowledge of breeding in the preceding hundred years. From then on, breeding records were preserved, more systematically for Thorough-breds than for humans.

One spring day I went to Los Angeles for a meeting. With dignity and restraint, I finished my part of the business by late morning, pleaded other work on the far side of Los Angeles County, accepted the praise of my colleagues for my devotion to duty, and took off for Hollywood Park, a few minutes by automobile from the Los Angeles airport. There I found my friend Edward. He sat that day with a group in a box.

The third race was for the babies of the racetrack. They were two-year-old fillies who were maidens—non-winners of any race other than a romp in the meadow. A filly named Stage Miss won and paid a reasonable price, which, as far as I could tell, was not collected by anyone in the box. We all, with a single impulse, glanced at our *Racing Forms* to see what we might have overlooked. In truth, the filly had a negligible record. No one in the box could claim even to have considered her.

I can add that overlooking her did not turn out to be a memorable error. She won no more races that year. She started

three times the next year, without success, and so far as I know
has accomplished nothing since. I am sure I would have forgotten the incident except that a few minutes later, inside the
grandstand, Edward and I encountered a young man, gaunt,
balding, with a close-cropped full beard. He wore sandals and
carried a clipboard with a fat sheaf of papers clutched against
his chest. He smiled cheerfully as he greeted Edward.

"I presume you liked Stage Miss," the young man said.

Edward looked at him sourly. "What was to like?"

The young man spoke precisely and with vast assurance.
"She had excellent works, Edward. Also, she is by First Bal-
cony, out of a Fleet Nasrullah mare. Speed on both sides."

"Sure," Edward said.

The young man nodded and walked away, still smiling, slew-
footed in his sandals, clutching his clipboard.

"That was Caleb Howe," Edward said.

"Bloodlines man?"

"Really he specializes in two- and three-year-olds, sprinting.
He clocks them himself in the mornings. I guess he pays attention to breeding. With two-year-olds there may be nothing else
in the *Form*."

I grew up on the chance-and-environment side of arguments
about heredity, and I cannot suppress my doubt when a horseplayer tells me that some horse "is a Crazy Kid, and you know
they have speed." In truth, I do not know, and I said so to
Edward.

"I can't argue with you," Edward said, "but I'm not going to
knock Caleb, either. He had the winner, and we didn't."

"Does he win often?"

"Look, I'm not his accountant," Edward said. "All I know is, I
see him here all the time. They tell me he used to be a painter.
Then somebody took him racing. It turned out he had a
memory—couldn't forget anything he saw on the track. Now
they say he makes a living here."

I can corroborate one part of Caleb Howe's story from my own
observation. Later that year I visited Del Mar and went early one
morning to watch the workouts. Howe was sitting alone in the
grandstand. He had binoculars in one hand, a stopwatch in the
other, and a tape recorder by his side. Presumably, he was
looking for true descendants of Herod and Matchem. I suspect

he only relied on bloodlines for a selection in the absence of hard information. But when he did, he was at least returning to basics that have endured in Thoroughbred racing and breeding for three hundred years. He and other specialists like him look to the Thoroughbred past for a projection of the future.

That day in Los Angeles I had some chance of catching a winner in the fourth race, but I would certainly have lost a bet if asked to predict my own whereabouts two weeks later.

As it turned out, I had to make a business trip, on short notice, to the University of Kentucky. The university is located in Lexington. Clustered about Lexington is the richest profusion of horse farms in the United States. Quite without planning it, I was going to the center of business and ritual in the breeding of the running horse.

Any one of two million farms in the United States might serve as a breeding place for Thoroughbred horses. Few do so. In all of Canada, the United States, and Mexico, fewer than 1,500 breeding farms are significant enough to be listed in the American Racing Manual. Nearly one-third of the total are in Kentucky. No other state comes close. Within Kentucky, no other area can touch Lexington for the number and importance of its studs and horse farms.

The country around Lexington is gently rolling, lightly wooded, grassy. Tradition holds that the quality of grass favors the nurture of horses. Perhaps it does; the point is hard to prove. It is hard even to find the color blue in the Kentucky bluegrass that gives the region its name. After several days, perhaps as a reward to the eye after much trying, perhaps because finally the light catches the blades of grass from just the right angle, the meadows do seem faintly tinged with blue. Local people wait patiently for you to see this, and encourage you, and reward you when you do report discovery to them, with the kindest of smiles and the farewell of reassurance: "Y'all come back and see us real soon, hear?"

Whatever the reason, the horse farms make up the tidiest, handsomest, most compact farming center to be found anywhere. The farmhouses, when they are close enough to the road to be seen, look substantial, sometimes elegant. The rich of a dozen Eastern states have moved in and bought up many of the farms. They live at least in comfort when they are in residence. The barns, however, literally overwhelm the houses. Bluegrass Kentucky barn architecture has called forth a social expression, executed by nameless carpenters, resembling on a lesser scale the cathedrals of France. Surrounding the barns are grassy paddocks and meadows, with clumps of trees to provide shade for grazing horses. Surrounding the fields and lining the roads are white fences.

Practically any of the roads radiating out of Lexington leads quickly to horse farms. With a little effort the traveler can work his way, on two-lane blacktop roads, all around the town. He will discover scores of farms with names famous in racing, finance, and romance.

The farms of Lexington and nearby Paris are beautiful. The barns, with their soaring cupolas, are works of art. Many of the people connected with the farms are pleasant. But none of this should obscure the fact that the buying and selling and breeding of horses are businesses.

Like bettors at races, people who sell horses stand a good chance of losing money. Again like horseplayers, some of them can win, too. For the winners, the stakes are big indeed.

Owners and trainers of Thoroughbreds enter them in races in the hope of winning purses. Horsemen accept purse money as willingly as bettors cash winning mutuel tickets. The largest rewards, though, come when a horse establishes a good enough record at the track to be used for breeding. Secretariat, on the basis of his racing record as a two-year-old in 1972, was sold for $6 million before he had run a single race as a three-year-old. His syndicators saw to it that he raced only one more year and then retired to stud. Had he raced seven more years, he could scarcely have won a third of his sale price in purses. The syndicate who bought shares in Secretariat could hope that the stallion would stand at stud fifteen years or more. In good years he might service, or cover, as many as forty mares. The syndicators, of course, ran the risk of the horse dying prematurely, or proving sterile or otherwise ineffective as a sire. A single service from Secretariat, in advance of any knowledge of his prepotency, surely would have been valued at substantially more than $20,000. Ounce for ounce, the semen of a champion stallion must be high among the most valuable biologic substances.

Most horses standing at stud cannot possibly be in a class with Secretariat—or with Ribot, Bold Ruler, Round Table, or Princequillo, to name a few outstanding champions among sires of the past. Each year since 1966 well over 20,000 Thoroughbred foals have been registered with the Jockey Club in New York, custodian of the American studbook. Most of these had undistinguished sires and dams, though all traced lines of descent in the same Thoroughbred register. A service from a respectable stud, with a good racing record, can be bought for $500. The price rises steeply, and is shrouded in secrecy by what is called "private treaty," for the handful of horses with the most outstanding records and most fashionable bloodlines. Here breeding farms like Spendthrift and Claiborne in bluegrass Kentucky come into their own. Most of the studs that command premium fees stand at the farms around Lexington. The gentle roll of the land, the elegance of some of the estates, the grace of the young horses running together in fields set off by white fences, all are secondary to the basic transaction for which the farms were set up—the transmission of a measurable number of ounces of remarkably valuable equine semen, from stallion to mare.

The group with which I visited one of the greatest farms, Spendthrift, included a man named Morton who had been in horse breeding himself, in the West. As we drove on side roads through the bluegrass, I asked Morton if he had owned a stud of his own.

"We had a couple," he said. "One was a pretty good Thoroughbred. We mainly bred him to quarter horse mares for a five-hundred-dollar fee."

I asked if he had enjoyed the work.

"It was my wife's idea," Morton said. "As far as I was concerned, it was hard work. Mucking out stables. That's a lot of horse shit. And waiting on horses, and worrying. Generally, I had to take my stud to the mare. You worry about getting him hurt. Or maybe he gets a dose of pseudomonas. It might as well be clap."

Morton shook his head. Nevertheless he had gone out of his

way to join the group traveling to Spendthrift.

There the stud holds court in splendor. The mare comes to him. As we entered Spendthrift, between sculptured stone pillars, and down a long, blacktop farm road leading into six thousand acres as well groomed as a city park, it appeared that—whatever the mares themselves felt—their owners at least were set at ease in every possible way.

Standard breeding contracts offer some protection to both buyer and seller, owners of stallion and mare. The owner of the mare undertakes to remove her hind shoes. He further guarantees that she is halter-broken and in good health. For his part, the owner of the stallion guarantees that if the mare comes to stay with him, he will care for and feed her in "a good and husbandlike manner." Above all, he guarantees, on pain of having to return the stud fee, that the service of his stud will produce a live foal, by which is meant "a foal that can stand up alone and nurse."

At Spendthrift, as at Claiborne to the northeast along the Paris Pike, the mare may be brought to any one of several dozen stallions of highest rank in the peerage of horses. We parked near a complex of handsome and immaculate barns. Each stallion in the stalls inside had his own brass nameplate, like a country lawyer awaiting clients. Across the road, alone in a paddock large enough to support a family if planted to crops, a burly old gentleman of a horse took his ease. It turned out he had earned his own acreage hundreds of times over.

A groom, like all the others we saw, a black man, had taken us in tow. He had the features of a pharaoh, and he offered an endless assortment of facts about the horses in his charge, with assurance and much practice.

"That's Nashua," he said, pointing to the stout and elderly horse grazing in his paddock. "He have put on a little weight, and he earned it. He is a millionaire. He's one of the first horses to be a millionaire. He weighs over thirteen hundred pounds these days."

"What was his stud fee?" Morton asked.

"If you could get in his book, if they was room for you," Pharaoh said somewhat severely. "Anyway, fifteen thousand dollars. That is Nashua."

"Just let your mind roll that one around," Morton said to the rest of us. "Fifteen K a pop. Thirty-five or forty engagements a year. Every year, for maybe fifteen years."

"Not no more," Pharaoh said.

"Well, it went on long enough," Morton said. "He earned his keep." Morton stared broodingly at Nashua.

In the paddock next to Nashua's, a much younger horse, a strikingly handsome chestnut, amused himself with a run from one corner to another and then looked inquiringly at Nashua.

"That Majestic Prince," said the groom who looked like a pharaoh. "He win the Santa Anita Derby. *And* the Kentucky Derby. *And* the Preakness."

"And broke down in the Belmont, because his people wanted to go for all three," Morton muttered.

Pharaoh stared at him steadily and said, "He have perfect conformation."

Another in our party said, "My God, a private field for each one. What would happen if you put them together?"

"They might fight," Pharaoh said. "They might hurt each other. They got more important things to do."

We turned back, across the road toward the barns, in time to see several of the grooms leading a heavyset, middle-aged stallion from a barn toward a large shed that stood apart with its doors wide open. The stallion was a sire of some note, Never Bend. The grooms led him at a quick walk, without fuss or bustle, giving him no room for decisions of his own. The stallion, for his part, seemed calm enough, and matter-of-fact, but altogether clear about what he was doing. As he walked, his penis—even as happens occasionally in the walking ring before a race—was descending and lengthening and flapping to and fro.

Inside the barn, we now could see, stood a mare, with her rump toward the door, and us, and Never Bend. As the stallion entered the mating shed and neared her, the mare sluiced a flood of urine. The stallion's penis now rose, extended fully, and assumed what were by human standards altogether improbable dimensions. It projected like a wagon tongue, as massive at the base as a heavy tree limb. The men in our group snickered in amusement and embarrassment—and some awe.

"Would you gentlemen like to stand inside the shed?" Pharaoh asked.

We followed him toward a side entrance. The one woman in our group followed, too, but Pharaoh turned immediately and stopped her.

"No, ma'am. No," he said. "I'm sorry. But no, ma'am. You can't."

"Why can't I?" the woman asked.

"I'm sorry," he said. He shook his head firmly. The woman was left to watch from the yard, through the open shed doors, while the rest of the party filed into a narrow side passage, mounted a wooden step running the length of the shed, and looked down through a high glass window at the coupling.

The mare stood, quivering slightly, her legs held in place by hobbles. Around her neck she wore a heavy protective collar of leather. Grooms stood on either side of her head to keep her firmly in place.

The stallion reared, plunged his penis into the mare, and made vigorous and rapid butting motions with his loins. He, too, was closely watched and held by grooms. He chewed in a perfunctory way at the mare's leather collar, and then, in startlingly few seconds, considering both costs and dimensions, completed the transaction and dismounted.

If the act was quickly done, it was also quickly repeated. As all the actors in the shed, the two horses and the several humans, quietly waited, the penis again rose and extended. This time a white man with close-cropped hair, wearing a long, white, moderately clean hospital coat, stepped forward and withdrew the penis as it was ejaculating. He caught the remaining semen in what appeared to be an ordinary Dixie cup. Then he drew the semen up into a long glass tube, inserted the tube into the mare's vagina, and injected the semen as directly as if by artificial insemination. Finally, he examined both horses' lip tattoos, took up a clipboard, and entered the particulars of the mating for the records of the breeders, the Jockey Club, and posterity.

Done now with his business for the day, the stallion wheeled and without protest followed the grooms across the yard to his own stall in a nearby barn. The grooms again led him briskly. They rubbed him dry and wiped his now diminishing penis with a rag. Their movements throughout were as quick, and deft, and businesslike as those of a good major league infield completing a routine double play.

We saw Never Bend later in his stall in a spacious barn paved with stone. He munched on hay and raised his head to look at us with the dignity and composure of a creature at ease with himself, his surroundings, and his job in life.

Horse breeders are convinced that bloodlines count. They think the best horses come from breeding champions to champions. In short, they believe their genetic experiments have been successful, or, in the language of statistics, significant.

It occurred to me that it might be worthwhile to seek a scientist's view of the genetic value of Thoroughbred breeding. During a visit to New York I went to see one of a group of outstanding young molecular biologists at Rockefeller University. My informant worked specifically in genetics—though, to be sure, not in animal breeding. He dealt with genes and nucleic acids and the nearly invisible stuff of life. I found the biologist willing to talk and clearly interested in all aspects of genetics, from invisible particles to racehorses.

"Let me tell you straight out," he said, "we're nowhere near the time when we can point to specific combinations of genes and say those are the ones that make a horse run fast."

I explained that I only wanted to find out if the records of horse breeding were to be taken at all seriously from a scientific view, and if the handicapper's concern with bloodlines was at all warranted.

"Depends what you mean by seriously," he said. "You're not dealing with mice from the Bar Harbor lab, or drosophilae, of course—"

"Drosophila?"

"Fruit flies. But good Lord, consider how many of those you can breed, and how fast, and with what controls to ensure breeding true. The records you describe for horses must be more voluminous and older than any we have for other large mammals. How long does a mare carry her foal—nearly a year, isn't it?"

I said it was about eleven months.

"The primate centers are doing very careful work with apes

and monkeys, but their records can't go back very far. And we're large mammals ourselves, and certainly our records are scanty. So, in that sense, I'd say you have to take the records of Thoroughbred horses seriously indeed."

I asked about the fragility of the Thoroughbred and the general belief that inbreeding for speed and running qualities might make for weaknesses.

"Absolutely. You can think of a couple of reasons for that. Now, you understand, I don't know anything about horses as such."

I assured him that I did understand.

"Well, then. You could argue that the qualities that make for speed might also make for brittleness. If you breed for the first, you get the second whether you like it or not. Suppose the horses who run faster have bones that are lighter compared to their musculature and the rest of their bodies. Of course, I'm thinking of birds here. But, over time, it could work with large mammals, too. Bones like that would break down."

The horse as you see him on the track bears out this idea, I remarked. He appears to be a graceful, powerful, rippling mass of muscles—suspended on skinny, almost spindly ankles.

"Another thing you're getting into is the matter of lethal mutants," the biologist said. "You see, you're trying to establish a special gene pool. The genes, you know, are what you inherit, the stuff of genetics. You want to be able to predict what you get from the matching of genes in a selected male and female. In other words, you're trying to breed out random characteristics. But if you get stuck with a lethal mutant, it may crop up more and more frequently in the type you're breeding for. The breeder is interfering with nature's way of getting rid of it. If the lethal or bad gene crops up in the same position in the male and female, you produce an animal which is homozygous for that lethal gene. End of the line. You see?"

I said it sounded dangerous and I asked about some other commonly held beliefs about breeding: "What about the idea that the male is more important in transmitting characteristics? And the idea some breeders have that the female line is more important? They can't both be right, can they?"

My friend laughed. "In a curious way," he said, "they might both be right. Or somewhat right. As far as the male line's importance goes, it's obvious that one male can impregnate a large number of females, so in that sense his line is more important, because you can choose to concentrate on just a few males. On the other hand, the female has a unique genetic contribution to make. Besides the characteristics you're breeding for—the qualities of a runner, in the Thoroughbred—there are some females who are better nourishers of the young. So you might very well want to concentrate on looking for those."

"You've mentioned the bones," I said. "Can you think of any other qualities you might want to look into, to see if they help make a horse run better? Yes, I know—you don't know anything about horses. But what kinds of things might you look for?"

"Well, not just the lightness of bones, but their proportions. And you'd certainly want to look at the kind of heart and lungs the successful racehorse inherits, his cardiopulmonary apparatus. And you might want to look at his alertness, the way his nervous system operates, too."

I said he was beginning to sound curiously like people in the backstretch. Some of them say the better racers also seem very often to be the more intelligent horses.

"One of these days I'd better see what a racetrack looks like," he said.

I said we would arrange it and continued on my way.

Just a dozen blocks from Rockefeller University, in a midtown Manhattan office building, is the Jockey Club. The club library has appropriate dark wood paneling. Hanging on the walls are conservatively painted portraits of famous horses, in heavy museum frames. Most of the club's floor space is turned over to its chief working function: the registration and certification of Thoroughbreds.

The club was set up in 1894 to bring order out of confusion in racing. It limited itself to just fifty members—all rich, all as a matter of course involved in racing, but none dependent on racing for a living. In its first eighty years, the club had only six chairmen: John Hunter, August Belmont II, F. K. Sturgis, William Woodward, George D. Widener, and Ogden Phipps. The club wrote rules for racing which still, though now informally, influence racing practices at most tracks. Until the early 1950s, the Jockey Club actually served as a licensing authority at the New York tracks, then and now the most important in the country.

In 1951 the club denied an owner's license to a well-known and successful horseplayer, Jule Fink, who also owned horses. Fink took the Jockey Club to court and ultimately won his case. The highest appeals court in New York ruled, in effect, that tracks were now chartered by the state, that the state derived income from the tracks and for that purpose regulated them, and that the state therefore had no right to yield any part of its licensing power to a private association.

Racing is now regulated by the states, but the state horse racing boards or commissions accept the authority of the Jockey Club in all matters having to do with the authenticity of the breed. No state permits any but Jockey Club authenticated and certified Thoroughbreds to run in a race for Thoroughbreds. The crowds gathered around the paddock at any track, shortly before the post parade, will see a paddock judge go to each horse in turn and lift its lip. He is verifying certification numbers tattooed on the lip, and these numbers in turn go back to the records maintained by the Jockey Club at its Park Avenue offices and at its statistical bureau in Lexington, Kentucky.

Foreign horses may race in the United States, but only after verification of their pedigrees. English, French, and Italian pedigrees are accepted here without question; the records of other countries are supposed to be searched, though in rare cases this does not happen. The minimum demand is for a record of at least eight generations and at least a hundred years of unblemished Thoroughbred ancestry.

The basic records here are maintained in dozens of volumes of the American Stud Book, published by the Jockey Club. The General Stud Book, maintained in England, serves as the basic source for all other studbooks.

The owner of an American stallion must report to the club all the mares his stallion may have serviced in a year. Owners of the mares, too, report to the club with a certified and dated report of the services rendered to each. When foals are dropped, they are registered with the club and the registration must be backed by the stallion and mare reports. Along with all the documents for the foal registration go a detailed physical description and photograph of the young animal. The owner of the foal asks permission to use the name he has chosen, and receives it only if it is not in use, if it can be written in eighteen spaces, and if it is neither ridiculous nor obscene.

What the Jockey Club and the breeders are protecting amounts to nothing less than a large-scale experiment in genetics and selective breeding. When the experiment scores an outstanding success, it may reward a horse owner with a stallion like What a Pleasure or The Minstrel, worth eight or nine million dollars.

From a horseplayer's point of view, the matter boils down to one question: Do bloodlines truly tell you anything about a horse's speed and the distance he can go?

In any single case, the bloodlines may tell you nothing. Horses called "royally bred"—because they had expensive or highly successful sires and dams—often do badly at the track or never race at all. At the other extreme, racing history is full of Cinderella stories of horses with undistinguished parents and grandparents who went on to become stakes winners.

Taken overall, the breeding statistics do begin to yield a pattern. In recent years less than a fifth of all foals have been dropped in Kentucky. Nearly as many have come from California, and Florida runs third.

As a consequence, Kentucky-bred horses make up only a small percentage of the entrants, in most races, at most tracks, around the country. But the percentage of Kentucky-breds goes up in the higher-category races, which offer the largest purses. In a state like California, with its own breeding industry, there may be no Kentucky horses at all in the cheaper races on a card, and then in the feature race, offering the largest purse and calling forth the swiftest horses, Kentucky-breds may make up half the field.

Owners and trainers send their horses where they have a chance to compete successfully. The best horses therefore go where the purses are biggest. The result is seen most clearly in the records of stakes races. Year after year the Kentucky stud farms, which may have only, say, 17 percent of the foals, produce about half the winners of the major stakes, offering purses of $50,000 or more, at all tracks in the country. Of the remaining major stakes winners, foaled in other states, many were sired by one of the great Kentucky stallions. The breeding farms in Kentucky retain much the largest share of the outstanding sires and dams. Whatever the effect of Kentucky climate, grass, and water, it appears that the biggest contribution comes from the gene pool carefully maintained at places like Claiborne and Spendthrift, and guarded by the registry system at the Jockey Club.

And what sort of creature emerges from this nurture? It is a handsome animal, full of muscles, beautiful in motion, and, above all, a runner. The Thoroughbred's urge to run, and run very fast, becomes more fascinating the longer it is observed.

Conceivably, some of the big cats—the cheetah in particular, it is said—can go faster for a short distance. Grizzly bears covered any distance between themselves and fur trappers in nearly no time at all. Or so it appears from the trappers' journals: fear may have clouded the clockers' judgment. At any event, no one ever saddled a grizzly and started it from a gate. Of all living things that have entered with men into the spirit of racing, the Thoroughbred is fastest and most marvelous to watch.

A quarter horse may break faster from the gate, and may stay ahead of the Thoroughbred for the first furlong or two. A burro clearly makes a more dependable companion for a descent into a canyon. A mule is a safer bet to get you home if you are lost in wild country. For the rest, the Thoroughbred does best the things his breeders hoped he would do. He runs faster than any likely rival at all distances from half a mile to four miles, on the flat or over jumps, on dirt or grass courses.

A good horse racing a mile on a fast track will average about 12 seconds for each furlong (or eighth of a mile). That works out to a rate of speed of 37½ miles per hour. But he will almost always run the first furlongs faster than the last. That means he may cover a sixteenth of a mile, at peak speed, in 5½ or even 5 seconds. His maximum rate, then, is between 40 and 45 miles per hour. The fastest human being can scarcely run at half that speed.

Sometimes the horse's urge to run seems unstanchable. Part

of a trainer's job with a horse is to teach him to conserve his speed and control his spending. Some naturally fast horses never do learn this and therefore fail to do as well as they might at the track. Anyone who goes reasonably often to the races will recall seeing a natural sprinter who dashes so wildly straight ahead from the starting gate that he can scarcely be persuaded to negotiate the first turn. This happens most often on standard one-mile tracks, in races at a mile, where the gate is close to the first, or clubhouse, turn.

Sooner or later, too, the racegoer will see the horse who runs to the point of death, or tries to. The fatal breakdown may happen on any kind of track. It can happen to a Ruffian, one of the handful of great horses, to a cheap horse, or to one called simply "nice." It can happen at daybreak on a training track or, before thousands of people, in the homestretch during a race.

A five-year-old mare named Bold Broad ran in a six-furlong opening day feature at Bay Meadows a few years ago. Most of the crowd gave her little chance to win. She went off at the long odds of 10 to 1. But horses cannot read the tote board. Bold Broad broke from the gate as if she were the favorite. All the way down the backstretch and around the far turn she led the field, fighting off challenges from other horses. In the homestretch she strained to keep her nose in front, but now her stride shortened and became choppy. A sixteenth of a mile from the finish, quite suddenly, she fell and rolled over on a shoulder. The rider, Wayne Freeman, jumped clear, hit the track hard, and managed to avoid other horses' hooves while he crawled under the inside rail.

Bold Broad, with a violent effort, struggled to her feet and made a gesture with her body as if to go on. The rest of the field had swept past. A great, collective gasp could be heard from the stands as the mare staggered, and it could be seen now that the bones of one of her front legs had snapped clean and had torn through most of the encasing flesh. Men from the gate crew ran to grab her reins. She whirled away from them, circling on three legs, her head tossing, the great muscles contorting in her chest and shoulders as she fought to keep her footing and continue running. She shook the broken leg until its hoof swung from a flap of skin.

While thousands watched in silence, a low, tractor-driven

cart very slowly came round from the far side of the track and stopped beside the mortally wounded mare. The horse's trainer and some of his helpers tried futilely to lead her up a ramp into the cart. Eventually, while two men held a long sheet of canvas in front of the horse, to hide her, more or less, the track veterinarian administered a fatal injection by syringe. Bold Broad was winched aboard the cart and the tractor hauled her away.

Horses were already in the paddock, being saddled and readied for the ninth and last race of the day, at a mile and a sixteenth, for $2,500 claimers. The starting gate was hauled into position at almost exactly the spot where Bold Broad fell in her stretch run.

Among Bold Broad's sisters in her race, several completed a successful meeting. Some have since been retired to breeding farms, to be sent to the cover of the most stylish studs their owners could afford, and to bear foals.

THE WONDERFUL BETTING MACHINE

Before the American Civil War a bet on a horse race was a personal transaction between two parties with a difference of opinion (though one of the bettors might be a President of the United States). The war changed the shape of American society. It set loose an industrial renaissance in the North and Midwest. It created a class of very rich industrialists and businessmen, some of whom—those not altogether bound up in the Protestant Ethic—could ape the style of the Southern gentry who had lost the war. The running horse fit very well into that style. And, when racing expanded in the post–Civil War North, more people could and did bet on the outcome of races. The newly prosperous of several classes made their way upriver from New York to Saratoga, while men were still fighting at Cold Harbor and the Wilderness, to take the waters, gamble in casinos, and bet on horses. The only thing lacking to create modern racing was a way to handle large volumes of wagers. The need, in short, was for a betting machine.

In 1871 an answer appeared in New York in the person of one

James E. Kelley, a bookmaker. A few years later the first of a number of English bookmakers arrived to take bets at American tracks. In effect, any reasonable number of people could bet as they wished, large sums or small, and modern racing was under way.

The English had already passed through the stages of personal wagers and auction betting to the booking of bets by bookmakers who set odds on all the horses in a field and took bets from all comers. The "Tattersall," or ring of bookies, became a feature of English racing meetings. Curiously, the Tattersall family, whose name was thus borrowed, had little to do with betting. For a century and a half, from the late eighteenth century to World War II, they bought and sold horses. Richard Tattersall, the founding father of this line of traders, came to London at the age of twenty-one and went to work in the stables of noblemen. Through the exercise of wit, personality, and a strong memory, he became a highly successful auctioneer. He established a selling place of his own at The Corner, in Hyde Park. He made himself an indispensable adviser to princes. The Corner became a meeting place for the Jockey Club—and for the settlement of bets among gentlemen. Eventually, a Subscription Room had to be set aside at Tattersall's Corner for settling day, generally Monday, and those who defaulted were ruled off the race courses by the Jockey Club. Bookmakers set up their small stands at the equivalent of Tattersall's Corner at each British race course. They do business in much the same way today.

The imported English bookmakers quickly put down their own roots in the United States. In less than twenty-five years, between the mid-1870s and 1900, the bookie made himself into a standard American institution. At the same time, tracks multiplied rapidly. So, too, did the breeding of Thoroughbreds, and modern racing, as a major public spectacle, took shape.

Just one year after James Kelley started booking bets in New York, the instrument that ultimately drove bookmaking off American tracks was being invented in France. In 1872 Pierre Oller, a businessman who evidently had a taste for gambling, devised the first parimutuel system. Oller, whose main business apparently had been the selling of perfumes and other toiletries in Paris, dabbled in running lotteries. As a sideline, he booked bets on horse races. It is thought that as a book-maker he was a loser and that he created the parimutuel system as a means of guaranteeing himself a profit. Oller took the form "pari" from the verb *parier*—to wager. "Mutuel" stood for betting mutually, among a group of people, by pool.

The first approximation of a parimutuel system can be seen in any office pool. Say twelve people join in a pool to bet among themselves on the outcome of a race with a twelve-horse field. Each person pays a dollar into the pool. Each receives, by lot, a ticket with the name of a horse. The winner takes all. In this crude betting system, the winner takes in $11 for the dollar he wagered: every horse in the field is held at odds of 11 to 1. Suppose, though, that one horse stands out in the field. Suppose it is a Secretariat year and the office workers bid among themselves until it is necessary for the holder of the Secretariat ticket to bid and pay $11 for it. The other eleven tickets, for which there is no very great demand, still go for $1 each. The pool now contains $22. Secretariat is being held at even money. That is, if he wins, the holder of the Secretariat ticket takes in $22, which means that he has gained an amount exactly even to the amount he bet, or bid, $11. Bidding up the price of Secretariat's ticket has automatically raised the odds on each of the other eleven horses to 21 to 1. Should one of the other horses win, the holder of his ticket also takes the whole $22 pool, consisting in this case of $21 profit and $1 as his original wager. The twelve anonymous office workers have reinvented, not the wheel, but the auction system of betting which in turn is the precursor of the parimutuel system.

Oller's idea was to sell tickets on every horse in a race, to anybody who wished to buy. The bettor could buy any number of tickets he wished. The total amount bet then constituted the mutuel pool for that race. Suppose 1,000 two-franc tickets were sold. The pool totaled 2,000 francs. Oller took roughly 10 percent as his commission. The remaining 1,800 francs was then distributed among holders of tickets on the winner. If, for example, 100 tickets on the winner had been sold, each ticket, costing 2 francs originally, was now worth 18 francs—a profit of 16 francs for each 2 francs invested, or a payoff of 8 to 1.

When a bettor visited his own bookmaker, the bookie set the odds and the rate of payoff was fixed at the moment the bet was made. The player who laid his bet by buying tickets from Pierre Oller found the odds determined by the sum of the actions of all the other players in the mutuel pool. The more money bet on a horse, the lower the odds on that horse would be; the less bet, the higher the odds. The odds changed with every bet. The betting, of course, had nothing to do with determining the ultimate winner of the race, but selection of a favorite by parimutuel betting somewhat resembled voting in a popularity contest. In fact, at tracks today, a novice horseplayer is sometimes heard to say, "I voted for number four."

An outstanding feature of Oller's creation, designed to please the French mind, was its objectivity. Oller, the manager of the pool, had no interest in who won or at what odds. He made his commission without regard to the number of players or the running of the race. He could afford to pay off on a long shot or a favorite with the same impartiality. It served his interests to run an honest game. He had thus opened the way for a unique form of gambling—as impersonal as a lottery, as full of calculation as chess.

In a poker game the showdown can be intensely personal, a confrontation among two or three players as a rule. At any game in a gambling house or casino the player's win is the house's loss; the encounter again can become highly personal and each side may, with reason, mistrust and watch the other closely. The bookmaker at the track, in distinction to the parimutuel machine, made a large series of individual bets with players. He took bets on all horses, usually, and tried to adjust the odds so that his loss on the winner would be more than balanced by his winnings from the losers. Such odds could only be approximate; the bookmaker could rarely afford to pay a truly long price, and in any case each transaction remained in the end personal.

With parimutuels, the payoff exactly reflects the state of the betting pool at the final moment before the race. The betting is a collective transaction among all the players; the individual, in a quite impersonal way, competes with the rest of the public.

Curiously, Oller wrought so well with his invention that in principle it has not been changed in a hundred years. The manager of the mutuel system at any American track today could have journeyed to Longchamps, in the Bois de Boulogne of Paris, in the fall of 1872 and immediately taken charge of Oller's wagon, a large ticket booth on wheels. The physical properties of the parimutuel system have changed, but only to take advantage of mechanical and later electronic calculating systems, so that the fluctuating odds on each horse can be shown at short intervals until post time and the payoff can be ready within a few minutes after the running of the race. The modern system in the United States conducts separate place and show pools. A place ticket pays off if the horse selected finishes either first or second. What is left of the pool, after the takeout (the modern and rather higher equivalent of Oller's commission) and the amounts bet on the first two horses are subtracted, is divided equally among the holders of tickets on the two horses. That is, the ticket holder gets back his own stake and his share of 50 percent of the profit. In a similar way, a show ticket pays off if the horse finishes first, second, or third. After the cuts from the top of the pool, the profit is divided by three. Necessarily, odds drop rapidly to place and even more drastically to show. Special pools, each separate from the rest, may be conducted for daily double, quinella, or exacta betting, and trifectas.* In every case, without exception, each pool is operated exactly along the lines laid out by Oller.

Oller's invention took root in countries throughout the world within ten years after he first sold mutuel tickets to the horseplayers of Paris. In the United States, in 1877, the parimutuel machines invaded the territory of the bookies at Jerome Park and Morris Park in New York. But the bookies already had close connections with track managements, wherever horses ran in America. The bookmakers succeeded in having the betting machines quietly removed from those tracks that experimented with them. The machines were stored in warehouses and, for the time being, forgotten.

The parimutuel machines might have moldered in the warehouse dust, until their very function was lost, except for a

---

*These are all forms of betting in which the player buys a single ticket designating two or more horses. In the daily double he buys a ticket selecting the winners of each of two races. In an exacta (or perfecta) he selects the winner and second horse, in correct order, in a single race; where the two horses may finish in either order, the ticket is a quinella. In the trifecta the player's ticket, to pay off, must designate the first three finishers in proper order.

calamity that threatened to wipe out racing altogether. The calamity was reform.

By 1900, after thirty-five years of post–Civil War industrial expansion, easy money, and steady infestation of crookedness in all branches of government, something of a reform movement took shape nationally. Some reformers recognized that crimes were committed for profit, against immigrant girls in sweatshops and pale children in coal mines and textile mills. Others strove to throw rascals out of city halls and to break up crime rings that bound together professional crooks and policemen. A few brave women, as late as the years of World War I, still had to lead a fight—unbelievable as it might seem half a century later—for women's right to vote at all. Still other waves of the reform movement did battle against giant industrial monopolies, and respectable business lawyers like Charles Evans Hughes investigated thievery in the insurance industry. And finally, since goodness and righteousness were much confused, early and late, with the Protestant Ethic and the patrolling of the inner borders of men's minds, one great wave of do-good broke over any game or sport that promised a moment of ease or comfort or release from the bleakness of honest toil.

Was man to be liberated from political bosses? Let him also be freed, whether he wished it or not, from cigars, booze, gambling, or whatever else gave him an unnatural degree of pleasure. A few of the clearest-eyed reformers—Lincoln Steffens, for one, on his way from muckraking to the study of revolution—saw the inherent contradiction between movements for liberation and repression. Most people did not, and racing, through a by-product of the improvement of the political breed, faced destruction.

By 1900, when the reform movement was in full bloom, bookmakers and track management were generally in league. In many places the sport was corrupt. Political reformers struck at it through the only betting mechanism it then had—private bookmaking.

The same Charles Evans Hughes who investigated the insurance business, and soon after won the governorship of New York, in 1908 sponsored a bill which temporarily brought racing to a stop in New York State—then, as now, the pivot of organized racing in America. The law shrewdly enough did not bar horse races as such. It simply prohibited betting. Similar laws were passed in other states.

The hold of the bookmaker as a result was permanently loosened from American tracks. The private handbook persisted, as a matter of course, and still does. But the bookie was never again the official instrument of betting at tracks (except for a period of a few years in New York itself). Racing did persist, and eventually it revived. Curiously, what made the revival possible was the use of parimutuel betting machines. They in turn had a chance to operate only because bookies were outlawed.

The turning point came in Kentucky in the critical year 1908. Churchill Downs a few years before had already been losing ground as a business organization. The directors persuaded Matt J. Winn, then in his early middle age, to take on the job of manager. Winn was, by his own description, a successful "merchant tailor" with no previous connection with horses except that he had grown up in Louisville and was an earnest horseplayer.

The crisis for Winn and Churchill Downs—a piece of the crisis facing all of racing in America—came about with the loss of a city election. As Winn described it in his memoirs through the voice of his ghost, Frank G. Menke, a new crowd in Louisville's city hall seized on betting as the weapon for striking at Churchill Downs. They declared bookmaking illegal. Bookies at that point held a monopoly on all betting at the track. No bookies, no betting, no racing.

Winn and the rest of the Churchill Downs directorate searched desperately for some legal way to allow the public to back opinions about horse races with money. They tried and rejected the old-fashioned idea of auction pools. Then they came upon "French pools," a term from the 1870s, which stood for—Pierre Oller's machinery for parimutuel betting. City Hall declared the French pools illegal, too. Winn and his fellows persisted in their search of the law. To their amazement and delight, they unearthed a thirty-year-old amendment to Louisville's gambling law, passed in 1878, which said specifically: "This act [forbidding use of machinery or contrivances for betting] shall not apply to persons who may sell combination, or French pools, on any regular race track during the races thereon." Evidently, during those first years when Oller's machines were tried out on a few American tracks, before the bookmakers succeeded in getting them thrown out, someone, long forgotten, had persuaded city government in Louisville to legalize their use. A fight over the amendment of 1878 was carried to the Kentucky courts. Churchill Downs won its case, and American racing had found a way out of the entanglement of blue laws.

Winn still had to find bank note paper that might hinder counterfeiters. Above all, he had to locate some of the original Oller machines, for use until new equipment could be devised. One genuine Oller antique, rusty and broken, was found in a Churchill Downs storeroom. Another was hauled from the back of a pawnshop. Eventually, search of warehouses from Kentucky to New York yielded six machines that could be put in working order. Parimutuel betting was installed in time for the Kentucky Derby of 1908. The system handled $67,570 in total bets that day, with $18,300 in wagers on the Derby itself. A long shot, the bay colt Stone Street, by Longstreet, won the race, at odds of 23.72 to 1—the betting machines having permitted precise reckoning of odds for the first time. Management and plungers alike went home happy. Winn admitted later that he expected the parimutuels to give racing merely a year's emergency relief. In fact, they remained permanently at Churchill Downs and, in the end, took over at all American tracks.

Following the lead of Matt Winn and the Kentucky courts, legalization came about very slowly, a state at a time, and then accelerated rapidly during the depression of the 1930s. Legislators searched frankly and hungrily for new sources of revenue. A public that was prepared finally to forgo the hypocrisy of prohibition of liquor could at least look aside as racetrack promoters put through bills legalizing racing. A few states experimented briefly with legalized forms of bookmaking. By 1940 all tracks were using the parimutuel system.

The effects of the transformation are still unfolding. Most obviously, parimutuel betting permitted a vast expansion of racing and Thoroughbred breeding. The number of tracks sanctioned by the state racing commissions never again came to much more than a third of the 350 or so which had spread about the country, like mushrooms after a rain, around 1900. But the number of people going to tracks, and the amounts of money they bet, swelled from year to year. By the 1970s admissions to racetracks totaled more than 70 million per year. The amounts wagered passed the $7 billion mark. Revenue to government came to more than a half a billion dollars. Except for single, highly publicized events like the Kentucky Derby, racetracks generally drew crowds far smaller than, say, the numbers at professional football games. But the major racing states, by the 1970s, were allowing several hundred racing days each. A constant horseplayer could, if he wished and if his skill or his bankroll permitted, go to the track as regularly as a businessman to his office.

The breeding industry also expanded in the 1950s and 1960s, directly in proportion to the swelling of racetrack crowds and parimutuel betting. A nine-million-dollar syndication of a successful racer, before he has been tried at stud, rests on a solid base of purse money—generated in turn out of the horsemen's cut from the parimutuel pool.

As a final bit of irony, parimutuel betting, in some measure at least, also helped the surviving bookmakers, including those who operate outside the law. They pay off at track odds, set through the mutuel machines by the crowd. If they hold too much on one horse, they can send it back to the track to be bet there and depress the odds.

A grandstand or amphitheater superficially appears to be a contrivance for seating spectators. Most structures, though, contain inner depths never seen by the public. At a racetrack part of the space within the stands serves for betting enclosures. Horseplayers see the faces of mutuel clerks through long rows of sellers' and cashiers' windows. Behind the clerks lies another, hidden part of the grandstand, and this the players never see at all.

On a racing day at Golden Gate Fields, on the eastern shore of San Francisco Bay, Kermit Henderson, the manager of the mutuel department, takes a last look at the morning sky as he crosses the parking lot behind the stands. Then he enters a labyrinth of passages leading to his own office. He will not see the sky again until evening—except for momentary glimpses,

when he is out among the customers, inspecting the movement of lines at windows, and then he is too engrossed to
notice.

His office is small enough to be well filled by a desk, a couple
of chairs, and some shelving. Not only does it have no windows,
it is at least two layers away from any part of the grandstand
which does have windows. The office could easily be converted
into a vault, and that is appropriate enough, because it is the
nerve center of a financial operation of surprising size and
complexity.

On the desk awaiting Henderson are some sheets of computer printout and several large manila paper–wrapped pack-
ages full of cashed mutuel tickets. The printout charts the
flow of money into the track. It breaks down the numbers of
tickets sold, by denominations and types, at each window at
the track, on the preceding racing day. Most of the tickets, the
losers, were torn or otherwise thrown away, until, at day's end,
all floor space at the track was littered with them. The winning
tickets made their way, via the cashiers' windows, where they
were exchanged for money, into the package on Henderson's
desk. And some appeared to vanish.

"The number of cashed tickets never exactly equals the
number sold," Henderson said in the course of one spring
morning at Golden Gate. "Some tickets never get cashed. Or
some people want to get a quick start for home, and they may
hold on to winning tickets for days before coming back to cash
them."

Henderson is a slim man of middle height, with the hands of
an expert card dealer or musician. He is, in fact, something of a
musician, and he was an expert mutuel clerk before he became
department manager. A good mutuel clerk is, above all, a person with manual dexterity. Alone among the men in his department, Henderson wears a business suit and tie. He would
not look out of place on the officers' platform in a bank in one of
the suburban towns along the San Francisco peninsula where
he lives. The rest of the mutuel department dress for comfort.
Their work is nerve-racking. It must be done fast and with
remarkable accuracy.

For the thousands of players at a track, the least slowdown by
the clerks, or diversion of their attention, makes a thundering

difference. The lines at the ticket sellers' windows slowly shuffle forward. As post time nears, muttering begins. In the last seconds people yell, "Hurry up! Don't take all day!" Inevitably, before most races, a few last-minute gamblers are left standing at the moment the starting gates, out on the track, fly open at the starter's signal. Nearly simultaneously, or at most a few seconds later, every ticket-selling machine in the stands locks. At most tracks the chief steward, in a booth high on the roof of the grandstand directly above the finish line, has pressed a single button locking the machines. The bettors left stranded with currency unspent groan and rush back to the track to watch the race, which will be run without their help. As a matter of course, a large number of them would have backed losing horses. They have therefore saved money, but the ones you hear from after the race approach you with pain in their faces, indignation in their voices, saying, "Did you have that one? I had the winner but I got shut out."

Remarkably few do get shut out and the reason for that is the skill of the clerks and the care with which the mutuel manager distributes his force among windows. Nine times on a racing afternoon the ticket sellers, working smoothly, without flurry and with absolute concentration, must accommodate as many bettors as possible. The cashiers, counting out bills to pay off the winners after races, have no fixed deadline, but they too must concentrate perfectly.* Neither sellers nor cashiers can afford a single error. As a condition of employment, they have signed a clear statement assuming full liability for any mistakes made at their windows. Has the seller punched the wrong key by mistake? If the bettor rejects the ticket, the seller must keep it and make good its price. He may sometimes involuntarily catch a winner that way, but rarely indeed. Has the clerk, whether as seller or cashier, made a mistake in counting bills? Again he takes full responsibility.

In the view of racetrack people, an average bank teller, protected several times over by special bonding and the bank's insurance policies, would flounder hopelessly in the tougher world of parimutuel betting.

*Advanced-technology ticket selling systems were under study in 1978 and 1979; they promised some conveniences and possible labor savings, without changing the basics of parimutuel betting.

Always in the background, with so many people handling such large amounts of pure, undiluted, untraceable cash, is the question of policing the cash flow. Every employee is cleared by a state horse racing board or commission, as a condition of employment. Bonding covers the clerks as a whole. Bundles of money are constantly counted and checked as they flow between windows and money room. The basic control comes from the ticket machines themselves, tied together electronically into a single computer system which not only punches out tickets at the customers' order and computes odds for every horse in the mutuel pool every ninety seconds, but also records the exact amounts taken in, for each race, at each window, for tickets of each kind and every denomination.

A related problem is betting by clerks. Supposedly, they do not bet. No one assumes that they can be kept from betting, if they choose to do so. The air at the track crackles with the prospects of gambling. Any conversation, from parking lot, to a sandwich stand, to press box, to steward's booth, to the track physician's infirmary, to the general manager's office, may contain some reference to bets made, won, or lost. The mutuel clerk in effect makes a bet, whether he wants to or not, whenever he punches a wrong key. Most track managements, therefore, without fuss or public declaration, follow a rule of tolerance and good sense: The clerks may not allow betting to interfere with their duties.

More subtle, and more serious, is the possibility of collusion between clerks and players. An experienced clerk in the course of time comes to know many of the bettors; others may approach him to learn what the most astute players are doing. Or clerks may be approached by bookmakers' rings. Tracks know that such things can happen. They watch for them. Evidently, they prevent them for the most part. When, in June 1973, five mutuel clerks and a saloon owner were arrested in Los Angeles and charged with operating an illegal betting ring at the Southern California tracks, the case had been at least a year and a half in preparation by the FBI. The case was also a genuine rarity. The six were said to have booked bets without recourse to the parimutuel machinery, thereby appropriating the 16 percent takeout for themselves. As an added service to their own patrons, they allegedly secretly handled "IRS tickets"—winning tickets, generally on exactas or daily doubles, where the payoff is at a rate of 300 to 1 or more. These high-payoff bets at the time were the only ones at the track for which winners had to show Social Security cards before cashing their tickets, and the track reported the winnings to the Internal Revenue Service. Obviously, most winnings at the track cannot be recorded.

If the track must worry about the conduct of its own people, it must also, in the pleasantest way possible, contend with its public. Bettors naturally try to win bets on horses, but some of them try to make the mutuel system work for them no matter what horse wins. At the kindergarten level the cashier must be alert for non-winning tickets mixed in among genuine winners—whether by mistake in the happy confusion of collecting on a winner or by design to extract a bonus from the money machine. At the graduate level the tracks, and behind them the companies that make and install the machines, have constantly to guard against counterfeits of winning tickets. American Totalizator Company, a subsidiary of General Instrument Corporation, operates the tote boards and calculating systems at most American tracks. It also provides the mutuel tickets, and strives mightily to make them as nearly counterfeit-proof as possible. The company uses special paper, with special printing devices, including weird, randomly arranged symbols that change for every race. Even so, the counterfeiters never stop trying. They lavish vast amounts of effort on their own product, and the tussle never ends.

The ultimate threat to the money machine, which always looms in the background though it has nearly always been fended off, is outright assault and robbery. No track management or the police force with which it works will give the details of its defensive alignment. All will acknowledge, sometimes reluctantly as if it were bad luck to talk about such matters, that preparations have been made and that they may well be called massive. It is a fact, obvious to anyone with an eye for larceny who happens to go racing, that the money machine accumulates rather staggering volumes of currency. A track of average size and no very great handle must count, stack, and transport some millions of dollars, purely in currency, every week. No bank adjacent to a track has anything like such amounts of cash on hand.

Each day at a track, during a racing meeting, begins before daybreak with grooms working with horses in the stable area. The day proceeds through morning works on the track. Later in the morning cleaning crews move slowly through the stands, picking up the leavings from the day before. By noon the mutuel clerks are assembling for work and the first customers are straggling into the stands. Then, for more than four hours of racing, perhaps eighty or ninety Thoroughbreds and their riders, and trainers and owners, and supporters in the stands, will have struggled and hoped and exulted or despaired. And at the end, at sundown, with the horses back in the barns and most of the people long gone, the distillate of all the effort remains behind in the form of a great pile of more than a million dollars, covering a table to a height of more than a foot, in sacks and cans of coin and great bundles of bills, counted, sorted, and labeled, in denominations from $1 to $100.

Leaving Golden Gate Fields one afternoon, I saw an old man standing beside an exit road leading from a parking lot. It requires a serious effort of will to pull off to the side of the road when cars are oozing forward and struggling for the right to join the freeway traffic jam. I did stop, though, and as he slowly, painfully, clambered in I understood my impulse better. He was small, almost as if recently shrunk, so that his bright-colored, nearly new sport jacket seemed two sizes too large for him. His old man's trousers draped around him and sagged to the ground. His head was round and nearly bald and appeared to roll loosely on his shoulders, as if he lacked the physical strength to hold it firm.

He was glad to be picked up, but not effusive. I thought it was a fair bet that he could not walk another hundred yards, yet he seemed placid enough and content. He had made his way to the track at midday by public transportation: a Greyhound bus ride from San Mateo, where he lived, to San Francisco; a ride on a municipal bus across downtown to still another bus station; a third ride, on a racetrack special, to Golden Gate. Altogether, the trip must have taken nearly two hours and would have been tiring as well as boring for a younger and healthier man.

It occurred to me this man must be among the most devoted followers of racing. We talked, and it appeared that he did indeed love the track and had gone frequently, but casually, through most of his life.

"My name is Mr. Joseph O'Hanlon," he told me, and he drew his coat about him with a touch of formality. He had worked in the office of a San Francisco judge until he was forced to retire. Yes, he still tried to come to the track a couple of days a week, most often toward the beginning of the month, when he still had his pension money. On some of the other days his wife took him to the Veterans Hospital in Palo Alto. I had noticed a tremor in his hand. He said he was being treated with something called "dopey."

Remembering a term from another connection, I asked if he had said "L-dopa."

He looked at me sharply and said, "That's right. That's what I said. Dopey."

We talked about racing. He mentioned things and places from a past I found attractive: betting commissioners off Market Street, and poker parlors, and the Bay City Grill and other places to eat. It seemed to me I should not let a source of racing knowledge go untapped. I ventured to ask O'Hanlon about his own approach to handicapping.

"I don't have no approach to handicapping."

"I mean, what do you look for in the past performances, in the *Form*?"

"I don't look for nothing in the *Form*. I don't have one." In truth, he was not carrying a *Daily Racing Form* or any other paper.

"If I may ask, what do you do?"

"I just watch the board," O'Hanlon said. "When they bet a lot, I bet a little, too."

I considered this, and risked one more question: "Can you win doing that?"

"Oh, no," he said, and he smiled cheerfully. "Mostly I lose. And I never win much."

He sat back at his ease, in the depths of his coat, swaying gently with the motion of the car. I took him to his building in

San Mateo. He lurched dangerously as he got out, and he staggered away toward his apartment.

A few days later I met an old racing companion named Spinoza at the track and discussed O'Hanlon's system with him. "Can you believe a man goes to the races for forty years and still doesn't look at a *Form*, or anything else except the tote board?" I asked.

"Why not?"

"He knows he'll lose," I said. "Why not pick his own losers?"

"I think you're forgetting something," Spinoza said. "Company. Pick your own and you stand alone. That can be scary. Watch the board. Wait for the big underlays. Catch the horse that was six to one in the morning line, and now it's two to one. You make your bet and you feel you're right in there with the smart money." He paused and then asked mildly' "You never did that?"

Of course I had. So, I imagine, have a majority of horse-players.

The morning line is a forecast, by a pricemaker working for the track, of the odds at which each horse is likely to go off. Morning-line odds appear in the official program. If the tide of sentiment in the crowd pushes the odds on a horse below the morning line, he becomes an underlay. When the crowd so neglects a horse that his odds rise above the morning line, he is an overlay.

The terms "underlay" and "overlay" can also be used in connection with the odds set by a skilled handicapper for himself. A handicapper likes a horse. He puts it on top of its field, with about a 35 percent chance of winning the race. The crowd has somewhat overlooked the horse; at post time the board says a ticket on the horse will pay 5–1 if he wins. The handicapper regards that horse as a distinct overlay—and an excellent bet. The winning horseplayer seeks the true overlay as earnestly as a crusader searching for a piece of the true cross.

Underlays and overlays reflect the fact that betting at the racetrack is a public act. A bettor must walk to a seller's window, in plain sight of other people, to buy a ticket. Effects of the sale of tickets are seen, within a minute or two, by everyone in the park, whenever the odds change. When the odds on a horse begin to drop—O'Hanlon's signal for a bet—a buzz of conversation goes up all over the grandstand. The same question is asked a thousand times over: Did someone know something? As the odds continue to drop, the attractiveness of an underlay can be powerful. Of course, a drop in odds on one horse in the parimutuel system means a rise in the odds on another. And now the market swings. The horse with rising odds may become just attractive enough to coax a bet from a bettor who liked his chances anyway.

The tote board is one of the basic ingredients of the world of the horseplayer. It is evidently also used as a tool, or substitute, for handicapping by players like Mr. Joseph O'Hanlon. For such players, a few rules of the game may make tote board watching more useful.

1. Following the betting action helps most if the player has done his homework and has already arrived at an opinion about the horses in the field. An unexpected show of action on the board may force him to take another look at a horse he has scanted.

2. Conversely, the board is most dangerous for people who have not done, or cannot do, their own handicapping. People who bet mainly on the basis of betting action seen on the tote board lose, generally heavily.

3. Unusual early action is at least interesting. Late action is largely something to talk about. There is no evidence that the late money is smart money, but even if there were, how can the player expect not to get shut out at the window if he waits for the last tote board clues?

4. A number of systems for interpreting the signs on the board may be had—for a price. All involve a double guess: Who made the bets that seem to signal action; and just how smart is the unknown signaler and what does he really know? The cost of guessing games runs high.

5. None of this says not to watch the board. To the contrary: all skilled players watch the board, all the time, sometimes without thinking about it. The board influences the best of players at least to the extent of making them ask themselves, Have I found an overlay? Am I getting a square price on the

horse I like? And, have I overlooked something about another horse?

6. Most horseplayers of any experience know that the morning line does not set out to pick winners but only tries to predict how the crowd will bet. Some players, though, then proceed to forget something which should be equally obvious: A morning line, for any use at all, is no better than the pricemaker who calculates it. The pricemaker, by the way, is not the track's official handicapper. That person is the racing secretary, who, among many other duties, assigns weights for horses entered in the relatively small number of handicap stakes. Among the scores of pricemakers whose morning lines appear in track programs, some are excellent, some abysmal. The player must decide for himself whether the morning line at his own track is well or poorly done.

A STATISTICAL NOTE

Readers allergic to numbers are invited to skip over this chapter with a glance at the final paragraph. I say this out of regard for my fellows, not to slight the chapter. Actually, the matter covered seems to me important. It states that the parimutuel machine makes it possible for some horseplayers to be winners. It tries to demonstrate this with statistics drawn from parimutuel operations.

The key points here are: (1) a horse race is not a random event (it is not like the spin of a roulette wheel); and (2) the player bets against other players, not against the house. In a house game (blackjack, roulette, craps, and the like) everyone, including you, must lose in the long run. Winnings at a casino come from the house. The house makes the rules. You may therefore count on the house to win more than you do, in the long run.

Winnings at the track come from other players. At the track, most players must lose; more goes into the pool than comes out, since the pool is cut from the top. But you do not have to be among the losers.

If you wish to see the reason for hope, visualize a parimutuel pool in which the bettors, as a group, get back everything they put in, without any cut from the top. In 1973 New York took $75 million out of the mutuels from Thoroughbred racing in that state. Suppose, now, that an oil sheik, as a fitting monument to Mr. Darley's Arabian, handed over $75 million to the state, saying, "Let the players enjoy themselves. For one year, do not cut the mutuel pool."

Overlook the consequences this rash act might have in oil markets or on traffic around Belmont and Aqueduct. Accept what seems to me obvious, that chance alone does not determine the winner of a horse race (simplest demonstration: favorites make up about 10 percent of horses, about a third of winners). Since judgment thus enters into selection of winners, make one last stipulation: some people have more or better judgment, some have less. It then follows to a certainty that after a year of operation of the Darley's Arabian Memorial Fund, the players would have sorted themselves into three groups: those who finished the year clearly ahead, those who just about broke even, and those who clearly lost. The more able selectors would have won their year-long contest with the poor selectors. Since all the money in this generously operated pool returned to the bettors, the winners would not only have won more than their share; they would have shown a clear profit. The losers, lacking for once the comfort of a large majority, might finally quit the game, thus bringing about the ruin of horse racing—but then any competent loser can find excuses for at least a year at the races.

The crucial question is how much must the pot be cut from the top (thus driving down average payoffs) before the winners can no longer show a profit? A takeout of only 3 percent, say, would surely bother very few. A takeout of 50 percent (if a horseplayer can allow himself to imagine a state that greedy) just as certainly must put an end to winners.

It is my contention that with a takeout of 17 percent (an average of what states, in 1978, were taking from mutuel pools for their own revenues, purse money, and track managements), while many players grumble, a rather small group of winners have not yet been wiped out.

The first evidence (not proof) that winners still survive the 17 percent takeout is a simple observation: no one I know of has reported any falling off among the racetrack regulars during the last five years. Bill Veeck, the sports promoter who ran Suffolk Downs in Massachusetts for a couple of years, made this observation, I think accurately. Veeck was in racing only two years. He did not claim to be an expert on parimutuel betting. But he is a shrewd judge of crowds at sporting events. He said in his book *30 Tons a Day* (written with Ed Linn):

> Roughly speaking, the fans [at a racetrack] break down into two basic types, the racing aficionados and the general run of sport fan. . . . At the very top of the aficionado list you have to place the winner. For despite mythology that all horseplayers die broke, it just ain't so. . . . I like to wander around the stands and talk to the people I saw there every day, and I can tell you that there is a surprisingly large cadre who follow the races from track to track—following the sun, as it were—and make a very, very good living. They all did it the same way. With a cold, businesslike approach to betting.

Such observations may be strongly suggestive, but they do not constitute proof. At best, a scrupulous observer can only certify a handful of players he knows, from the closest observation, to be consistent winners.

In a strict sense, statistical proof that some players win consistently is impossible. Proof will remain impossible until something like a thousand skilled players, in several parts of the country, agree to keep detailed records of their betting and to turn these over to an umpire. I suppose they would also have to be shadowed, to make sure they do not sneak off and make other bets in secret. Since I do not expect to see this happy experiment performed, I have done what I can to squeeze some answers from known facts about parimutuel pools. Curiously, while the facts are scarce, they all point in the same direction: toward the probability of a number of consistent winners, over the long haul, in a parimutuel pool.

The starting point is a commonplace device in elementary statistics, a frequency distribution. This is an arrangement of a large number of items (a universe) grouped in numerical order, according to some important quality or characteristic. Thus all army recruits might be grouped according to weight.

And it might be found that the largest number clustered around some midpoint, or average—say, around 150 or 160 pounds, with small numbers in the groups at either extreme. Very few, for example, would be found to weigh more than 250 pounds or less than 100 pounds.

Imagine, then, a frequency distribution of horseplayers grouped according to the percentage of the total bets which they won or lost. To be sure, most of the true numbers are unknown. So we have to deduce them and test the results by how much sense they make (something known as "model" building, in technical jargon).

The midpoint in the horseplayers' distribution is known. It is minus 17 percent, representing the average loss, of an average player, in the long run. If the distribution is anything like normal, the greatest number of cases will cluster around the center, at −17 percent (calculated as a loss on the total of all bets made by the player). At one extreme, the scale might approach −100 percent, representing those unfortunates who lost all they were ever able to bet. At the other end, the scale will include those players who lost less than the average, and may even have won.

To fill in gaps along the scale, a number of assumptions must be made. So far as I can see, they do not bias the results.

1. I have assumed that all players bet the same amounts. This is obviously not true, but it simplifies the analysis and I think it makes little difference. (Among other things, players who go to the $100 and $50 windows are no more likely to be winners than $10 bettors.)

2. Also for the sake of simplicity, my model embraces all players covered by the same parimutuel system, with all players staying in the game long enough to iron out the role of pure chance (presumably a year or more). Each player is assumed to follow his own style of betting consistently. Again, the last assumption is unrealistic, but I do not think it produces a bias.

3. Finally, and most important, I assume that horseplayers' winnings and losses conform to a normal or "bell-shaped" curve of distribution. Statisticians I have discussed this with agree with me. It is the *kind* of distribution which produces a normal curve. I can see some reason to expect it to be somewhat lopsided, or "skewed," but no more so, say, than curves of

income distribution, or shoe sizes of army recruits, or school test scores.

Three key facts about the parimutuel pool are well known:

1. Favorite players, if they bet all favorites or a random selection of favorites, and nothing else, lose about 10 percent of the total amount they wager.

2. From the average prices paid by winning favorites at most tracks, it may be deduced that favorite players contribute a little less than a third, on the average, to the total mutuel pool.

3. A loss of 17 percent must be the midpoint of the model distribution if the curve is anything like normal.

One deduction of crucial importance emerges immediately from these few numbers. If roughly three out of ten players (those who play favorites) lose only 10 percent of their total bet, and the average loss is 17 percent (or the amount of the takeout), then it follows as the day the night that *some considerable number of players must lose more than 17 percent.* They sit and stew and consult the *Form* and tout sheets, and proceed systematically to lose more than the legendary little old lady who stabs at her program at random with a hat pin. As a matter of fact, if the distribution is indeed normal, then roughly three out of ten lose about 25 percent of the sum of all their wagers, thus keeping the curve symmetrical.

The second major step in the analysis is to visualize which players contribute, and how much each group contributes, to the 17 percent takeout. Assume the mutuel pool embraces 10,000 players and each bets one unit over the year (a unit can be anything you wish: a year's wages, a small farm, many quarts of life blood; I simply wish to equate each player with one unit bet). If 10,000 units are bet, the takeout accounts for 1,700 units.

Of the 1,700 units of takeout, the favorite players in any distribution will contribute 300 units. They constitute 30 percent of the players, therefore bought 30 percent of the tickets, or 3,000 units, and, since they lost 10 percent of their total wagered, made a contribution of 300 to the takeout.

Conceivably (though I believe this is false), no one loses less than the favorite players, and in that case there can be no winners. The takeout might then be composed as follows: 300 from the favorite players; 731 from the average losers, if they amounted to 43 percent of all players; and 675 from the heavier losers, if indeed no group lost more than 25 percent on the average and those losers accounted for the remaining 27 percent of the players. The takeout would thus equal 1,706, and the same total could be arrived at with minor variations with similar arrangements.

But this pattern has at least one fatal flaw. I can introduce one more valid number, based on study of charts of results from several tracks over a period of four years. Some players *lose more than 25 percent.* In another chapter (on money management) I cite extensive workouts based on results from betting solely and indiscriminately on leading jockeys, and also from betting on the longest shots in each field. All these workouts registered losses in the range of 30 to 40 percent. The same exercises (and the experience of horseplayers) make it reasonable to assume that the extreme losers (showing a loss of around 35 percent and more of the total bet) amount to about 10 percent of all players.

Making allowance for the heaviest losers leads to the final conclusion, and the most important of all: it demonstrates the presence of a small group who actually finish ahead. The whole takeout is now accounted for by roughly 90 percent of the total players in the pool. Any number of combinations are possible, but they all add up to about the same result. For example: favorite players, 30 percent of the pool, with an average loss of 10 percent, contribute 300 to the takeout of 1,700; average or random losers, if they happen to represent 20 percent of the pool, contribute 17 percent of their total bet, or 340; heavier losers, 30 percent of the pool (to correspond, symmetrically, to the favorite players), lose 25 percent of their total bet and thus contribute 750 to the takeout; and the heaviest losers, 10 percent of the pool, with an average loss of 35 percent, make a contribution of 350. These contributions then add up as follows: 300 + 340 + 750 + 350 = 1,740. But the number of players contributing adds up to less than the total of 10,000: 3,000 + 2,000 + 3,000 + 1,000 = 9,000. The remaining 1,000 players contribute nothing at all to the takeout. That is to say, they lose nothing. In fact, they gather in the slight balance of 40 in their favor.

Thus a group of 10 percent of all players at least breaks even.

And, consistent with the rest of the distribution, assuming that this 10 percent divides into more and less successful halves, its more successful half—5 percent of all players— actually shows profits, ranging from modest to downright generous.

Anyone sufficiently interested can experiment with other variations in this arithmetic exercise. Given the premises, they will all show a small group of winners. The exercise is far from proof, but it seems strongly suggestive, based on what is known about the parimutuel pool.

One or two long-term winners out of every twenty players may seem a small number. To me, it seems substantial enough to demonstrate that Thoroughbred racing is indeed unique among all forms of organized public gambling.

TWO

Tools of the Handicapper's Craft

ABOUT HANDICAPPING

The parimutuel system, uniquely among the forms of public gambling, rewards judgment. Still it is merely glib to say the best horseplayers win because they have the best judgment (or, as we say at the track, because they have a good opinion). It is something else to describe how they arrive at a better judgment.

The basis of a horseplayer's judgment is handicapping—a craft halfway between art and science.

Some experts on racing write as if handicapping alone makes winners. This sadly misleads the unwary. In later chapters I will try to demonstrate why qualities of character and personal discipline are just as important. And the ultimate secret is to make probabilities work for you. Without doubt, though, handicapping lays the foundation for winning.

The principles of handicapping are old. Just how old, no one can say. It is certain that Pittsburgh Phil (a historical, not a legendary, figure), around the turn of the century, used many of the handicapping ideas in vogue today. But the art has grown. The principles can better be put in words. And, most important of all, it is possible, with some effort, to go behind the principles, to tell *why* they work and even *when* they are most likely to work and when they probably will not. In short, it is possible to show how the master player uses handicapping principles—which is to say, intelligently and with due respect for the equalizing injustices of luck.

I myself must have seen in writing, or heard, more than a hundred handicapping rules. These, stated baldly and taken one at a time or in clusters, make up the handicapping systems that are sold with promises of quick wealth. In that form they are largely frauds. They are copper bracelets for the arthritis of greed.

If the rules are traced back to principles, and if the principles are studied in depth and with an eye to exceptions, the methods of winning players begin to emerge—and can be followed.

THE INVISIBLE DIMENSION

The handicapper at the racetrack confronts a world with an invisible fourth dimension, not dreamed of in Professor Einstein's philosophy. The invisible dimension consists of matter that fills the air at the track and passes for information—a wild mixture of hard fact, spongy fact, and the stuff that dreams are made of. It surrounds the player at all times. He breathes it. He struggles with it. He uses it if he is able, and if he is unlucky he is swamped by it. But like it or not, information is the necessary starting point. The handicapper will use information as the seedbed in which he grows a crop of bettable opinions.

By far the most important source of information for horseplayers is the *Daily Racing Form*. Breeders, trainers, owners, officials, and bettors: all, alike, use it as their trade paper. For some it is the only paper they look at; the *Form* makes a bow in their direction by inserting, in its first few pages, a few capsules of general news. When a broker or banker refers to "the *Journal*," he means, of course, *The Wall Street Journal*, but he probably reads several other business publications, daily and weekly. In the world of horse racing there is only one *Form.*

For the handicapper in particular, by far the most important parts of the *Form* are the past performances. These, without distracting prose, contain a staggering amount of information. The past performances for all the horses entered on one day's program at a single track consist of about 900 lines and a total of between 25,000 and 30,000 bits of information. At least 95 percent of this mass of data comes from the daily charts of races. The charts in turn are the work of a single man, or of his fellows at other tracks. And yet, in spite of the paramount importance of the charts, an overwhelming majority of horseplayers have never heard of the chart maker at their track.

On a fall day at Bay Meadows, I watched a tall young man cross the mezzanine enclosure. He was a pleasant-looking fellow, informally dressed. He conveyed no sense of haste. Certainly, he was not avoiding attention. No one spoke to him, and he spoke to no one as he made his way to an elevator. The people he passed simply did not know who he was. I am reasonably sure that a large majority of those he passed would not have recognized his name.

The man's name is Darryl Hove. He was, at that time, the *Daily Racing Form*'s chart maker for northern California tracks. (He has since become a columnist for the *Form.*) Among other duties, Hove did public handicapping for the *Racing Form* under the name "Trackman." His picks appeared in a box beside those of four other selectors, never identified, who bore such noms-de-course as "Sweep," "Hermis," "Analyst," and "Handicap." Horseplayers with an eye for by-lines might also have noticed that Hove's name appeared over daily articles analyzing races to come. Between reporting, and handicapping or selecting, it might have been supposed that Hove kept himself busy enough. In fact, however, it was his third task—chart making or calling—that was his chief duty.

The chart for a single race, as it will appear in the *Form* a day later, fills a space two columns wide and several inches deep. The condensed version in some metropolitan dailies uses just a quarter of that space. Encoded in the chart is all the information that will ever be recorded officially about the race: conditions for entering the race and distribution of purse money; the weather and the state of the track; times made by the leaders at points along the way (points of call) and by the winner at the finish; and the distances between the horses all along the way. Do you want to know how the bettors regarded each horse's chances? The odds for each entrant are shown, as registered by the totalizator a moment before the race started. You can learn the names of riders, and of owners, the weights carried, age and special equipment for each horse, and the trainer and lineage of the winner. Given, too, are the values of $2 win, place, and show tickets on the first three finishers. At the bottom of each chart comes a narrative putting into words the qualities shown by horses, or the trouble they met, as they advanced or fell back, jostled for place, tired or held on strongly, in the course of the race.

The rules for encoding all this information make up a common language for the racing world. As with any language, time sets the mold. I have looked at a *Racing Form* chart book for 1911. It showed, for some races, much the same information, set forth in much the same way.

From today's charts, each horse's performance is later condensed into one line. About ten such lines, in chronological order, make up one horse's past performance. That is, each line reveals what the horse did in a single race. After each further race a line is dropped, another added. The past performances, grouped for each horse in each race, fill many pages in the *Form*. Here, in numbers and symbols, lies the codified history that the player pores over to decide his bets, that owners and trainers equally intently study to determine the merit and value of a horse. All of it starts with the observations of one man, the chart caller, recorded under pressure, in the time it takes to run the race.

To do his job as a chart maker, Hove had to be at his station, generally in a booth on the grandstand roof, well before first post time. I visited him there. Among all the thousands at the track, only the stewards had as sweeping and Olympian a view.

The 90-odd horses on a single day's card are drawn from perhaps 1,400 stabled at the track. From constant use and familiarization, Hove was able to recognize nearly all the names of the entrants. He remembered something of their records and running styles, and knew some by sight. But now he had to add to his memory in a concentrated way. Perhaps ten minutes before the horses entered the starting gate, he retired into himself as an actor might in learning a part. He held that day's program nearly concealed in a large hand, peered at it intently, muttering under his breath, and memorized the field for the race about to be run. He had to memorize the list of horses by name and number and by the colors of their jockeys' silks.

As an experiment I asked a linguist and a musician, both trained in graduate schools, both obviously able and successful people, to memorize the fields for a single race with eleven horses entered. Neither was a horseplayer. One, the older, needed slightly over twenty minutes to commit the names of eleven horses to memory and to associate with each, correctly, the number that would appear on each horse's saddlecloth. The other needed about twelve minutes. A chart caller would have found both amounts of time hopeless. As a further experiment I asked a horseplayer, also university-trained, to memorize the same list. He was also a chess player of moderate strength. I mention this because chess players often have uncommonly strong memories. He needed five minutes to absorb the list. This, at least, was a nearly feasible amount of time, but in it he had only memorized names and numbers. The jockeys' silks, with their variety of colors, patterns, hoops, bars, and insignia, and the added differences among caps, remained a jumble in his mind. Hove, in about the same time, with no show of exertion, had prepared himself to recognize every horse in the field through his binoculars, at long distance, by the numbers or by the riders' silks, or by whatever clue flashed before his eye. This considerable feat was, of course, being duplicated, equally routinely, by chart callers at every track in the country covered by the *Racing Form* that day.

Now the starter's crew loaded the horses, one and two at a time, into stalls in the starting gate. Hove stepped forward into his booth directly overlooking the track and focused his glasses on the gate. Behind him stood his partner, the chart taker, a slim, quiet young man who had materialized without fuss or waste motion from a corner of the press box. The partner held a clipboard with a sheet of paper, ruled in tabular form, with abbreviations prepared ahead of time for each horse, on which he could write down Hove's calls as fast as he made them.

A quarter of a mile away, at the starting chute for a six-furlong race, the small figure of a man in green work clothes could be seen holding up a bright orange flag. The horses sprang from the gate and Hove began speaking, in a rapid, low-pitched monotone that never ceased until the last horse had crossed the finish line. Contained in Hove's low, almost muttered chant was a recitation of the order in which the horses came out of the gate and then passed each of four points of call along the way to the finish, where his judgment would be confirmed by the evidence of an automatically triggered camera. Five times over he called off the list of horses, by name, in the order in which he saw them. At every point of call, too, he gave the distances separating each horse from the one immediately following.

The average horseplayer, caught up in the emotion of a bet and the excitement of the race, may see only his own horse in the pack charging around the course. The more experienced racegoer tries to see the whole field and can give you, after the race, the highlights of what happened to perhaps half the field all along the way. The chart caller must somehow record on his eyeballs the exact order and gaps among the field several times over, as if they were running, not continuously and very fast in a shifting, surging pack, but on a tape which he stopped and read off at intervals. The distances between horses are given in "lengths," meaning the approximate length of a horse's body in motion (perhaps nine feet in actuality), and in fractions of lengths, down to such small fragments as a "neck," a "head," and a "nose."

Assuming the running order of the horses is captured correctly and called in full detail, the distances separating them can only be approximations—particularly when the gaps are very small or large. The miracle is that they are caught at all. Even the sheer recitation of each item in the call—later to be recorded in the printed chart and stored in the vast warehouse of racing information in the past performances—is difficult enough.

As another experiment I myself tried reading aloud from an existing chart, as rapidly as I could, the names of all the horses in a twelve-horse field, in the order in which they passed each point of call, with the gaps as given in the chart. All I had to do was disentangle the order of the horses at each point. I did not have to stare through glasses at the shifting patterns among a mass of racing horses. After some practice I managed to read aloud a chart for a six-furlong race in a little more than 123 seconds, or, as track language would have it, "two-oh-three and change." The actual time of the winner of the race was 1:11, or 71 seconds. If the chart caller had needed the amount of time it took me to read the chart, he and his partner, the chart taker, would have pieced together a chart by peering dimly backward into history at about the time the leader was returning to the winner's circle to have his picture taken.

The silent partner in chart making, the chart taker, clearly must also perform the writing chore without flaw and in great haste. Darryl Hove's chart taker some of the time was a charming young woman who was trained to help other people learn to write. She was, in fact, Hove's wife, and she held a California high school teacher's certificate. Young teachers, of English and most other subjects in California in the early 1970s, were left stranded by a failure in the baby boom. But Mrs. Hove offered no complaint. She looked out at the world from a racetrack press box with every appearance of pleased surprise and seemed to prefer chart taking to remedial reading courses.

When a race has been run, the noise in the grandstand quiets to a buzz for a few moments while the stewards view a rerun of the race on videotape. Then, except in cases of inquiry, an "official" sign is posted, the mutuel payoff prices go up on the tote board, and the player who is sufficiently interested can watch the rerun on closed-circuit television.

The videotape gives the chart caller his only mechanical support. During the rerun, Hove crouched over a television set in his end of the press box, rough chart in hand, making slight adjustments in his observations. This done, he turned reporter once more. He moved to his typewriter and composed his prose accompaniment to the block of numbers that renders the struggle just completed on the track below: "JUNE'S LOVE raced close up early with little need of urging, responded after being settled into the stretch and wore down PORT OF GLORY to win in full stride. The latter broke alertly to set the pace and gave way late. DOC THOMAS, without early speed, maneuvered in traffic to get clear, then rallied late . . . " The narrative style is as firmly set in mold as if handed down from the storytellers' guild of Homer's time. The anonymous scribe who preserved the running of the first race at Butte, Montana, on August 15, 1911, heard the same rhythm in his ear as he wrote: "ELECTRIC got away flying and simply ran away from the others, winning in a canter. FIRST FASHION, also off quickly, ran in nearest pursuit throughout and held LADY MINT safe . . ."

Chart and accompaniment move along at once by wire to the *Racing Form*. The chart caller for his part can stretch, look at the sea gulls in the infield, compare notes with a press box visitor—and, in a few minutes, prepare once more to record another race.

Can a chart made under such stress accurately catch everything that happened during a race? The answer is, the charts capture a great deal with astonishing accuracy. But, of course, they must err. This is the chance the able handicapper waits for. He hopes to profit by catching for himself the gaps and flaws in the charts used by everyone else.

On one trip to Los Angeles I found myself still mulling over chart making. I was impressed. Making charts seemed to me then, and it still does, a considerable feat. Yet I had to wonder about the horseplayer who uses past performances—derived from charts—as if they were sacred writ, making all sorts of calculations and deductions, some of them ingenious, all assuming the absolute reliability of the small numbers.

Can any chart caller's vision, no matter how sharp or quick, in the least fraction of a second truly measure the distances separating each horse in a field? For that matter, can he invariably record on his eyeballs the exact order in which the horses passed each point of call?

I was thinking about all this on my way to Los Angeles and that day's assembly of horseplayers at Hollywood Park. There I found my friend Edward, the expert handicapper. He sits in a group of argumentative players where no opinion goes unchallenged. Edward uses the voice, accent, and manner of his fellows, but he has an altogether different and, in fact, excellent mind. When I had a chance to talk to him alone, I told him what I had learned about charts. It turned out that he, who had used the *Racing Form* all his adult life, had not known how charts were made.

"That's interesting," Edward said. "Do you remember what I told you about Al Winderman?"

"Who's that?"

"The Brain. I told you about him. He said once—I wish I could remember exactly—but it was something like 'I don't mean to lose a bet on somebody else's typographical error.' "

I was reminded of the great chess master Tartakower, who remarked of the position on the board before a piece has been moved: "All the mistakes are there, waiting to be made."

"That's why Al made his own charts," Edward said. "Or practically did. Harry will remember. We used to sit with the Brain and his people, high in the grandstand, at Belmont, twenty or more years ago. Let's find Harry."

Harry is a mutual friend, a former athlete turned businessman. He is wiry, active, and intense. Among the first-rate handicappers I have met, Harry seeks a long price most avidly. I have seen him bet, and win, on a horse going off at 5 to 2, but his eyes light and he seems to hum when he gets a bet down at 10 to 1 or better. We found him in the clubhouse, pensively looking back and forth between his *Form* and an odds board.

"What was the name of the guy who sat with the Brain and held a stopwatch for him?" Edward asked after we had attracted Harry's attention.

"The Sailor. He had two stopwatches, one in each hand," Harry said, and his eyes drifted back to the odds board.

"Oh, come off it. What's this two stopwatches?"

"You asked me, I told you."

"The other guy, on the other side of him, did he chart the whole race?"

"Just the horses they were interested in, or that caught their eyes." Harry's voice went flat and staccato. "Red wide at three-eighths, blocked by blue at the quarter. Four big move on inside, almost hit rail, took back, Ten came over at eighth pole, green and white going best after finish, Seven pulled up after finish before clubhouse turn, looks spent. That sort of thing. What you read in the charts, but more of it on a few horses. Did you tell him about the pictures?"

"I forgot about that," Edward said. "He had guys all over the stands—"

"Not all over the stands. He had two guys with cameras. One at each end of the stands, for the clubhouse turn and the far turn, and the starts. Great long lenses, both of them."

"And then the photographers would rush out after the races, and develop the pictures and get the prints to the Brain, at home, the same evening," Edward said.

"What did he do with them?" I asked.

Edward and Harry looked at each other.

"Studied them," Harry said.

"Looked for horses in trouble," Edward said.

"Why were they in such a hurry?" I asked. "None of the horses in the pictures was going to run again in less than four to five days—or much longer."

They both shrugged. "That's the way the Brain did things," Edward said. "Coming back with us, Harry?"

"I've got to see a man," Harry said, and we went off in different directions.

As we returned to our seats, I observed to Edward: "I suppose Winderman had a file card on every horse he was following, and maybe that's why he wanted to get the work done each night."

"I don't know," Edward said. "I never asked him, he never told me."

"Must have," I said, "if he was paying a crew for all that information."

I had one more question to ask Edward, but this time he could not help me. I wondered if Al the Brain had his own clockers at early morning workouts. Edward said he himself had only started to watch occasional works since coming to California. He added, "At least they're fun to watch."

In the following months I, too, watched the horses at their early morning exercises at several tracks, from grandstands and on the back side—in the clockers' shed and from the rail itself near the gap where horses enter the track from the stable area. The morning works provide another major source of information to fill the atmosphere at race time.

The backstretch at a racetrack resembles a small town with

perhaps 3,000 inhabitants. Town limits are vague, but they include the far side of the track itself, service buildings and sheds, and enough rows of stables, at many tracks, to house about 1,400 horses. The horses, of course, represent the largest, and most important, and most stable part of the town's population. During a racing meeting they have nowhere else to go. The other inhabitants consist of miscellaneous animal pets, stable ponies, and various humans who come and go but carry on their chief business at the track. This census makes no count of the birds who look over the activities from stable roofs or waddle close up on the ground and are the only creatures who derive an easy living from following the horses.

The broad sandy spaces between stable rows are the town's streets. Rush hour in the stable area starts a little after daybreak and continues until about nine o'clock in the morning. Riders, dressed like ranch hands in jeans and quilted jackets against the cold of dawn but wearing jockeys' protective helmets, guide their horses between the stable rows. Many of the exercise riders are girls with long hair streaming back under their helmets. In front of each stable as the morning goes on, grooms lead out horses who have already exercised and bathe them, steam rising from glistening flanks in the pale early light. The bustle and movement seem random, but actually the horsemen all head toward one point, the gap in the rail, leading onto the track. Near the gap, generally, is the true focus of the morning work, the clockers' shed, with windows along its entire front. Here the clockers sit to watch and time the workouts. The works continue for hours, in an unorganized, hit-or-miss procession. The clockers must somehow produce a record, which ultimately appears in the *Daily Racing Form*, listing horses alphabetically for each distance run that day, with the time for the distance to the fifth of a second and with a notation presumably telling how hard each horse ran.

At some tracks the trainer gives the horse's name and the distance he is to work as he comes through the gap. These facts are then relayed over the loudspeakers. At many tracks, though, the clockers receive no such help. They must go about their job through a welter of confusion thicker than the morning mists. The riders wear no silks. The horses bear no numbers or other insignia. Some of the horses, with exercise riders up, simply gallop around the track for conditioning, without regard to time. Some, riderless, are led onto the track by a mounted trainer and then are ponied around the track at a canter. Hundreds of horses may come onto the track for exercise before the rest of the world has cleaned up from breakfast. Sometimes only eighty or ninety of these run a set distance to be timed. The distances vary—unpredictably. The horses start their timed runs from different points around the track, some from a starting gate for drill, some from a warmup canter as they pass one of the track's main poles. All this happens under the eyes of the clockers, and from it they must produce some sort of order.

Of a few legendary clockers, it is said they knew at sight every fit horse stabled on the grounds. Russell F. Brown, who in his eighties was chief steward at Longacres, was such a one. Most clockers need, and are happy to get, some help along the way.

At Bay Meadows, on a brisk fall morning, Rusty Brundage presided at the windows of a dusty green clockers' shed overlooking the backstretch. Brundage is a stout man who has been watching horses run for more than forty years. He wears a quilted windbreaker and with it a wide-brimmed felt hat that would have looked familiar on the streets of San Francisco in the time of Dashiell Hammett's Sam Spade. The shed itself, which could be an engineer's office on a construction job, seems to date from the same period.

"We rebuilt it some few years ago," Brundage said. "It was full of cracks. My God, how we froze—two electric heaters and they couldn't keep us warm. The wind blew right through. I guess it's still full of wind." Without raising his voice and with no sign of haste, Brundage turned to his assistant, a silver-haired, smaller man sitting beside him at a narrow shelf running the length of the shed's windows. "Who's the bay filly, Bob? She's going with one of Hixon's. I don't know who Hixon's got."

Bob made no immediate answer, but he had already caught the filly on his stopwatch. Both men held watches in one hand, secured by a leather thong around the fingers, at all times. A pencil was always in the other hand and notebooks and work sheets lay before them.

On the track in front of the shed, trainers sat their ponies in a row, at their ease in stock saddles, while the horses exercised on the track. One of the mounted trainers leaned in at a window to say, "We're going to go three-quarters from the gate." Brundage nodded and made a note.

Bob said, "What did I give you on that Offield? Thirty-five and one?"

A horse passed, head down, snorting, tugging at his bit, the rider standing in the stirrups and hauling back on the reins. One of the trainers remarked, "That goddam horse is so ugly he's good-looking. He's a nice colt, too, until that crazy Billy gets on him." Others in the row of riders had been encouraging Billy to make the horse perform. The trainer said, "The colt got him down once and like to stomped him to death."

Bob made a notation and at the same time called out to a woman trainer passing on the track, "What have we got, Kathy?" Kathy replied, "Out Till Dawn." Brundage asked another trainer, "That one of yours, Lefty?" The trainer said, "I got the quarter pole." Another trainer said, "That you on the outside?" Lefty turned to the clockers and said, "I got thirty-eight flat." Bob muttered, "Yeah, I had my split on another horse, the one with the left hind stocking and the narrow stripe, it's one of those new ones of Battles'."

In a pause in the stream of workouts, Brundage showed me his watch. It is a refined piece of apparatus, with a split sweep hand that can be started and stopped separately from the main hand. "With the split, we can catch as many as six horses at the same time."

Bob asked, "What was that one?"

A trainer answered, "Bold Air."

"One word, with an *e* on it, Boldaire?"

"Bold Air. Like the stuff you're breathing."

Bob said, "That horse went in forty-seven and one. That ought to be worth a stall. I had six horses on my split that time. The last was forty-nine and one."

A slim girl rider passed, startlingly good-looking, hair blowing behind, Diana mounted in the early light. No one made any comment about her. I asked if girl riders had less trouble than men in making weight. "They're pretty heavy in the can, some of them," Rusty said. "Weigh more than you think—and more than they say." A woman trainer galloped by, working a stakes winner named Big Jess. A little later she passed again, ponying another of her horses. Brundage noted with approval, "She works hard, that woman."

A trainer leaned in at the window to ask his horse's time. "A minute and a fifth," Bob said. The trainer stared at him and moved away. Under his breath Bob said, "Don't look at me, Jack. I didn't ride him."

Brundage said, "Get that one out of the gate, Bob. I think it's a quarter horse."

"Yes. He came out of there bouncing. He's pulling up already. I made it eleven-six."

Inside the shed men contemplated the past performances in that day's *Form*. Under the windows two of the trainers, mounted on their ponies while the racers galloped, also examined the *Form*. An elderly trainer, who earlier had complained that an ineligible horse had crept into the entries, returned from the racing secretary's office to say he'd had the horse declared out of the race.

A man said, "If you'd been second to him, you'd have got the pot. Did you ever think of that?"

The elderly trainer shrugged and said, slowly and unconvincingly, "Yeah, I thought of that."

Some of the works ended close to the clockers' windows. Others, though, finished some distance down the track. I asked how such times could be caught. One of the clockers pointed to a pole an eighth of a mile down the backstretch. "See the sun on the inside rail by the half-mile pole? Horse makes a flick of a shadow as he goes past."

Most of the trainers carried stopwatches of their own. One stopped by to ask his horse's time for six furlongs and then argued that he had really run faster. When he left, another trainer said, "He's trying to sell that horse to Larry."

By nine o'clock the last of the timed works had been run. Full sunlight brightened the empty grandstand across the track. For the first time that morning I noticed in the background the tops of buildings in downtown San Mateo and the wooded hills beyond. The clockers leaned back in their chairs and looked over the track, empty now except for sea gulls roosting in the infield grass.

"We missed our crow this morning," Bob said. "We missed our Plymouth Rock sea gull, too."

> *"Show me the man who can class
> horses correctly and I will show
> you the man who can win all the
> money he wants, and he only
> needs a dollar to start."*
> —MIKE DWYER,
> *according to Pittsburgh Phil*

A MATTER
OF CLASS

Servius Tullius divided the Roman people into six orders, or classes, for purposes of taxation. The word "class," with its many meanings, seems to date from this invention.

The sentimental use of the word "class" is common in writing about most professional sports. Thus in connection with baseball it is said that Ted Williams was the best hitter of his time, but Joe DiMaggio had the most class. "Class" in this sense may replace "courage" in Hemingway's remark about "grace under pressure."

A certain amount of pinwheel rhetoric flourishes around horses, too. According to romance, a wizened old Kentucky Colonel picks a winning horse because he sees "the look of eagles" in his eyes. Or it is sometimes said of a stakes winner that "his regal bloodlines show in every lineament." I should note in passing that after looking with more than friendly interest, close up, at a good many thousands of horses, I have yet to tell the blueness of the blood from the hide.

But no matter: where betting is the chief business of the day, a certain realism has to prevail. Around a racetrack, the serious use of the word "class" has to do with horse trading and winning bets. And then the unit of measure is not the look in the eye, but dollar value.

It is obviously true that some horses are better than others. They prove their superiority, or higher class, by beating the others on the racetrack. The horseplayer who can detect a horse of higher class among a field of middling opponents wins more than his share of bets.

But how does the player go about classifying, or selecting the classiest horse in a race? The question has engaged the attention of handicappers for at least a century and a half.

Among a thousand slightly different ways of forecasting the winner of the next race, the serious approaches can be reduced to two: one based on class, the other based on time (or speed, as shown in the record of a horse's past performances). Class and speed handicappers may argue. Actually, each group borrows from the other's tool kit. Still, it is useful to study them separately. And classifying has to be considered first, if only because gauging the class of Thoroughbreds was being done, and well done, before the invention of the stopwatch.

The father of class handicapping was an Englishman, Admiral Henry John Rous, born in 1795, second son of Lord Rous of Henham Hall, Suffolk. Most curiously, a naval disaster in 1834 launched Rous on his true career as first in the line of master handicappers. Rous commanded the thirty-six-gun frigate *Pique*. While cruising in fog in the tricky waters off the coast of Newfoundland, the *Pique* ran onto rocks which stove in her side. Rous had served well and survived the Napoleonic wars, starting as a midshipman at the age of thirteen. Now, in peacetime, the Lords of the Admiralty took a dim view of damage done to a ship from other than cannonade. Rous was cleared of specific wrongdoing in the accident. He saved his ship and brought her home across the North Atlantic by a considerable feat of seamanship. Still, Rous had the feeling the Lords had welcomed him back with something of the warmth and pleasure of a man opening a gift package of well-aged, dried mackerel. As speedily as he properly could, Rous retired from active service and did not refer to the incident again for twenty-five years, until he talked about it at a Jockey Club dinner.

The Jockey Club had become Rous's career. He had married the daughter of a wealthy man, J. R. Cuthbert of Grosvenor Square, London. He was able to devote himself single-mindedly to racing—not as an owner, scarcely at all as a gambler, but as a lawmaker. And why did racing need a Solon?—to settle bets, if not amicably, at least fairly and without bloodshed.

The accepted view of nineteenth-century racing in England reduces the sport to a sort of bucolic pastiche of good fellowship. The fact is that gambling bulked as large then as now, as much on the hallowed turf of Newmarket as at Aqueduct or at the Ferndale County Fair. The amounts bet among the gentry a hundred years ago would cause anyone standing in line at the $100 window at Hollywood Park to turn green with anxiety. They literally staked patrimonies on races. And feelings ran correspondingly high if anyone failed to pay, and particularly if anyone interfered with a horse or gained an advantage by sharp practice.

Out of countless stormy disputes—some bringing him threats of libel action—Rous evolved a set of principles which he set down in his book, *The Laws and Practice of the Turf.* The book appeared in 1850 and Rous kept revising it for another fifteen years. The result proved as durable as the constitutions of most countries. The rules were picked up by the American Jockey Club and are still followed by American state horse racing boards and commissions. Stewards and commissioners at tracks all over the country, whether or not they ever heard of the Admiral, daily execute his will.

Settling debts was relatively straightforward, though not necessarily easy for a loser. Here, curiously, Rous's fellows thought he tended to favor the bookmakers. He did not associate with bookies; a frosty quarter-deck style stayed with him all his life. It is said he never sat down at his own dining table with a jockey or trainer. He simply thought losers should pay.

But how to assure fair races? This was trickier. In attacking the problem, Rous invented the first approach to modern handicapping. His masterwork was the Jockey Club scale of weights.

It had long been known, perhaps it was always known, that if you put enough weight on a horse, it will slow him down. Around American tracks today, the bromide is: "Enough weight will stop a freight train." It was also known that males carry somewhat more weight than females (or are likely to run slightly faster under equal weights) and that horses of both sexes generally gain in strength from the time they first come to the track, at two, until they are four and a half or five years old. The weight carried by a horse consists of the rider, his tack, and enough lead to bring the total to a required amount. Rous worked out the theoretical differences in weight-carrying abilities and reduced them to a table, or scale, which is still regarded as largely accurate (see Appendix).

Rous did not then rest from his labors. The scale of weights only suggested average differences among horses of different ages and sexes. The true differences among individuals are far greater. Rous in his prime years served as the Jockey Club's official handicapper—*handicapping* the horses in a particular race by adding to, or taking from, a horse's scale weight. Presumably, the individual weights would equalize a field enough to assure a fair race. Otherwise, a few superior horses might win every purse in sight. Among other things, for lack of difference of opinion betting would languish.

A specific weight assigned to a horse, as a variation from scale (two pounds off, three pounds on, and the like), became the bettors' first clear-cut, numerical sign of class. If a gambler thought he had reason to disagree with the opinion of the official handicapper, so much the better. The horses could settle the question on the course. Incidentally, British racing still has many handicap races; American racing, a few. In the overwhelming majority of American races today, weights are set by the conditions of the race, with weight off or on depending on the horse's recent performance.

Rous, of course, was likely to add to a horse's weight every time he won. He also snooped about the training courses looking at the fitness of horses who conceivably were being readied for a betting coup which might ruin the gentlemen of the Jockey Club. The honorable members seem to have stepped lightly around the forbidding figure of the Admiral. If done by anyone else, in the words of one English historian, "watching the private trials of race horses was regarded as an atrocious crime."

The question remains: Did the weights actually bring the horses together at the finish line? On this point we can cross the Atlantic Ocean and pass to the other end of the social scale to take the testimony of Pittsburgh Phil. He was probably the most successful horseplayer of his time in America, from the 1880s until his death in 1908. Phil did come from Pittsburgh, but his name actually was George E. Smith. He had been a cork cutter by trade. Phil went to New York, worked out the principles of handicapping for himself and terrorized the bookmakers. On the matter of weight and class, his biographer, Edward W. Cole, quoted him as remarking: "One of the mysterious rules of class that I cannot understand is that a real high class horse and a positively common horse cannot be brought together by weights within the handicapper's reason."

Phil's judgment told him that something more than assigned weight was needed to help in classifying horses. That help came, one step at a time, through development of the system of claiming races which made it possible to classify by means of price tags.

Claiming races make up a majority on most cards at American tracks. In these races all horses entered carry a price tag—or claiming price. If a race is for horses "entered to be claimed for $5,000," each entrant may be claimed—or bought—for $5,000, with no further negotiations, by means of a claim properly submitted in the office of the track's racing secretary before the race. To be sure, this marketplace is tightly restricted. A spectator, lucky enough to win a large bet on one race, cannot claim a horse in the next. With a few exceptions, the buyer, or claimant, must already own horses stabled at the track. Incidentally, if a claimed horse wins a piece of the purse, the winnings go to the original owner. But the claimant holds full title to the animal from the moment he steps onto the track. And if the horse breaks down during the race? The man who claimed him owns him, and his trainer must get the horse off the track. Whether for bettors or horsemen, the racetrack is no place for backward looks, second thoughts, or renegotiations.

Clearly, owners sometimes lose good horses to a claim, and regret the loss bitterly. In the early years of claiming races, during the late nineteenth century, the rules were so loose that an owner could hold on to a horse presumably claimed from him. The claimed horse was put up for auction after the race; the claiming price merely represented the first bid, entered by the claimant. Auctions permitted collusion. Sam Hildreth, a racing man who owned, trained, and bet on horses from the 1880s well into the 1920s, told in his autobiography of having horses of his claimed, and then saved for him by wealthy friends who outbid the claimant in the auction.

At smaller Western tracks before 1900, claiming rules were sometimes simply ignored. In those years one Harry Stover operated a track, long vanished, at Petaluma, north of San Francisco. Deeply suspicious by nature, Stover was a man who distrusted banks (he kept his savings in cans buried in a horse's stall) and thought it downright unfair that an owner might lose a useful horse to a claim.

Another horseman asked Stover one morning how to go about making a claim, since claiming races appeared in the program.

"File it with the racing secretary," Stover said, and he motioned toward the empty stands.

The man searched, found no one, and returned to Stover. "He ain't there," the man said. "All I saw was an old collie dog lying in the sun."

"That's the racing secretary," Stover said.

Modern racing secretaries can and do accept all valid claims, and claiming price has thereby become the single commonest measure of class.

The theory behind claiming races seems clear enough. And it introduces the matter of trainers' intentions, yet another problem for handicappers to study.

The backstretch at a track is like a small town in which everyone keeps a close eye on everyone else. Claims are made, on behalf of owners, by trainers who spend lifetimes looking at horses. The best and shrewdest of trainers know value. Put your $10,000 horse in a $5,000 claiming race, and he may well win the purse for you but someone will probably grab him. On the other hand, put a $5,000 horse in among $10,000 racers, and he has practically no chance of winning anything. Meanwhile, his board bill runs on.

In theory, therefore, a $5,000 claiming race attracts horses that are worth just a little more or less than $5,000 and thus are well matched. But reality, as so often happens, does not altogether match theory. A glance at the past performances for any claiming race reveals that horses constantly move up and down the claiming scale—as if restless, or dissatisfied with their stations in life. To fathom the reasons for such moves, the handicapper must put himself inside the mind of a trainer.

Has the stable entered the horse at too high a price? Perhaps the owner is an optimist, or the trainer thinks the horse is improving—or he wants to give him some healthy competitive exercise without danger of a claim.

Or is the horse apparently dropping down in class? The past performances show that the horse ran reasonably well and recently for $4,000. Today he is in for $2,500. The student of form pounces on the change, or dropdown, when he first scans the *Daily Racing Form*. At the track, before the race, he keeps looking at the tote board to follow the horse's changing odds—and then stews in a welter of anxiety. With the minutes passing, and the tote board changing, and the horses warming up in the backstretch, soon to load into the starting gate, the player asks himself: Is this a horse with a big hole in him? Do they want to sell him at any price? Was that honest sweat I saw in the post parade, or is the horse too nervous? Or, maybe, hope rising again, is it a hungry stable? Do they want very much to win the purse and possibly a bet? The odds are dropping. Is that smart money pouring in? Or are the bettors just fools like me, chasing the dropdown?

A nice mare named Mythical Summer ran for a $16,000 claiming price at Bay Meadows one November several years ago. She had won at Santa Anita a month before when entered for $20,000. Incidentally, the comparable claiming prices in 1978 would have been at least $5,000 higher.

My friend Mike the Baker and I discussed this apparent dropdown as we stood at the paddock watching the saddling. Mike is a Slovene who, through the fortunes of war and depression in the 1920s and 1930s, grew up by stages in several countries. He had to learn at least four languages as he went, English last and least well. His accent embarrasses him. His friends know him for an honorable man, highly intelligent and particularly shrewd in the ways of racetracks. Mike rubbed a big thumb under the mare's name in his program.

"Why they do that?" he said. "Why they sell horse for sixteen thousand when she already won sixty-three thousand this year?"

Neither of us bet. As the race was run, Mythical Summer lagged in the starting gate, was last in the field, a full ten lengths behind the leader after a quarter of a mile. She gained steadily from that point, closed like a fire truck in the stretch, and just got up in time to win.

A winning bet passed is not quite so aggravating as an outright loser, but it will do until the next genuine loser comes along. I consoled myself with the thought that the local trainers had also been suspicious of the horse; no one claimed her, and she was led back, looking calm and gracious, to the stable she had come from.

One last question of intentions must also be considered: the horse's own. An aged $2,500 plater, remembering days of glory, may wake up feeling good one day and, showing a touch of old class, win against better. Or, more often, the horse, like any other athlete, may feel off form and decide not to make a supreme effort against lesser horses. In either case, the horse most likely cannot read his own claiming price.

Among the horses stabled at a track, a certain number are not for sale—at least not for a claiming price. These horses run in allowance races. The best of them run in stakes, featured races with the largest purses.

The allowance horses as a group may be a little superior to the highest-priced claimers, though this is not always so. They may not yet have demonstrated where they truly belong on the class ladder, and until they do, their stables are protecting them from claim.

The track's racing secretary keeps a record of perhaps 1,500 horses at the track. For the nine races on each day's program, he must devise conditions which will permit all the fit horses to find a suitable race once every week or two. If he has mainly claiming horses in the stable area, he will program mainly claiming races. For example, of 180 races held on 20 consecutive racing days in March 1978 at Golden Gate Fields, 70 percent were claimers ranging in price from $2,500 to $25,000. During the same period at Santa Anita only 45 percent of the races were claimers and the claiming prices were substantially higher. At Santa Anita higher purses (based on greater attendance and more money bet) evidently attracted more expensive horses—most of them not for sale at claiming prices.

In allowance races (as in claimers) all entrants, in effect, start with the same weight, and pounds are then taken off, or added, depending on races the horse may or may not have won in recent months. Generally, the high weights are carried by horses that have won something recently. But weight differences in an allowance race do not give the horseplayer enough information to warrant a decision to bet. In a few stakes races the racing secretary himself, acting as the track's handicapper in the tradition of Admiral Rous, assigns individual weights. For most non-claiming races, weight offers only unclear signs to the player.

The handicapper therefore looks for another sort of price tag, one that fits allowance races. He looks at what the horse has earned, or come close to earning, in purse money. Thus a horse that has finished close to the winner of an allowance race with a purse of $8,000 may be more impressive than the actual winner of a $5,000 purse. Purse size, incidentally, does not appear in past performance lines. It appears only in charts, and the handicapper must save these.

Much ingenuity has been expended on methods for extracting a class rating from a horse's earnings records. These are set forth, step by step, in the Appendix.

The final word on classification properly belongs to the horses themselves as they race against each other daily. Since from 400 to 500 horses will appear on your own friendly neighborhood track each racing week, an elephantine memory helps. In the absence of a capacity to retain and recall the qualities of scores of fields, a good collection of charts and your own notes will do nicely. Thus Horse A, which interests you today, ran a close second to Horse B a couple of weeks ago.

Horse B since then has beaten a substantially stronger field. Your opinion about Horse A is consequently firmer.

In the sixth race at Golden Gate Fields on March 30, 1978, Mike the Baker liked a horse named Bokobo, though the favorite was White Sprite, a recent visitor from Santa Anita. Mike liked Bokobo for a number of reasons, but the most important was that in his last race the horse had run a good second, several lengths in front of the third horse. The horse that won that last race, Three Bits, was good enough to run in the feature on March 30. In the running of the sixth race, Mike's horse, Bokobo, went to the front at once, led all the way around, and paid $6.80 to win.

I cannot refrain from mentioning one small triumph of my own (in which luck led me by the hand to a successful guess about class). During the 1977 Bay Meadows meeting I was looking at a nondescript allowance horse's rather uneven past performance lines. The last line in the past performances represented a race some months before in which he had finished out of the money, beaten by four lengths. But in the small type at the end of the line were the names of the first two finishers in that race: Crystal Water and Vigors. It seemed to me a horse that could stay fairly close to the two best handicap runners on the West Coast during that year could surely handle the field he faced today. He did. And I was rewarded.

(Note: See Appendix for step-by-step treatment of claiming price and earnings data, in order to rate horses by class. The Appendix also contains further material on classifying horses by the company they have kept.)

> *"O, what excuse will my poor
> beast then find,
> "When swift extremity can seem
> but slow?"*
>
> —SHAKESPEARE,
> *Sonnet LI*

 CONCERNING TIME

Of all the signs the horseplayer probes for in the past performances, time is the most frustrating. On the surface, the recorded time for the running of a race seems to be the truest and most objective of all handicapping factors. Yet, when *comparing* times, as he must when he rates a field, the player runs into unanswered questions at every turn. As the questions pile up, they become discouraging. Besides, speed handicapping has a bad name—like playing favorites. Catch a player looking at speed ratings and he will claim he is really a classifier.

I believe it can be proved that speed numbers are extremely useful—probably the single most valuable handicapping tool—if calculated properly and used only where they make sense. And to understand this, it is necessary to see where speed numbers *do not* make sense.

Several years ago I had the good fortune to spend a spring afternoon at Newbury, an hour's train ride west of London. I recall in particular watching a field of fourteen two-year-old fillies being saddled in a huge and grassy paddock, seemingly half the size of a polo field, dotted with riders, trainers and their lads, and little clusters of English horse fanciers in stout tweeds. The fillies themselves were a lovely lot, beautifully groomed and nicely handled. The breeding notes in the program bore the names of sires likely to catch the eye of any handicapper: I find in my notes such names as Bold Lad, Runnymede, Ballymoss, Round Table. The fillies ambled onto the deep grass of the race course, warmed up, and then ran a five-furlong race down a more or less straight chute. The winner's time was a little more than a minute and three seconds.

I recall the race because it permitted comparison with American distances. If, by some engineering miracle, a perfectly graded American dirt track had been built beside the Newbury course, good young horses running on the new track would most likely have finished in rather less than fifty-nine seconds.

Over a distance as short as five-eighths of a mile, four seconds is a huge difference. Do the times suggest that American horses are faster than British? Scarcely. The difference lies in the racing strips, and the times cannot be compared. The band of elegantly groomed fillies at Newbury ran down a chute that was straight enough but kept some of the original roll of the land. The grass, not by chance, had been left so long that it seemed fetlock-deep. To compare times made by similar horses over the same distances at Newbury and, say, at Hollywood Park (where, among other differences, the race would have been run around one turn) would be nonsensical. Actually, the British tracks differ among themselves nearly as widely. And since British racing meetings are short, lasting only a few days at each location, the speed handicapper could never deal with enough races to make valid comparisons of racing times.

A somewhat similar situation faced players like Pittsburgh Phil at American tracks in the 1890s. Over the years tracks have become more standardized—as to shape, distances, and running surfaces. Comparing times remains an intricate problem. Nevertheless, it can be handled.

The key word is "comparison." The beginning student in statistics grapples with the subtleties of the idea that data must be comparable. The best of the handicappers, with no formal training at all, do remarkably well at reinventing this wheel for themselves. And I suppose this should not be surprising: Cardano, the Italian who invented probability mathematics four hundred years ago, was a professional gambler.

Before confronting the difficulties, the speed handicapper can take reassurance from two positive points:

1. The recorded times themselves are reliable. Times at the finish and at the points of call along the way register electronically as the lead horse flashes past a photoelectric cell.

2. Overall, the times do make a difference. They are not matters of chance. Through all the complications, one simple fact emerges: Better, or, if you wish, classier, horses do run faster.

Any horseplayer at all serious about improving his craft should confirm these points with a straightforward experiment. He needs only patience, a slight facility with numbers, and a file of charts for an entire meeting at one track (say, eighty days).

Take the distance most commonly run at that track; most often, the distance will be six furlongs (three-quarters of a mile). Sort the times into four groups, by class of race: cheap claimers, middle-priced claimers, allowance races and high-priced claimers, and stakes races (jumps of only a thousand dollars in claiming price would thin out the data too much and only confuse the results).

Clear differences in average times will soon emerge. Some races for cheap horses will be won in faster times than better horses clocked on the same day. Equally, good horses will occasionally win in what seems poor time. Overall, as they accumulate, the numbers will cluster around a different middle point for each group. Furthermore, the differences will be substantial—three-fifths of a second or sometimes a full second (for six furlongs) separating one group from the next. On the track that much difference translates into an easy win.

As for the difficulties in comparing times, the most obvious are: horses make faster times on some tracks than on others; on the same track, horses run faster on some days than on others; times for different distances cannot be compared directly; and, as a catchall, a horse's time may vary with shifts in weight, or jockey changes, or switches in post positions, or simply in racing tactics from one race to another.

All the problems of comparability can be handled, in one

degree or another. Handling them requires techniques, which are spelled out in the Appendix. But the principles behind the techniques must first be understood.

Consider an example of the differences among tracks: Two horses ship into Bay Meadows during the fall. They have run only in allowance races; you cannot take a quick glance at their claiming prices. One flew in from the East, where it recently ran six furlongs at Aqueduct in 1:11⅗. The other vanned up from the Fresno County Fair, where it did six furlongs in 1:10⅗. Does that mean the Fresno horse will run a second faster at Bay Meadows than the Aqueduct horse? A handicapper of any experience would assume the opposite. The Aqueduct horse will almost certainly run faster. The differences among the tracks make unadjusted time hopelessly misleading. The tracks are designed differently and use different materials in their racing strips, and horses of different class run on them.

It is possible to buy tables that translate times from one track to another. In my opinion, such tables should be used sparingly, if at all. By the time the numbers reach you in print, they cannot be less than a year old. They probably are much older than that. Meanwhile, the running surfaces themselves may have changed. Still, the player who does not have time to keep records for several tracks simultaneously does have one easy way out: no law requires a bet on every race. Did the contending horses in the next race at your track drop in from all over the country? Pass the race, and move on to the next.

The variations in the speed of the running surface of your own track are another matter. They must be calculated, scrupulously and daily, by any player who hopes to use speed numbers sensibly. Some ways of making a daily track variant are given in the Appendix. I can report that the simplest of these takes me no more than ten minutes a day and seems to me to give adequate results.

Some of the reasons for variation in the speed of a racing strip are obvious. Times are slower after a rain, faster after a dry spell. But apart from weather, work by the maintenance crew on the strip can make it run faster or slower. Hence the variant must be calculated daily to make speed numbers meaningful.

Finally, suppose the handicapper must compare times for

horses that have been running different distances. He has another set of number problems to solve. Suppose a horse ran six furlongs in 1:12, or a total of 72 seconds. The horse averaged 24 seconds per quarter of a mile. But it would be a terrible mistake to assume that the same horse could therefore go on for another quarter of a mile and complete a whole mile in 96 seconds (72 + 24), or 1:36. Actually, he would do well to finish the mile in 1:38 and a fraction.

Most Thoroughbreds, if encouraged to run, will generally run fastest in the first stages of a race, progressively less fast as the race goes on. Usually, the horse that seems to be closing strongly, charging through the stretch like a runaway train, has done his fastest running half a mile before. At the finish, he simply has not slowed down as much as the rest of the field; he passes them with a rush because they are struggling to finish. For the horseplayer, his own psychology heightens the dramatics of a stretch duel: the horses are closer to him than they were in the backstretch; the noise of the crowd swells around him; and he may have a bet on the outcome. In actuality, the horse that runs faster at the end of a race than at the beginning is a rarity—most often a first-rate stakes horse.

Times for different distances can be translated into comparable numbers by speed charts. The Appendix describes how the serious handicapper himself can make speed charts (or parallel time charts) for the tracks he follows. Here another cautionary note is needed: Horses cannot read speed charts.

Horsemen speak of some horses that run "short" and others that run "long." The confirmed sprinter that can go six furlongs in 1:10²/₅ should finish a mile and a sixteenth in about 1:43, according to the speed charts. But the horse may simply be one that spends all its energy in six furlongs, has nothing left, and quits cold at the longer distance.

To be sure, some sprinters can make the distance switch, or "stretch out," particularly if they get out in front and are permitted to stay there in overdrive. Determining which horses can stretch out is one of the subtlest and most interesting problems in handicapping. Numbers are useful, but no number system takes the place of the handicapper's art—the sense of which horses, though quick out of the gate, have a steady way of going and have something left at the end of six furlongs.

The past performance lines in the *Racing Form* give, in addition to the final time of the winner of a race, the times made by the leading horse at points of call along the way. These times, called "fractions," make possible pace analysis.

Suppose two horses ran in separate six-furlong races at the same track on the same day. The handicapper need not worry about the track variant or switches in distance or between tracks. Presumably, the finish times can be compared directly. Both horses won, and in the same time, 1:11 flat.

In one race, though, the leading horse was timed at the half-mile in :46, while the half-mile time in the other race was :45⅗. The pace handicapper prefers the race with the faster half-mile fraction.

He reasons: If the horses finish in the same time, but one field of horses had to use up more energy early in the racing than the other, theirs was a more impressive effort. The pace handicapper gives a higher number for a faster early pace, thereby further refining raw speed numbers.

The value of this refinement is one more debated point among handicappers. But concerning one use of fractional times there can be no argument at all: the fractions permit the astute analyst to visualize, in advance, how a race is likely to be run—which horses, on the basis of fractions, are most likely to be in front at each point along the way.

The handicapper who in his hunt through past performances comes up with a genuine, and unopposed, speed horse—one fast out of the gate and most likely to be well in the lead after a quarter of a mile—rejoices. Given anything like equality in class and condition, the horse running unopposed on the lead has all the best of it. In addition to all other advantages, the fast-breaking horse stays out of trouble. All sorts of bad luck, not necessarily of its own making, can afflict the horse that comes from behind. The closing rush through the stretch produces fine dramatic effects, but the serious player willingly does without these. Therefore, some expert handicappers concentrate, insofar as possible, on speed horses in relatively short races. They may even carry the specialty a step further and concentrate on races for two- and three-year-olds, on the grounds that these have fewest infirmities and more often win on the basis of speed alone.

Unfortunately, life rarely assigns simple problems. Having found one speed horse in the entries, the handicapper more often than not will find one or two others that from the study of fractional times seem poised to contest the early pace. What then?

The handicapper at this point has landed in the middle of a distressingly complicated problem in the physiology of extreme effort.

The speed horse, when successful, gets out ahead of the pack and stays there, running easily. The pace of the race allows the horse to expend its effort both suddenly and smoothly. But horses, too, are competitive athletes. If two speed horses go out together, one, or both, may strain to put out an extra amount of effort. Instead of being left alone to relax on the pace, your candidate may simply try harder without going appreciably faster and thereby exhaust itself within half a mile. Among the horses stabled at any track are some which, if they get clear at the start, cannot be beaten except by a genuinely good horse but will falter if challenged early. People at the track dismiss such horses as quitters, lacking in what humans choose to think of as courage. What, if anything, horses themselves think about such matters is not revealed. It seems at least possible that the horse who quits, who spits out the bit, when another horse hooks into it, may actually be too eager to please, or too eager to win. This horse may thereby exhaust himself in wasted effort.

The pace handicapper may convince himself that both pacesetters—or, as he might put it, "all the early speed"—will quit. In that case he may look for a horse able to close strongly, from off the pace. Should he find one, he may score a most satisfactory win. But he does not always find the winning closer. One of the speed horses may in fact refuse to quit.

The horse who does not quit, when head to head with another, does more than win races. He supplies the simplest answer to the baffling question of class. He has superior class because he continues to produce his best effort when subjected to severe pressure. And so speed handicapping comes full circle and returns to class handicapping. A speed handicapper, considering a bet on a match race, may be familiar with every number bearing on the performance of the two horses, but in the end he will only risk a wager if he thinks one horse can beat the other—because it is simply classier.

(*Note:* See Appendix for step-by-step treatment of times to produce speed rating numbers.)

> *"There's a dry stump at the turn of the road . . . two white stones are set against it . . . and the land round this is smooth for horses . . . and now Achilles has fixed it for the turning point of his race. Drive your car close, almost grazing the post. . . ."*
> —NESTOR TO ANTILOCHUS,
> *Iliad, Book XXIII*

WHERE THE RACE IS RUN

Seen on a map, a typical English race course looks like a heap of rope, or an enlargement of the digestive tract of an insect.

The plans for the clusters of more than a dozen tracks in the Bois de Boulogne near Paris are full of lovely, swooping, crossing lines, like something done by an engineer with drafting instruments to distract himself from a toothache.

A typical American racetrack, seen in diagram, looks simply like an ellipse with its sides flattened, and with two arms or chutes extending, in opposite directions, one on each side.

No doubt someone who set his mind to it could squeeze from these bits of information some significant truths about national character. For the serious handicapper of horse races, the matter is simpler. He asks one question: How does the shape and substance of the track affect the speed of the horse? The horseplayer faces the question, one way or another, whenever he goes to the track.

Many of the first race courses in America were village streets. According to the folklore of a number of cities and towns, the name "Race Street" refers not to the varieties of human beings, but to the running horse. Horse racing in the streets a century or two ago apparently had the same effect on citizens that automobile drag racing downtown had in the 1960s. They did not like it. In Lexington, Kentucky, for example, an ordinance of 1793 banned street racing. As a result, horsemen who wished to settle a difference of opinion about the speed of their mounts moved to the cleared space on the outskirts of town. Since cleared space cost much labor and was hard to come by, the horses ran around a closed circuit, generally oval, with sharp turns. Most racing in the United States since then has been around one or two turns, with racing on a straightaway reserved for relatively short dashes or for a few tracks which could be particularly lavish with space.

The point of racing is to compare horses, whether for breeding purposes or for betting. Accordingly, track operators everywhere try to offer horses a familiar running surface. Several dozen tracks of the more than one hundred in North America measure less than a mile around. Most of these, known sometimes as bullrings, measure half or five-eighths of a mile, and all of them are regarded as minor league. The rest, ranging in class from middling to major, measure exactly a mile around, except for Belmont Park, which is a full mile and a half in circumference, Aqueduct, which has a circumference of a mile and an eighth, and some half a dozen other tracks, which measure either one and one-eighth or one and one-sixteenth miles. All these tracks consist of some sort of dirt, but an increasing number of tracks also have a grass course, more often than not along the rim of the infield, inside the main, dirt track. As for the composition of the dirt tracks, the official descriptions, over and over, use the same words—"sandy loam."

Given the apparent similarities of size, shape, and running surface, it is remarkable how different, in fact, the race courses are from one another. Most obvious are slight differences in shape which can produce important differences in the running of a race. Turns can be more or less tight, homestretch and backstretch can be shorter or longer, on standard one-mile tracks The style of a horse can be helped or hurt by the differences. A horse with early speed may do well where the homestretch is short. A horse that closes strongly may favor a track, like Churchill Downs, with an uncommonly long stretch. At a few American tracks—Santa Anita, for example—part of the running may be downhill and the shape of turns out of chutes on grass courses can be downright eccentric.

A more important difference, and one generally not visible from the stands, is in the composition of the main racing strip itself. Conversation with trainers and above all with the bosses of the crews that maintain racing strips reveals that "sandy loam" covers as many mixtures as can be found in a cookbook. Sand, at least, generally means what people think it means. It is a mixture of fine rock particles containing no organic matter. But loam is not all that clear. According to most dictionary definitions, it is friable—which means it crumbles easily—and it contains some clay, some organic matter, and some sand. The prime ingredients of loam can be mixed in different proportions. And, since one of the ingredients is sand itself, a "sandy loam" may really consist largely of sand.

Some trainers, and it seems to me they are mainly trainers of the old school who want their horses to run on a racing strip as earthlike and natural as possible, object even more when the cushion, the upper layer of the track, is thin and the base below the cushion has packed down hard.

As with everything else in racing, arguments rage over the differences in racing strips. Some horsemen, and racetrack managements, like the fact that horses run unusually fast on sandy, thin-cushioned tracks. On such tracks cheap claiming horses may run three-quarters of a mile, the standard six-furlong race, in little more than a minute and ten seconds. Time like that on a deep track—one of the New Jersey tracks, for example—would do for stakes horses. The equivalent time for cheap claimers on a deep track might be 1:13 or 1:14.

Some tracks, particularly in the Southwest, are notorious for hard surfaces and fast times. At least two other Western tracks—Longacres, near Seattle, and Del Mar, near San Diego—seem to produce fast times, but horsemen agree that those racing strips do not damage their horses. Longacres and Del Mar, occupying the two remotest Western corners of the United States, are among the most attractive and pleasant tracks anywhere. Their racing strips are frequently said to be "springy." Del Mar is literally a bow shot from the ocean, assuming the metaphorical archer has strong arms and a following wind. People generally credit the fast times to the fact that the water table lies close beneath the surface at Del Mar. In fact, one theory holds that the track runs faster or slower depending on whether the tide is in or out. Longacres, 1,500 miles to the north, is somewhat farther inland, but heavy annual rainfall makes the grounds handsomely lush and produces a high water table, too. Racing is full of unproved legends, but it may well be that Longacres and Del Mar really do provide springy cushions and that Thoroughbreds respond gratefully and without damage to their fragile legs.

No matter what the nature of the track, damage to legs is always a threat. Conceivably, hard tracks do the most harm, but it is a fact that horses go lame, and break down, daily, on tracks of all sorts, in all parts of the country. Most of the casualties occur among sore, old claimers—but then, as Lincoln remarked of fools, there are so many of them. The quality of the horse is insufficient protection. Hoist the Flag, who looked so promising early in his three-year-old year that he might have duplicated the feats of Secretariat in 1973, Seattle Slew in 1977, and Affirmed in 1978, broke down during a routine work. Most tragic of all, the great filly Ruffian had to be destroyed after breaking a leg during her match race with Foolish Pleasure at Belmont Park in 1975.

The man responsible for keeping the running surface as safe as possible for horses is generally known as the superintendent of the racing strip. He comes as close as he can to accomplishing the impossible feat of pleasing all the many varieties of trainers, owners, racing officials, and horseplayers. It seemed to me it would be useful to see at first hand how someone went about a job like that. On a raw spring day in northern California, when one rain had just passed over and another was on the way, I went to see Ralph Barnes, who was then superintendent of the racing strip at Golden Gate Fields.

The job seems clearly impossible—and correspondingly interesting, for a reporter if not for the man doing it. Accordingly, I went looking for Barnes in the track's corporation yard, a compound tucked away at the north end of the field, just beyond the far turn of the track. I saw sheds and shacks and an array of heavy earth-moving equipment, but nothing that suggested the superintendent's office. I asked directions of a man slogging through the muddy yard in rubber boots. He waved his arm in the general direction of the track and said, "Over there. Don't you see?"

I did not see. He pointed again, saying: "Look. Green shed, striped canvas, looks like an Ay-rab tent."

I saw it then, and it did look like an Ay-rab tent. It looked like something grown up from the earth, or like a curious oasis in the midst of the business of the track, or like something improvised, a little at a time, and weathered over the years. A trail of corn kernels, cast about for the birds over the mud in what might have been the front yard of a frontier cabin, led to the entrance to the superintendent's office. Plywood sheets extended the office in random directions. The remnant of an old Quonset hut seemed somehow embedded in its midst. And, at the rear, directly adjoining the track at the quarter pole, striped canvas, very like a tent in the desert, enclosed an outdoor eating place, furnished with a big picnic table.

Signs picked up at random festooned the front of the shed: ENTER AT YOUR OWN RISK, PUBLIC TRAINER, and NO DOGS ALLOWED. Inside, Ralph Barnes, the superintendent, and several of his men sat at a rough table, bulky in quilted jackets, waterproof pants, and wide-brimmed hats. They looked like field hands just in from ploughing in the early spring—or, like what they more nearly were, a road maintenance crew at rest. On the table in front of Barnes rested a small black cube. This turned out to be a radio, tuned permanently to one frequency broadcasting weather reports at all hours.

"I can't ever be far away from this," Barnes told me, resting his hands on the tiny set. "This time of year you never know what to expect. Other night I woke up about four o'clock. Pitch-black. I don't know what made me wake up. But I turned on this thing. And it said rain was coming. I come over here in a hurry to seal the track. But I was too late. The rain beat me."

"What would you have done if you got there in time?"

"Like I said, we wanted to seal it."

"Sealing a track" is one of many phrases used freely around racetracks with little comprehension of meaning. The phrase creates the picture of men going about with buckets and brushes to paint some sort of sealing compound over the whole of the track's running surface. Of course, this is not at all what is done, and in fact it could not be done. The expanse of a one-mile racing strip is deceptively large. It occupies, including the main oval and the two chutes at opposite corners, but not including either the infield or the surrounding grounds, about twelve acres.

"Dragging" more accurately conveys the meaning of sealing. Barnes led the way outside to demonstrate his yard full of equipment. "You see that there float? That's what we seal with."

The float consisted of half a dozen massive timbers, three by twelve inches and fourteen feet long, bolted together to make a sort of sledge. A fifty-gallon barrel of water rested on the top of the sledge as a weight. Barnes had three such floats at Golden Gate Fields. Before the first race he and two of his men hitched their big-tired tractors to the floats and dragged them smoothly, moving in echelon, over the muddy surface of the track.

Water and some surface mud are pushed aside and packed down. The track in theory gets less soggy. In any case, the horses do not have to run through the thickest sort of muck.

Rain was simply the main variable in Barnes's working life. For the rest he had only to worry about the constant factors— like unending arguments among horse people who want the track faster and those who will feel favored if it runs slower. Barnes had tended to the condition of northern California racetracks for nearly thirty years and he no longer worried greatly about the differences in opinion. He merely resisted, silently and pleasantly if possible, angrily if pushed too hard, any radical change.

"I started working at Bay Meadows in Bill Kyne's time," Barnes recalled. "I was fresh out of the Navy—the Seabees, you know. I was hitchhiking along the old Bayshore highway, near San Mateo. A man picked me up. Said he was looking for somebody who could handle a big team. Hell, I grew up on a ranch, handled all kinds of stock. In the Navy I used all kinds of heavy earth-moving stuff. Well, that man came from Bay Meadows. I went to work for them and that's been my work ever since, at both northern California tracks, though it's a long time since we used a team of eight to drag a harrow over a strip."

The ground the horses race over at a track like Golden Gate consists of three layers. The track sits on reclaimed land at the very edge of the eastern shore of San Francisco Bay. Old nautical charts identify the spot as Fleming Point, a bit of nomenclature long since lost under the press of racing and its followers. The fill consists of broken hunks of red rock. Barnes himself had seen this bottom layer only rarely, when, for example, a deep trench had to be dug for drainage pipes. Next comes what horsemen think of as the track's base: a foot and a half to two feet of hard packed clay. Is anything done with this base? "Not really," according to Barnes. "It just sits there year after year. We keep adding and working on top of it."

The work of Barnes and his crew, then, concerned itself largely with a couple of inches of added matter known as the cushion, the surface the horses actually run on. In dry weather, for Thoroughbred horses, the cushion is about two inches deep. Before each race on the bright, clear days, the men of the racing strip crew piloted their tractors in echelon, dragging harrows instead of floats. Barnes himself brought up the rear, smoothing out spots that may have been left too rough. The harrows consist simply of vertical iron rods, in eight rows, set to cut the required depth into the cushion. Among them, the three harrows cut into and smooth out every inch of racing surface before each race. In effect, the three-man crew cultivated a twelve-acre farm ten times a day, in a total elapsed time of scarcely over an hour, performing their work before some thousands of people in the stands who were scarcely aware of them or what it was they did.

At intervals, sometimes weekly, Barnes said, they had to blade the cushion. "That's in the morning, of course, to get it spread around right. Otherwise, it moves downhill on you, toward the rail. Or that damn north wind. I hate it worse than the rain." He jerked his thumb in the direction of San Pablo Bay to the north of San Francisco Bay. "That wind from up there, it just sucks the water out of the cushion. Then we have to water it, and roto-till it good, cut down maybe four inches and let the water get in. And then sometimes we have to put on new cushion."

The last time Barnes had done that, he ordered no less than fifty-two trucks and trailer loads of sandy loam, twenty-five tons to the load. "We dumped twenty-six loads all round the inside by the rail, and the other twenty-six loads all the way around the outside. It took us a couple of weeks, working every day before the meeting began, to get it in right. The stuff we used was mainly Antioch sand, about eighty percent or so, and maybe twenty percent top soil. The sand comes from near Antioch in the San Joaquin River delta."

On the bright days at Golden Gate, Barnes's crew and a few backstretch people who may have come to see them, and the ambulance driver and his wife, who parked their vehicle next to the Ay-rab tent, all joined around the lunch table enclosed by the striped canvas. The track is a place where people live. Barnes and his people had a couple of bunks in one of the outbuildings within the corporation yard. Most of the stables have stalls set aside for grooms who sleep there. Like a sprawling garrison army, the track people develop separate mess halls for themselves, the mutuel clerks cooking on hot plates in the inner depths of the stands, the racing strip crew preparing meals in their tent, stable people eating in places of their own.

By first post time the tractors hitched to harrows are ready to move out onto the track. Nine times after that, following each race, they will go out to restore the racing strip. Before each race, as the horses saunter by from the post parade and go into a canter to warm up, the crew are sitting by the outside rail to watch. On a day when I visited Barnes and his men, a rider in the procession before one race eased his horse over toward them. It was Roy Yaka, a Japanese-American, perched on his mount like a compact samurai, armed with a whip instead of a sword. Yaka pointed to the track emphatically, several times, and called out in passing, "Too hard! Too hard!" He was grinning as he spoke. Evidently, the complaint was a standing joke between him and Barnes. But from some of the trainers the complaints were more serious.

"Bitch, bitch, bitch," Barnes said. "You can't please them all. I watch the times of the races every day, and I try to set the harrows and the watering, to keep the strip running just about the same. It doesn't always work. Then a few of the horsemen may get pretty mean. One man offered me a hundred-dollar bill to fix the strip to favor his horse. I told him to stuff it."

On the track, in a starting gate halfway down the backstretch, the horses, a field of two-year-old maidens, leaped forward. They came toward us with a rush, straining and crowding around the turn, clods of loam jumping behind the hooves, jockeys' whips popping, one horse now clearly in the lead and drawing away.

"That looks like the outside horse, The Bureaucrat," I said. I had reason to notice the outside horse. "I had a little push on him this morning," I added.

We had a fine view of the rear end of the horse rapidly moving away from us down the stretch.

"Kind of late for that," one of the men in the crew said.

The Bureaucrat won, easily. The men who work on the racing strip, like everyone else at the track, know something about bets and bettors. They looked at me keenly, almost kindly, to see how I reacted to a winning bet not made. Then they mounted their tractors to harrow and smooth the track once again.

When the player has done worrying about the effects of the shape of the track, the composition of the racing strip, and the shifting of the track's cushion down toward the rail, he is ready to consider the wind. The wind, too, has a marked effect on horses' speed, and affects some more than others. The wind plays a particularly big part at a track like Golden Gate Fields, located at the edge of San Francisco Bay.

At Golden Gate Fields, as an example, a cold winter wind is likely to come down from the north, straight at the horses as they leave the starting gate for a six-furlong race. Later, the spring wind is more likely to come from the west. The west wind catches the horses full force as they come around the far turn. This is particularly tricky for the horseplayer, because sitting in the stands he may not be fully aware of the wind unless he looks aloft and sees the pennants whipping briskly on their poles.

One man I see at the northern California tracks is a retired regular army man known, inappropriately, as Halsey, because of a fancied resemblance to the Admiral. Halsey is a reasonably sound handicapper but a perpetual loser. As he told me wistfully one day, "I can't bear to pass a race." He shows up at the track every day until he goes broke, whereupon he goes home to recover from the damage and wait for his next pension check. Halsey came originally from the Pacific Northwest, first saw racing at Longacres, and is most likely to be tempted to bet on a horse that has shipped into California from Seattle. Above all, he will always bet, so long as he has a few dollars in his pocket, on what he calls a "wind horse." He has the notion that some horses like to feel the wind, are stimulated by having it blow into their faces. He won a couple of bets, on windy days, on a horse called Wild Melee. The horse then lost ten races in a row, in fair weather and foul, but Halsey never lost faith in him.

Whether in fact any horse actually enjoys the wind has never been revealed to me. Clearly wind does affect the running of a race. Any player who has not observed this for himself should note that the winner of a race for human runners may not claim a new record if wind velocity approaches five miles per hour—a faint breeze for horses at a bayside race course. At collegiate track meets, under National Collegiate Athletic Association rules, a wind gauge must be in place and operating before every running race, and records may not be claimed if wind velocity (translated from meters per second) exceeds 4.473 miles per hour. I suspect my friend Halsey may be confused as to the true effects of wind on horses. But I do know that the thoroughgoing horseplayer, who attends daily and observes everything on, beneath, or around the track itself that may influence the running of the race, can profitably make notes about the wind. At some tracks the wind is no factor at all. At a track like Golden Gate Fields the player can see the wind's action for himself, with or without gauges, if he looks up at flags or observes the wind scallops on the water as he approaches the track along the bay shore. He will pay closest attention to the effect of the wind on a horse's normal running style. For example, a wind blowing straight down a six-furlong chute may ruin the chances of a horse with early speed that might expect to be well in the lead after a quarter of a mile. The same horse entered later on a windless day might do much better. The player with such information in his notebook can comfort himself in adversity: the information appears nowhere else.

An increasing number of major tracks have turf courses in

addition to the main dirt track. Where I have observed the maintenance of the racing strips, a separate crew takes care of the grass course. And here, too, the player must observe carefully, for himself, because no one will do the looking for him. Turf courses, as much as the familiar "sandy loam," are subject to all sorts of nearly invisible changes. Some get-rich-quick guides to handicapping so despair of calculating the state of the grass that they recommend passing all races on turf. Turf, like dirt, has a different consistency when damp. When downright soaked, most turf courses are not used at all, and their races are rescheduled for the main track. But even when presumed dry enough for racing, a grass course may still be slower than it will be after weeks of baking in uninterrupted sun. Still another variable is the length of grass. Also, the shape of grass courses differs from the main course, sometimes sharply. Altogether, times on the turf often cannot be compared with each other, still less with times on the dirt. Here, too, the player who has recorded his observations in a notebook is building a substantial advantage.

Late in his study of a race the handicapper may have winnowed the field. He has compared the horses for class, and for time and pace. He has reduced the apparent contenders to two or three. And at this point he may well find that one of the qualities of the track itself tilts the balance finally and points to one bettable horse.

(*Note:* A summary of handicapping factors to consider in conjunction with the different aspects of the track appears in the Appendix.)

> *"Yes I do know something. I can
> tell when flies are in the milk.
> One is white, the other black."*
> —MASTER FRANÇOIS VILLON,
> *Dispute with His Heart*

THE LONG TRAIL

When I want to find Mike the Baker or
Bill the Pipe Fitter, I go to the pad-
dock between races. Usually, I can see them at a distance. Bill
wears a blue windbreaker. Otherwise, he is nondescript: bulky
and middle-aged, lantern-jawed and dark, one of many standing around at the track or stopping off for a beer at his neighborhood saloon on the way home from work. Mike stands erect.
He is tall, broad-shouldered, and white-haired. He came originally from Dalmatia, but he speaks Italian as well as Serbo-
Croat, English least well, He carries himself like a Commenda-
tore.

Many people come to the paddock for the one obvious
reason—to look at the horses while they are being saddled and
led around the walking circle. Bill scarcely glances at the
horses. He does not know how a horse should or should not
look, and he says so. Mike adds, when Bill is not near, that the
Pipe Fitter cannot even read a *Racing Form*. Mike himself does
know what he is supposed to look for. He can, if he wishes,

recite conventional wisdom about the minute signs whereby a horse reveals the state of his health. But I have rarely seen him use such knowledge. In truth, he has little faith in it. Mike has a hardheaded, unsuperstitious respect for facts. He tests facts as rigorously as anyone, inside or outside a research laboratory. If a racetrack source tells him something, with every appearance of good faith, Mike may walk back and forth the length of the grandstand and patiently invest fifteen minutes in finding out whether the source truly meant what he said.

Therefore, when Mike stands at the paddock rail, he seeks in his own fashion to learn something about the fitness of a horse that interests him. But he does not expect the horse to give him the clue. He watches the human beings connected with the horse. In each saddling stall in the paddock a cluster of people stands around a horse which submits more or less patiently to being saddled and having its equipment adjusted. A groom (or "swipe," or "guinea") has led the horse there from the backstretch. A trainer tightens the girth and adjusts hoods and blinkers; working with him, on the opposite side of the horse, may be an assistant trainer. With them may be owners or friends. Somewhere in this gathering, Mike reasons, is information about the horse's condition. To extract that information, to sift it out and compare it with what he already knows, Mike employs the arts of the trailer. So do lesser players, like Bill, who are trying to unravel the same puzzle. The long trail starts at the paddock.

The theory is simple. People at the track bet. Betting is a public act, visible to anyone standing near a ticket seller's window. The bettor who buys a ticket while you watch says in effect that he thinks his choice has a shot—a reasonable chance of winning. If that bettor happens to be one of the connections of the horse you like—preferably the head of the stable, the trainer himself—you may conclude that the stable deems the horse fit enough to run well.

The trailers assemble at the paddock. When the paddock judge gives the order "Riders, up!" and the trainers boost their jockeys to the saddle, and grooms lead horses and riders in single file onto the track, the trailers come to life. Silently, unobtrusively, they blend into the crowd, each on the trail of someone they picked as a target at the paddock. The trailer follows his quarry wherever he can, all about the track. In the course of the chase, the trailer may pick up and examine a menu in a clubhouse restaurant, or lean against a post near a bar, or hover about near a hotdog stand, or unnecessarily urinate or wash his hands in the men's toilet, as he waits for the trainer, or groom, or owner, to declare his opinion at a ticket seller's window.

My source on the theory of trailing is another of the people Mike sees at the paddock, a youngish man named Rudy, plump and long-haired, with sad eyes and a bushy mustache. Neither would be flattered by the resemblance, but Rudy looks rather like a nephew, say, of Albert Einstein. Rudy has no nickname that I have heard; among other things, no one I know can say what other jobs he may work at. Rudy is articulate. His words tumble over one another when he talks and his eyes dart about. He does some handicapping of his own. In fact, I think he handicaps quite well, but he has little confidence in his own work. He believes that trainers often know what is going to happen on the track, and therefore, above all, he wants to know what he supposes they know. To find out, before each race, he follows the trainer of his choice with the zeal of a narcotics agent pursuing a pusher to a schoolyard.

Mike the Baker also wants to know what the trainer thinks of his own horse—when it is the horse Mike is thinking about betting on anyway. But Rudy looks avidly for any number of opinions. For that reason he often acts as a sort of trail dispatcher when the group assembles at the paddock.

"You take the Five," I heard Rudy say to Mike one day. "Okay? I'll get the Three. Porter don't bet much but when he does, watch out. That's a pretty good guinea with the Five. You going to take him, or the trainer?"

"I follow guinea," Mike said. He is an agreeable fellow. He does not like to disappoint Rudy, and in any case he constantly adds to his already extensive knowledge of other people's betting habits. But, as I then suspected and later verified, he had no intention of betting on that race.

A "good guinea," incidentally, as Rudy uses the term, is not necessarily one who skillfully calms an unruly horse, or who treats his parents or his children kindly, or who pays his debts. He is one who bets, preferably on some sort of sliding scale from which Rudy can deduce the strength of his opinion, and best of all one who walks straight to a window and bets, without delay or attempt at evasion.

Rudy looked about impatiently, then fixed on me. "How about you taking the Four?"

"Do you figure the Four has a chance in this race, too?" I said.

"Sure I do," Rudy said. "You've got to give him a shot. He's a Ruken out of an Indian Red mare, and you know they love this distance. And I'd like him a whole lot more if I saw that guinea with him bet. You know who that is? That's Garcia's brother. If he likes the horse, he'll bet him pretty good, twenty easy, maybe more."

I must confess I was reluctant to join the trailers, but in the end curiosity overcame embarrassment. After the riders mounted I waited by the rail until Garcia's brother led his horse, the "Four," onto the track and turned him over to the rider on a lead pony. I had already noted, with some coaching from Rudy, that the groom wore a broad-brimmed gray hat and a bright red sweater. I dutifully dropped into stride, some thirty feet to the rear, and followed the red sweater from the rail, through the crowd, across the concrete apron to the ground floor betting area. I quickly discovered that I was not alone. Man Friday in this case revealed himself, not by a footprint, but by interposing himself quickly between Garcia's brother and me. He was short and stout, elderly, and he wore skid row clothes topped by a battered straw planter's hat whose brim sagged in great eccentric dips. He walked with a purposeful duck waddle. The planter's hat stayed as close to the red sweater as a neurotic dog scurrying at his master's heels. It occurred to me that trailing was a good deal less than invisible.

The groom stopped to talk, in Spanish, to a group of friends. The straw hat stopped and, superfluously, ducked behind a pillar. I continued walking slowly, and stationed myself between Garcia's brother and the betting windows. I found myself edging closer and wishing I understood Spanish, as if the outcome of the race hung on what they were saying. The red sweater walked on, and our procession formed again. I was reminded of the boy in a fairy tale who walked through town with a goose under his arm and with a string of townspeople stuck to the goose and to each other behind him. The red sweater stopped to reach for his wallet in his rear pants pocket. The straw hat moved still closer. But the red sweater stopped this time at a food counter for a beer. Finally, he joined the line at a seller's window. Within a couple of minutes he came to the window himself, and at that point two other men whom I had not noticed at all jumped forward, jostling the small man in the planter's hat and others in line, and all three craned and stared, over and around the groom, at the moment that the mutuel clerk punched out tickets.

I had been told to rendezvous at a $10 window on the mezzanine floor, three or four minutes before post time. Rudy was there ahead of me.

"Did he bet?" Rudy asked.

"First he stopped to talk to some friends, and then he had a beer, but yes, he did bet."

"What did he bet?"

"I don't know what horse he bet on. I couldn't hear, and I couldn't see. But the clerk hit a key at least a couple of times, and it was a five-dollar win window."

Rudy shook his head, but he did not bawl me out. "Well, we know he likes something. The trainer with the Three didn't do a thing. Went right to his box and he's still there."

Mike reported in. The swipe with the Five had bet—on the Eight. Mike passed the race. Rudy said he was going to bet on the Four. I made a small bet on a long shot that finished far back. The Three, the horse whose trainer Rudy had followed, won in a close finish.

Mike rarely sits down. We watched the race standing at the clubhouse end of the mezzanine. As we slowly walked back, I remarked that you practically had to stick your head inside the window to be sure of what someone had bet. Mike grinned and nodded.

"But what if it had been a trainer?" I asked. "Do you look to see what tickets they buy?" I was aware, as I spoke, that the Jockey Club rules, and the rules of state racing commissions, require a trainer to bet, if at all, only on his own horse.

"No." Mike shook his head emphatically. "They can't take chances. They bet other horse, somebody sees, they lose license. You see them at the window, that's enough."

The other trailers agree. I have only once heard one of them say he had "caught" an assistant trainer betting on a horse from another stable.

The trailer's art calls for a specialized body of knowledge of its own. In the case of intelligent players like Mike the Baker, who is a first-rate handicapper, and Rudy, who could be, the amount of special knowledge is formidable. As a bare minimum, they know the layout of the stands and surrounding areas, foot by foot. They know how long it takes to cross any section of the floor, and they can estimate the speed with which the line before any window may shuffle forward. They know every trainer and assistant trainer and nearly every groom by sight. They know who associates with whom. They know friends, wives, and girl friends. They know who stops for a drink, who habitually visits the urinal after the horses reach the track. Above all, they know betting habits, large and small, and constantly probe for ways in which bets may be concealed.

The trailers use their stock of information in different ways, based on the firmness of their opinions. Mike the Baker is always interested in what others find out, even if he later tells me, "I had no intention to bet this race." He lays the information aside for future use. But he already has his own opinion. Therefore, when he says, "I want to see money go down," he is talking only about the trainer or swipe with the horse he likes. He is verifying his own opinion. He will probably bet anyway, but if he sees no action, he may cut the amount. Rudy suffers from an affliction common to many horseplayers who know something of the art: he has too many opinions. He sets a posse of trailers afoot in the hope of reinforcing the right opinion. Bill the Pipe Fitter, strictly speaking, has no opinion at all about horses. He vaguely tries to rate the horseplayers. He does trailing when someone like Rudy asks him to. Otherwise, he hangs about the betting enclosure, watching for people he knows by sight as they approach the sellers' windows.

When I see Bill striding purposefully across the betting enclosure, I assume he has learned something. I stopped him once and he ducked his head and told me, out of the corner of his mouth, "Maxie Gee just give me the Two horse." Maxie Gee is a bartender. Bill was unable to give the Two horse purse money: the horse finished a well-beaten sixth.

Both Rudy and Bill are losers. Bill stays away weeks at a time while he heals his wounds. Rudy is generally back in a week, suffering and complaining and blaming his misfortunes on the cleverness of a trainer or owner in hiding his intentions. Because they are looking for endorsements, the more the better, Rudy and Bill more often than not find themselves betting on favorites, though Rudy can be snide about what he regards as confirmed "chalk players." Betting all favorites, all the time, at any track, loses about 10 percent of the total wagered. Would Rudy and Bill do any better or worse if they sat down in comfort and bet on a random selection of favorites, whenever they happened to feel like it? I cannot prove it, but I suspect the results would be about the same. In Rudy's case he would lose the sense of belonging, of being privy to secret information, which must be what brings him to the track.

Trailing is just one part of the information network that sweeps up literally everyone at the track who either asks a question or answers one or in any other way indicates an opinion. But the trailers recognize each other as a group somewhat apart. As a rule, they know each other only at the track, and it does not matter where the track is. One of them can go to another track and find the trailers there before two races have passed. Rudy, in fact, did that when he came to California from New York.

My impression is that the most successful of trailers (leaving out someone like Mike who is above all an excellent handicapper) are those who frankly give up having opinions of their own about horses. Instead, they do systematically what Bill the Pipe Fitter does hit-or-miss: they handicap the horsemen. One such player was pointed out to me at a Los Angeles track. He followed a number of trainers and other horsemen to windows and kept records on *their* results, not his. He settled on three or four who he concluded were the soundest judges of their own horses (and who bet where he could see them). Now he trails those few he regards as "good." When he sees them bet, he bets. He gets relatively few bets, but he claims he turns a modest but steady profit. His greatest tension comes from the fear that one of his regulars will turn over his money to someone else to bet for him. In one such case, a trainer he was following sat down in a box. The trailer waited. The trainer remained seated. Post time was approaching. Finally, a woman left the box and went to a betting window. The woman hobbled. She was elderly and heavily draped in furs, though the day was mild. Anxious and in doubt, the trailer nevertheless followed her. At the window he literally thrust his face over her shoulder to make sure she really did bet on his trainer's horse. She turned to stare at him in some disbelief, and said, with a marked foreign accent: "Even on a three-to-five horse you gotta look over *my* shoulder?"

The horsemen, and other regulars at the track, have always known about trailing. The practice is at least as old as the time of Pittsburgh Phil. He said, in connection with his own betting operations with bookmakers at tracks: "I knew by sight every betting commissioner on the race tracks, whom he represented, and how heavily he bet. . . . If I had watched them, I knew they watched me."

One day, on the way to the paddock, I remarked to Mike that it seemed to me easy for any trainer who wished to conceal a bet to do so.

"Maybe he don't care," Mike said.

"And about the guineas," I said. "Suppose one doesn't bet. How can you tell what that means? Maybe the horse really did go bad. But what if the guinea simply was broke?"

"Look," Mike said. "Pardon me." He put one hand on my arm to stop me, the other over his heart. Then with a thumb he underlined the name of a horse in his program. "Horse like that. I like him. I bet. But I like better when I see the money go down."

Behind the theory of trailing, as described by Rudy and practiced by Mike, lies the third major problem in handicapping: judging current condition. After weaving his way through past performances, charts, and his own notes, the player may feel he has established basic class and has deciphered the code for speed and pace. Now he must satisfy himself that the horse he likes is fit to run his best race. This problem, too, was well known at the turn of the century to players like Pittsburgh Phil. He remarked that a fit horse of lesser class might beat a stakes horse that had not yet rounded into form. But in this case the modern player probably has a right to complain that matters were never so difficult as now.

With 50,000 horses racing, the proportion of unsound ones has probably increased.

Faced with the problem of condition, the handicapper goes back to past performances. And he uses prescriptions which Pittsburgh Phil probably used, too.

Any number of kindly souls are prepared to sell the player systems of handicapping and betting. The fees are modest, at least in comparison with the wealth promised. These and other forms of racing philanthropy will be examined in the next chapter. Here let it be noted simply that the best of the systems actually does give the beginner somewhat better than a random chance, and that practically all systems include a condition factor, based usually on how recently a horse last ran.

The system's rules may say: Eliminate all horses in claiming races which have not raced within the last two weeks. The time limit may be ten days, or seventeen days, or three weeks, according to the author's philosophy. It is the commonest of rules, and one of the most useless.

Most systems give every sign of having been worked out backwards. That is, the analyst looks at the past performances of winners, after they have won, and tries to find out what they had in common. One thing most winners have in common is that their last preceding race was fairly recent. At this point any reasonably good student in elementary statistics would ask, "How recent compared with other horses?" A slightly more advanced student, if showing off, might ask the same question in the words, "What's your denominator?" Both questions mean: What percentage of *all* starters has run recently? The answer comes back: About the same percentage as the percentage of winners. In other words, this test of fitness resembles the most infallible of all rules for handicapping. Bet only on Thoroughbreds. One hundred percent of winners are Thoroughbreds. One hundred percent of starters are Thoroughbreds, too. So the rule is infallible, and also worthless.

As with most handicapping factors, the truth about condition or fitness lies well below the surface and must be chased down through several layers of confusing and conflicting data. Overall statistics seem to make mockery of a recent outing clause. Yet every handicapper looks twice for an explanation, if in fact the horse has not raced recently. He knows, or senses, that the statistics lumped together may conceal all sorts of contradictions. Therefore, before he risks a wager, he tries to deduce why the trainer kept the horse away from racing. The handicapper may conclude the horse was so gimpy that the trainer would not let him compete lest a leg fly off. Just as often the handicapper may dig into the past and conclude that lack of recent racing is irrelevant to this horse. He may even find that the horse runs particularly well when fresh, which is to say, when returning from a layoff.

Some systems use workouts as an offset for lack of recent races. Few players could fail to have misgivings about a horse that showed neither races nor workouts in the last three weeks. If such a horse won anyway, and some do, the player who passed the race would no doubt curse earnestly to himself, or aloud if he deceived himself into thinking he had a sympathetic listener, while he wondered how fast the trainer was galloping the horse on days when he recorded no workouts. As seen from the clockers' shed, recording workouts cannot be an exact science. In any case, workouts may obviously be a positive factor. The player feels happier when his selection shows, for example, three good works in the last two weeks. He will feel still happier if the workouts were at distances of four furlongs or more. He may become positively euphoric if the times of the works look good, try as he will to remind himself that workout times mean little enough at best.

Many players will draw a line between "fitness," meaning a state of robust, athletic good health, and "sharpness," meaning keen form, or readiness to win. In other words, a horse just back from freshening at the farm may be as fit as he is ever going to be, but he may not be sharp enough yet to win. When it comes to gauging sharpness, the handicapper finds himself peering through the murk and gloom of past performances, looking for literally dozens of possible clues in the combinations of small numbers which the wise men of horseplaying have decreed signify the onset of sharp form. In short, the player who worries about the condition of the horse he likes is not merely a neurotic. He has something substantial to worry about.

The Thoroughbred is a fine athlete, weighing half a ton or more, full of muscles, but as subject to ailments as, say, a football lineman or a coal miner. Most football players carry their ailments into the game with them under an armor of tape. The horse equally carries his ailments with him into the starting gate and, unfortunately, can say nothing about his condition. No spectator in a football stadium has to tear up a mutuel ticket when his favorite tackle gets beaten a length at six furlongs.

Many horsemen claim that hard tracks and lengthened racing meetings have aggravated the problem of conditioning Thoroughbreds. The number of off-form horses racing does seem to increase as the year wears on. The player carries away from the wet, gray days of fall racing the impression of more horses breaking down or going lame. The charts bear out the impression: they show, from a recent sample I examined, three times as many horses dropping out of races lame at a fall meeting as at a spring meeting at a corresponding track.

Nothing in the rules of racing says that any prescribed percentage of favorites must win. It can be said, however, that when higher percentages of favorites do win, form is holding up better, for at least a plurality of players. Assuming that horseplayers do not grow progressively more stupid or indecisive when the leaves turn color, it seems to be significant that spring and summer meetings show markedly higher percentages of favorites winning than do meetings toward the end of the year. For example, in recent years form held up better at Golden Gate Fields in the spring than at Bay Meadows in the fall. The two tracks serve the same area, with very much the same crowds betting on horses drawn from the same pool and conditioned by the same trainers and ridden by the same jockeys. Specifically, according to official statistics for each of the seven years from 1970 through 1976, Golden Gate Fields had a higher percentage of winning favorites than did Bay Meadows. In 1977 the percentage was about the same for the two tracks. The same difference can be noted nationwide: form holds up slightly better in the spring than in the fall. In 1976, comparing only spring and fall meetings at major tracks, the meetings held exclusively in the first half of the year showed about 32 percent of favorites winning, while in the last half of the year less than 31 percent won.

The ailments that erode the strength and form of the running horse as the year progresses are as many and as varied as human afflictions. Some of them are very like human ailments—including infectious disease and heart attacks. But two important differences must be noted. The weight of the horse and his great speed and strength must all be borne on legs which seem, and are, downright fragile. It is said of all athletes that the legs are the first to go. The Thoroughbred horse carries the rule to ludicrous extremes. The second crucial difference is that the horse cannot describe his symptoms. As a result, people responsible for a horse must fuss over him like a young mother whose firstborn has a fever. And, since the legs are the most vulnerable part, horsemen, whether in the backstretch or at the paddock, constantly look at horses' legs in action, to catch any new peculiarities of gait.

The people like Bill and Rudy, who follow trainers about and then bet according to what they see, attribute almost magic powers to trainers. All trainers I have met quickly deny they have anything like such powers. The trainers do have one substantial advantage. More than any other group—more, probably, than veterinarians, who in any case are not numerous enough to rock the tote board—they can judge the condition of a horse from appearances. Over the course of a year they spend far more hours with horses than teachers do with students. To them, horses really do look like recognizable individuals, more so, say, than pink-skinned, big-nosed Europeans do to Chinese. Anyone who grew up in a town of 2,000 knew at sight most of the townspeople. I went to a university that at the time had an enrollment of 2,400. By my junior year I could greet at least half the people I saw in passing on campus. In the same ways, an experienced trainer knows not just his own horses but a majority of the 1,500 or so stabled at his track. Knowing what the horse normally looks like, he can instantly, without thinking about it, spot abnormalities.

The best of handicappers has advantages of his own. He has no bias in favor of particular horses until he bets on one, and then it is too late to matter. He is in a better position to observe what goes on during racing and he keeps far more and better numbers than any trainer. But the handicapper is struggling and scrambling to keep up when it comes to judging a horse's fitness by looks. He reminds himself of standard recipes: Is the horse wearing bandages that he did not wear before? Is he sweaty? Is he fractious? In the post parade does his walking gait show stiffness or irregularity? Is his coat blooming with health, or is it rough and is his eye dull?

For most players, unless they have the wealth of experience at trackside of a Pittsburgh Phil, or a latter-day, real-life equivalent to Phil, like Jule Fink, the answers are rarely clear. They can even be downright misleading.

I, for one, like to see a horse well groomed, and fussed over in the paddock with an atmosphere of tension and expectancy among his attendants. I have sometimes bet on such horses, if I liked them anyway, and won. Just as often, I must confess, I have read the signs wrong and lost. I came to the track one day having decided to bet on a mare named River Crest. I watched her while she was being saddled and was depressed to see her looking altogether lackluster, with downcast head and rough coat. (When I remarked on the incident later to a trainer friend, he grinned and nodded, and said, "Sure, like her coat was turned inside out.") Feeling every bit the resourceful handicapper, I adjusted my thinking and bet on another horse. As a matter of course, River Crest came out of the gate like a tiger, went around her field on the far turn, and won going away.

Some handicappers I know protect themselves by restricting their bets to the best-quality horses on the grounds, entered in races for which they are clearly suited as to class and pace, distance and footing. They assume that the more valuable animals will be scratched if not fit and that suitable races for them are too hard to find to be wasted. But most players, not patient enough to wait seemingly forever, do the best they can with the horse's vague signs of fitness. They develop a fondness for special signs of their own devising. Did the horse dump manure in the post parade? Was his tail waving briskly or drooping? They can interpret such symptoms any way they wish, depending on momentary whim.

A hardheaded realist, like my friend Mike, knows his own limitations. I cannot blame him for seeking any help he can find along the long trail.

At some points at the racetrack, the trails divide and scatter. The trailer who cannot spot someone important at a betting window sniffs about for other scents. Even if he is not a hand-icapper in the true sense, he may have recourse again to his *Racing Form*, and at the least he will resume his study of his program.

He is constantly on the watch for what touts call "secret trainers' angles." In the language of hard sell, the trainer is supposed to be "readying a betting coup," or preparing for a "crackdown." The player therefore looks through his past per-formances specifically for a recent letter *c* before a claiming price, indicating that a stable thought enough of a horse to buy him for a claiming price. He studies a horse's progress up and down in recent claiming prices and hopes that a drop in price means a coup is at hand. All this has some realistic basis, except that it overlooks other explanations. The stable may drop the horse into a lower claiming price as much to sell it as to win a purse. Or the horse may move up a notch, not as part of an intricate maneuver, but simply because the condition book offered the trainer no better spot.

Having run out of clues in the *Form*, the player now turns to his program for signs of stable intentions. He may, for example, operate on the theory that certain riders do their best work for certain stables. His eye stops at any horse with such a rider-trainer combination. In some cases, the player becomes in-terested in the combination only when the horse is likely to go off a favorite; or, equally, he may be most interested if the horse is not favored. For whatever it is worth, this kind of thinking has enough currency so that some racing commissions and tracks have kept records of the percentage of wins with favor-ites for each trainer. Presumably, this suggests that the player has some right to his suspicion that a horse may be held back if the price seems too low, the better to win a purse and a bet at higher odds another day. To me, this reasoning appears dim. Purse money is not all that easily won at will. Particularly at tracks of middling quality and upward, it is hard to conceive that a horseman would often take the chance of maneuvering his horse not to win, in the hope of winning at some indefinite time in the future when the horse may actually be less fit.

The trail of allegedly inside information thus leads from trainers to jockeys. Fortunately for the information seeker, guards keep him out of the jockeys' room. Riders are remarka-

ble and courageous athletes. The best of them have the musculature of boxers, reduced to steel wire, with negligible rear ends
and hands both sensitive and strong. They risk serious injury
in every race. In the face of danger they must exercise cool
judgment as to pace and in weaving a course through a field.
With all that, nothing requires jockeys to be good handicappers, most of them have the reputation of being poor ones.

This does not deter the players who hunt for information as if
each tidbit were a buried truffle. If jockeys are barred from their
view between races, they keep an eye on jockeys' wives, jockeys'
girl friends or mistresses, sisters, mothers, and friends. When
he has achieved greater sophistication, the player also watches
out for jockeys' agents. And here he is on slightly more fertile
hunting grounds. The agent seeks the best mounts he can find
for his clients. If the rider has a good reputation, the agent's
task is easier. Given a choice of mounts, the agent can decide
on the basis of his own handicapping. The most successful of
agents therefore has a clear notion of the quality of horses at a
track. When a player is reduced to handicapping the handicappers, he may find good ones among the jockeys' agents.

Through all this, the nature of information being sought has
subtly changed—as a freight train starting from a siding in
open country passes through villages, towns, and suburbs,
and finally comes to the outskirts of a metropolis. At the trail
head, where the trailer who is truly a handicapper starts from
the paddock, the information sought is simply: Is the horse I
like in fit condition? Where the trails divide, and as post time
approaches, and the information seeker casts about in all
directions, the question has become: What do they know?
or, What are they betting?

In the end, players may be reduced to cadging information—from each other. I can still recall my own sense of
astonishment the first time I saw someone dart to my side to
stare at the tickets I had just bought. Equally, I know how often
I have had to wrench myself back to reality, at the ticket seller's
window, to call out the number of the horse I myself have
selected, rather than the number I just heard said by the person ahead of me in line.

THREE

The Winning Player

CHARITY UNLEASHED

The horseplayer is a solitary in a noisy crowd. His sole protection against the tides and currents of sentiment around him is his opinion. But before he learns to rely on his own opinion, and thereby takes the first great step toward winning, he must find out whether it is possible to buy an opinion. In truth, any number of kind souls stand ready to press on him, for modest fee, opinions, systems, and secrets guaranteed to bring him wealth.

At the gates of every track I know, philanthropists with loud voices sell tout sheets. They beckon with sheafs of magic cards. They shout promises of winners in every race.

The cynic will say at once: Why don't they take their cards inside and get rich themselves? Let it be said that some of them try. I see them at the sellers' windows. They may not get rich, but they care; they read the *Racing Form*, like the rest of us, and they do try.

Most of the serious players I have met scorn the selections sold at park gates. They would suffer embarrassment if caught buying one. Yet most of them will glance at a card with frank curiosity, if given the chance. No one can evade the flood tide of information. The player's only protection lies in his own capacity to listen and reject. As a whole, the cards sold along Charity Row—for prices ranging generally from $1 to $2—give plausible selections. They cannot all agree, else they could not compete. They cannot all be right—but they can be uniformly wrong. In these respects they closely resemble the public handicappers in the metropolitan dailies published near tracks and in the *Daily Racing Form*. All, whether sold in a newspaper for 20 cents or for a dollar at the gate, suffer from overwhelming drawbacks. They offer selections for every race, a feat which every player of any experience knows to be impossible if tried day after day. The newspaper and *Racing Form* handicappers, operating in many cases behind fictitious names, must make their selections a day ahead, with only sketchy information about jockey assignments and scratches, and sometimes without having past performances at hand. The cards sold at track gates just before first post time at least reflect all but last-minute scratches and jockey switches, and their authors can, if industrious, study the *Form* as any studious player would.

Generally the selectors do not offer a record of their selections. This is understandable. In well over 90 percent of cases, the choices of any public handicapper followed blindly, regardless of odds and for every race through a whole meeting, will produce a substantial net loss. An occasional newspaper handicapper in an occasional year claims an overall profit for all his selections, but the feat is a rarity. (It is the kind of rarity a statistician would expect among a random distribution of results achieved by 50 to 100 selectors.)

With all that, the public handicappers as a group do a difficult and sometimes useful job. A few are far better than the average; a few, far worse.

In the several editions of the *Racing Form*, the handicappers using the name "Sweep" are veterans of their trade who must be taken seriously. Among other things, they offer a plausible price line—an estimate of the odds at which horses are likely to go to the post. So do a few of the best newspaper selectors. Also in the *Form*, selections appearing under the name "Trackman" sometimes reward study. Trackman, as reported earlier in this work, is the chart caller. Alone among selectors, it can be guaranteed that he watches all the races, every day, from a vantage point atop the grandstand roof. He may or may not be one of the great handicappers, he may or may not have the temperament of a first-rate gambler. But he knows the horses on the grounds, and it is sometimes worthwhile for the horse-player to find out from charts and past performances if Trackman's selection in a particular race may have been influenced by his seeing a sharp horse blocked or otherwise unfairly bothered in his last race.

Some of the cards sold along Charity Row are distinguished chiefly by typography carried over from 1910 and by a legend, "None genuine without a photograph of the founder," which points to a smudged mug shot seemingly picked at random from police files. A few are clearly serious productions printed daily by industrious and knowledgeable racing men.

Friends of mine whose word I accept tell me that Clocker Lawton's card, at the New York tracks, at least during some periods, was excellent. At the Southern California tracks, I can report from my own experience that Bud Baedeker's *Guide* is in a class by itself. I do not know what results the Baedeker card would give a beginning player who followed it blindly, though a flat bet profit for every race over the course of a whole meeting would be nothing less than remarkable. But I do know that Baedeker, unlike the authors of many cards, is visible at the track, in his own person, watches every race, circulates among knowledgeable racing people, and maintains his own files for nightly study. I first saw Baedeker toward the end of an afternoon at Del Mar. To get a fast start from the track, a friend and I watched the ninth race from a hill overlooking the backstretch. Near us I saw a tidy-looking van. The man beside the van, watching the ninth through his glasses before driving away in his mobile office to begin his evening's work, was Baedeker. He is a large, distinguished-looking, middle-aged man. He resembles a senior partner in any established business. His public manner would serve well at a Rotary lunch. In fact, he does sometimes hold public handicapping seminars. He is perfectly willing to talk about handicapping methods, and he makes no pretense of having bought secret information from unnameable sources in the backstretch. Two sons and a third young man—all of them cheerful, restrained, and well dressed—man the booths along Charity Row. They do no whooping, hollering, or sideshow barking, and the soft sell has evidently given them a prosperous business. While the elder Baedeker looks like a successful businessman out for a casual day's racing, he actually has spent his whole adult life around tracks. He came from the Midwest and settled in Southern California more than twenty-five years ago. He has published his *Baedeker's Guide* regularly ever since.

Also in a separate class, and offered only at and for the Southern California tracks, is William W. Saunders' *Racing Digest*, published daily during racing meetings. So far as I know, nothing like Saunders' *Digest* appears anywhere else. The *Digest* does not make selections—though its information may sometimes point toward one horse more than others. It consists of fifteen to twenty multigraphed pages closely packed with information. At first glance, it might be thought to duplicate parts of the *Racing Form*. Actually, Saunders' strong suit is that he observes and records details left out by the *Form*. For example, editions of the *Racing Form* from Chicago westward, in the past performance lines, used to give final times of winners but not fractional times. Saunders filled this gap (doing what careful handicappers did for themselves): he printed a running tabulation of fractional and final times at California tracks, by day and race. At the end of 1974, Western editions of the *Form* began to show fractional times, after the fashion of the larger Eastern edition, which in turn had taken over from the defunct *Morning Telegraph*. Could Saunders' *Digest* have had anything to do with the change? Of course, it is impossible to say, and the battle, if it occurred, was on the scale of a very large Goliath opposed by a tiny David.

Saunders himself is a keen and aggressive businessman. A relative of his, he says, established the first rental car company. By his own account, he came to racing, after a successful career in conventional business, because he found handicapping intriguing and a challenge he could not leave alone. He developed, and then sold, generally unavailable information which he regarded as vital to handicapping. He conducts the business, including the production of the *Digest*, from a pleasant home within walking distance of the Santa Anita track. Like Baedeker, he runs an open operation, and willingly tries to explain how he calculates some of his rather complex numbers.

Saunders maintains files on some 10,000 horses that are likely to appear on California tracks. He attends the races in Southern California daily and has observers at the track who keep notes on horses that were fractious, or washy, or appeared for the first time in bandages. For each race at Santa Anita, Hollywood, and Del Mar, he uses an entire page in the *Digest* to give comments on how each horse looked and acted last time out as well as numbers which rate the quality of opposition the horse faced and the all-around quality of the horse's own performance. He also calculates daily track variants. People I know in Southern California do not much like his variants and produce their own, but in fairness I should add that I do not know anyone who likes the *Racing Form*'s rather simple variants for Eastern tracks. Brewing such numbers is as much art as science; it may be that no one's numbers can truly please anyone else. Finally, for anyone not prepared to do his own handicapping, Saunders offers an analysis of the probable pace of the race.

Against the overwhelming weight of information offered to the player at a moderate price, what happens to the handicapper's law: You've got to have an opinion? Nothing happens to the law. You still have to have an opinion.

The simplest proof I know is the case of a player who, in vain search for certainty, bets only one horse a day, the single best-bet consensus choice of the five handicappers in the *Daily Racing Form*. Here the player clearly has no opinion of his own. Neither does he rely on any other single, legitimate opinion. Rather, he seeks comfort in company, using an average which cannot be better than one valid opinion and may well be worse. The results are exactly as bad as logic suggests. Playing the consensus best bet, he wins about as often as he would betting on all favorites, and at prices that are even lower. To document the point, though it needs no heavy-handed proof, I looked at twenty-five random days from a Golden Gate meeting and at another random twenty-five days from the preceding Bay

Meadows meeting. In one sample the consensus produced nine winners (36 percent), which is not at all bad, but at an average price of $4.35 for a winning $2 ticket, or an overall loss of 22 percent of the total bet. In the other sample only six of the twenty-five consensus best bets won, this time averaging $4.83 with an overall 40 percent dollar loss. It should be remembered that random play loses the amount of takeout from the mutuel pool, in this case 17 percent. The bettor playing safe, following an average of expert opinions, lost more than he might have by stabbing the program with a pin or taking post position numbers from birthdays, license plates, or dream books. Incidentally, if you look for it, you can easily find a month when the consensus best bets would produce a net profit. I guarantee that with an effort you can find some one month at any track wherein your aunt's birthday used for exacta numbers yields a sensational profit. But I have also found a run of twenty-five days at a major track during which the consensus best bet won only three times, with one unbroken series of fifteen losses. Such vagaries are commonplace in the handling of volumes of numbers. They demonstrate the weakness of most so-called "workouts" used to prove the value of a betting system.

After all this, why bother to separate useful from bad information?

Assuming the player has enough toughness of mind to cling to his own opinion, information is useful if it challenges him.

You have been studying the *Form*. You think two horses, A and B, stand out. Now someone you respect says, "What about C?" Whether you want to or not, you pause and take stock. With luck and some effort, you hide your confusion. You must surely be the gainer if your own opinion does stand up to sharper scrutiny. You will probably be the gainer, too, if you pass some races after a second look convinces you that your ideas were shoddy or that the race is truly wide open.

Finally, information has to be useful if it plugs gaps in the past performances. The only limits are that the player must have time enough to process the information, and he must not confuse himself. As for a good price line, or forecast of probable odds, that is indispensable to good handicapping. It is probably the most neglected factor in writing about handicapping, although it was stressed, clear and plain, by Pittsburgh Phil.

The subject of price, and money management, is so important that it must be examined at length (see Chapter 15).

Another and quite different class of benefactor stands ready to make the player's fortune: authors of books about handicapping. For players who read books, a large number of writers stand ready with the key to the absolute in horseracing. It should be said at once that the books vary widely in value. The best of them constitute a genuine bargain, particularly in comparison with other forms of friendly help to the handicapper. All, of course, claim that they can tell you how to go about handicapping successfully. Some do contain useful information. Some are palpable frauds. Some are so badly written that it is nearly impossible to find out if they might offer any sort of help to the reader. As a rule, the greater the claims, the more fraudulent the books.

The pioneer among the writers of handicapping manuals was Robert Saunders Dowst. His first book (written in collaboration with Jay Craig) appeared in 1934. At that time state legislatures were beginning to look approvingly at racing and the revenue it might produce. The sport was reaching out for new followers, and Dowst helped them find their bearings at the track. His first book ran through thirteen printings, and other titles of his were being sold well into the 1950s. Dowst apparently was a lawyer and an amateur handicapper. His writing conveys some sense of a testy, conservative personality. Not only was he the first writer to offer handicapping advice for the purchase price of a book, but for thirty years he remained the most literate and one of the best. The essence of his advice was to look for consistent horses—those that win or finish in the money in a high percentage of races. Followed today, his precepts would very often put you on favorites, at low odds, but with a high enough percentage of winners to keep you out of serious trouble.

A number of handicapping books appeared during the 1950s. None offered a serious threat to the *Iliad* as literature, and it seems unlikely that they produced a crop of rich horseplayers.

Around 1966 a man calling himself Tom Ainslie wrote *The Compleat Horseplayer.* When I first read Ainslie, I had not seen a book for horseplayers since first looking at Dowst, more than twenty years before, and *The Compleat Horseplayer* at once struck me as being in a separate category. That impression has only been strengthened as I have since waded through dozens of books dealing, more or less, with handicapping. To start with, Ainslie was obviously not simply literate but a clear and thoroughly professional writer. It also seemed to me that he made sense about handicapping.

None of my handicapper friends had read Ainslie, or at least none of them admitted it. On an impulse I asked Bud Baedeker what he thought of Ainslie as a handicapper. He replied with a somewhat puzzled look: "Why, he's a writer." Since that seemed to him to dispose of the subject, I let it rest.

Ainslie later let it be known that he was indeed a professional writer named Richard Carter, the author, to my own knowledge, of two books about medical affairs. The book-reading part of the racing public evidently was ready for sensible ideas about handicapping set forth clearly. Four other Ainslie books appeared by 1970. All of them cast at least some further light on the problems of the horseplayer. In the course of them, incidentally, Ainslie's own ideas about handicapping appeared to be changing. Ainslie later took up a possibly more profitable venture, the sale by private subscription of horseplaying systems or methods.

Naturally, I have no way of knowing how many readers of Ainslie books became successful horseplayers. I suspect the author could not make an accurate count, either. But I am sure Ainslie added to many people's *understanding* of handicapping (which is by no means the same thing as beating the races), and I also suspect that if some of Ainslie's readers actually became winners, his books must have cut their learning time by at least a year or two.

One other writer should be singled out. Andrew Beyer's *Picking Winners* came out in 1975. In one way, Beyer is unique among how-to writers. Most of the handicapping recipe books make the art seem easy. It is not. Beyer admits this; in fact, he proves it. He is good on the importance of detecting biases in a racing strip. He is excellent on the need for an intimate knowledge of trainers and their habits. He emphasizes the complications of calculating daily track variants and speed numbers for each race (though he might be surprised to find something very like his own approach in an article written years ago for *American Turf Monthly* by someone called Pat Cabell). Beyer treats pace in a confusing way—but that is my opinion. The point is that anyone reading Beyer can see how complicated the problems of handicapping are, and then he may—just may—come to the most important conclusion of all: that he must do his own thinking, make his own observations, develop his own approach, brew his own numbers, and come up with his own selections.

With the few honorable and interesting exceptions, most of the books on handicapping make outrageous claims. Yet in truth a published book provides its own antidotes. The reader can browse through it while standing at a book counter. With a little practice, he can spot outright fraud as quickly as he can the first copulation scene in a best-selling novel. Where imagination takes over is in the direct-mail sale of systems.

Dozens of simple systems for selection and betting can be bought for the price of a single book. One collection briefly summarized is in an Ainslie book, the *Complete Guide to Thoroughbred Racing*. The most representative collection is in *A Treasury of American Turf*, edited by Henry D. Bomze. Bomze's book consists of forty-six systems, which at $10 for the book works out to a little less than 22 cents per system. The average, hard-sell, direct-mail offering goes for about $20—for a single system. The hundred-fold increase in price pays mainly for the lavish use of imagination with which the direct mail, or private subscription, item is peddled.

Someone whom I shall call Reagan wrote me once, offering for a modest fee to send me a system that would make my fortune at the track. The letter had such a friendly tone, such a ring of sincerity, such a clear appeal to simple greed, that I could not resist it. I asked for the system. The sales pitch was the best I ever read. Unfortunately, the system was one of the worst. No matter. The prose was worth it. And my order entitled me to a second pitch, which I keep at hand to remind myself that there is such a thing as innocent charity. In his second letter Reagan told me that he had obtained the "$5,000 Challenge System" from a man "77 years old and now retired." He quoted from the old man as follows:

> I still have this system and believe that if you can find another one, it probably would cost you a few thousand dollars. You can learn this system by heart in ½ hour and this system never pays less than $15 mutuels and often pays 10–1 to over 30–1. It has made many a millionaire. You do not play all the races, only those picked by the system. I am wealthy now and am giving you the chance to make yourself some easy money. Now this is the only letter you will ever receive from me, now or ever.

Reagan described his tense negotiations with the aged philanthropist and then offered me a copy of the "$5,000 Challenge System" for only $25. I managed to pass the offer. The tax consequences worried me. But I cherish the prose.

In time my name made its way onto many other mailing lists, and some dozens of other benefactors offered to make me rich. Typical was the letter that told me, "the SUPER PROFESSIONAL MONEY-MAKING METHOD that I am about to introduce to you, has been acclaimed by a privileged number of Horsemen to be the most lethal method of uncovering WINNERS that they have ever seen or heard about." The writer realized that I might wonder why I was given this chance. He explained:

> My winning reputation has been such that for years I've been besieged nationally, with countless lucrative offers from racing enthusiasts, to divulge the WINNING MECHANICS of my SUPER PROFESSIONAL MONEY-MAKING METHOD. At this point in life I have nearly everything I could possibly want or need, except children with whom I could leave my skills. Therefore, after much thought I have consented to oblige the numerous requests for this SUPER METHOD on a strict quota limit basis. Now, here for the first time ever, you will have that one BIG CHANCE to put my winning knowledge and vast racing experience to work for you. For what will merely be a token part of your future winnings, just $30 complete, I will permit you to share privately, my one and only SUPER PROFESSIONAL MONEY-MAKING METHOD. . . .

It would be pointless to search through the pitches of system salesmen to single out the most spectacular claims. They all have their virtues. One otherwise modest and rather sensible offering caught my eye with the assertion: "This new automatic speed handicapper can spot a winner in 20 seconds—and win big money for you immediately." Perhaps this interested me because after much practice I can hardly tear loose the pages of my *Racing Form* in less than twenty seconds. For sheer optimism and upward reach, the prize must go to a plastic calculator named for a venerable university. For this the promoters asked $100—just like that, without discount or offer of money back if the device failed to work. And poetry, too, appears in the literature: one product, which instructed you to do without a *Racing Form*, to deal "only with the general and *never* the *specific*," included the incantation "Give me your hand, and let me guide you on a serene and unimpeded parade of progress toward greater racing profits together with the elimination of the irrational. . . ." I did not buy that man's system, but he could have sold me a cemetery plot if he had tried.

In the end, I did buy a number of systems; sometimes they were called "calculators" or "computers," but these were generally counting devices used to dress up a packaged system. The results surprised me. A number had more to offer than the charm of the sales pitch. Among the more respectable, I found that all had at least the kernel of a good idea. It can be stated categorically that no one should take any system to the track without first testing it thoroughly on paper. I doubt that any system will, by itself, make a winner of an otherwise losing horseplayer. But I think the serious student can get useful ideas from a number of the systems (though always for far less money from the better books). For example, the Kel-Co Calculator produces relatively good class-rating numbers, useful in many intelligent handicapping approaches; the same idea appears in an article at page 56 of the Bomze anthology and requires only paper and pencil. Similarly, the pace calculator sold by Amerpub, publishers of *American Turf Monthly*, has on its reverse side tables which permit calculation of quite a good daily track variant.

Four of the systems I examined offered money back if a workout failed to show a profit. With the first, I was too busy, or lazy, or disorganized, to make the trial. I suspect this must be the chief reliance of the salesmen. With the other three, I pulled myself together and went through the required exercise, daily, with the *Racing Form*. One of the three systems showed a slight profit and the other two lost, but not heavily. I sent the workouts to the two losers and asked for the return of my money. I was prepared to run the test to its logical end by appealing to the postal authorities, but that proved unnecessary. Both system sellers sent me checks in return, and both checks were good.

The public handicapper offers you what he says is an expert opinion. The system salesman says he will make you your own expert.

A third group, equally warmhearted and generous, also stand ready to enrich the player. They are touts in the purest sense. For a relatively modest price, they propose to give advance information of an impending betting coup. What is more, they claim to be privy to such coups regularly, every week, and sometimes daily.

Some years ago I suddenly found myself on the mailing list of someone calling himself an "ex-jockey." I suspect the list was built up from license plates spotted in the parking lots at Bay Meadows. I have been on the list ever since, and though I do not use the service, I cherish the hope it offers.

One letter began:

> To you who have little money and would appreciate a chance to make THOUSANDS OF DOLLARS IN A SINGLE AFTERNOON, SATURDAY, APRIL 14TH SHOULD BE THE BIGGEST WINNING DAY OF YOUR LIFE!!!

The letter said it knew of three horses running that afternoon

> that are POSITIVE AS POSITIVE CAN BE TO BE WINNERS!!! All 3 of these horses are not just ready and geared to hit the winner's circle, but the price they figure to pay should stagger the imagination! Fortunately, TWO OF THESE HORSES WILL BE INVOLVED IN THE 1ST and 7TH EXACTAS AND WHAT'S MORE IMPORTANT, THEY COME FROM THE SAME STABLE THAT GAVE US PAST WINNING EXACTAS, ALL PAYING BIG PRICES!!!

Letters in this genre always guarantee not only winners but high odds, though how mutuel prices are to be predicted is not revealed. They also hint darkly of large payments to "stable connections" for information that reveals a deeply contrived betting scheme. As for the cost of these "winning releases," after dizzying talk of a "$50 wire special" and a "$1,000 BLUE RIBBON PARLAY," the pitchman says he will offer a special bargain rate, Saturday only, of $15. The buyer is to telephone on Saturday morning for his winners.

Offers of specific winning selections have also come to me in the mail. My favorite injunction came in a letter from Los Angeles. After telling me how rich it could make me in "good old United States currency," it said:

> Just one word of caution: DO *NOT* PLAY ANY OTHER RACES. DON'T BE TEMPTED TO TRY AND PICK YOUR OWN WINNERS!!!!

Someone I know tested such services twice by calling on Saturday morning and giving a name taken at random from a phone book. The caller was prepared to argue indignantly—if told that his name was not on the list—that the mails must have gotten fouled up, but this turned out to be unnecessary. The magic "releases" were given matter-of-factly and without question. The selections, incidentally, were consensus choices. One of four won, and it paid low odds.

It can be taken for granted that stable information will *not* be sold by high-pressure direct mail. Of course, such information does exist. The backstretch (or stable area) is as full of the cross currents of opinion as the grandstand. Sometimes the word from a stable connection is useful; sometimes it is not.

A friend working in downtown San Francisco telephoned me one morning to ask if I was going to Bay Meadows. As it happened, I was. He asked me to make a bet for him. A friend of his had called from Los Angeles about a horse running that day at Bay Meadows. The horse was held at 8 to 1 in the track program morning line, was bet down rapidly, and went off as a short-priced favorite. The horse won. My friend and I later worked out the route by which the information reached his friend, 400 miles away. The word passed along through at least four people, and originated, we concluded, with someone who knew an assistant trainer in northern California.

Rather more often I have heard certified backstretch information that pointed to a loser.

The lure of backstretch opinion is powerful. It is strongest when it conveys an impression of wrongdoing, of a fix or a boat race. Some players assume they will never be handicappers. They go to the races just the same. They assume the sport is crooked, and they hope to find their way to the inside of the crookedness. Knowledge of just how crooked racing may or may not be is therefore one of the ultimate marks of the handicapper's art.

> *"I just found out who They is. He's a little guy from Texas in a big white hat. I saw him bet $2,000 on the Four."*
>
> —GERRY OKUNEFF,
> *handicapper, at Del Mar*

THEY: OR, PARANOIA IN THE STANDS

Among people one meets away from the racetrack, a fair number assume that racing must be crooked. It is hard to carry on an argument with them. They cheerfully admit to ignorance, but facts do not bother them. I find that the only way to capture their attention is to remark that many horseplayers agree with them.

The crowd at the track can be likened to a volcano that pours out emotion instead of lava. It erupts full force nine times daily, as the horses run through the stretch. Feelings switch rapidly from hope, to despair, to rage. A spinning color wheel may give the blurred impression of a single gray or brown; in the same way, the emotional uproar at the track adds up to one massive case of paranoia.

If ten horses run, nine will lose. Scarcely any backer of one of those nine will admit that his jockey ("his," mind you; a mutuel ticket conveys a sense of ownership shorter-lived but nearly as strong as the deed to a house) gave him anything but a stinking ride. The finish may have been close. Then, when the numbers go up, the yells of pain and outrage may go on for a minute, before they subside into violent suspicion.

One player demands of another standing beside him: "Did you see that? Did you see how They worked it that time?"

They. Always They. The accusing arm sometimes points toward the jockeys' room; They equals the riders. Or a loser may point toward the stable area, or vaguely toward the stewards' box. Because stewards, owners, track managers and officials, and even trainers are less visible, the fire centers on the jockeys. They perform publicly, watched intently through thousands of binoculars. In one of the uglier moments at the track, a losing rider walks through a barrage of curses from the scale back to the jocks' room after a race. He has staked his career and possibly his life in the race; nevertheless, the holder of a single $10 ticket shouts at the hurrying jockey who is already pulling open the snaps of his silks to change for the next race, "You rotten bastard, you! You dumped me again!"

The mass paranoia in the grandstands poses two questions, both basic to understanding racing:

Why does anyone bet on a race if he thinks it is fixed? and Is racing really crooked?

The first question answers itself. The chronically suspicious player is actually the most naïve of pigeons. He hopes to get on the inside himself and share in the swindle They have arranged. He listens for rumors. He tries to read the message on the tote board. He mills about in the betting enclosure looking for signs of action at the sellers' windows.

The second question is far more difficult—and crucial. If the game is crooked, handicapping ability is meaningless. The bettor wins only by guessing Their intentions, or sneaking into Their hidden circle. At best, the handicapper would have to be lucky enough to guess when the fix was *not* in and he might therefore have a chance to use his skill.

The straightness, or crookedness, of racing therefore seems to be the ultimate handicapping factor, which must be grappled with before analysis of class, speed, recent form, track variants, and the rest makes any sense. And if it is hard to measure the speed of a racing strip, how much more tricky to assay the honesty of riders, agents and valets, stewards, placing judges and clerks of scales, trainers and grooms. mutuel clerks and racing secretaries.

My own conclusion is that racing is essentially honest, more honest than most business. Without doubt, some people around racetracks (like people in many other places this side of paradise) would like to be crooked and aspire to be crooked. In some cases, they even think they have succeeded in being crooked. Yet I think that in fact they succeed surprisingly seldom. Among the reasons for this, perhaps the most important are (1) many people are paid to watch the would-be crooks, while (2) among the crooked themselves so many are suspiciously watching each other.

The evidence for all this needs careful sifting. A useful starting point is in the state of benign paranoia in grandstands.

It might be thought, for example, that violence constantly threatens in a crowd erupting with anger and suspicion. Curiously, a racetrack crowd is remarkably nonviolent. Racetrack concessions sell beer and booze, but drunkenness is far rarer than, say, at football games. I have rarely seen brawling at the races. Compared with a crowd at the fights, a convocation of twenty thousand horseplayers is like a nursery school picnic. I talked about this once with Captain Gordon Hall, of the San Mateo, California, police. He and a rather small detachment of uniformed men maintain order at Bay Meadows. He agreed that the track seems to present only moderate problems of crowd control.

The sports promoter Bill Veeck agrees with Captain Hall and me. After a colorful career as the head of a baseball team, Veeck was brought in to run Suffolk Downs near Boston. He had a stormy time and lasted only about two years. But in his book *Thirty Tons a Day* he pays his respects to horseplayers and he, too, comments on how generally peaceable they are through all the hubbub.

At bottom, it seems to me that some of the paranoia at the races goes off in sound, while much of the rest works itself out in fantasy. Fantasy is another ingredient to weigh in the stories of fixed races.

At one track I visit I see a woman called Cleo. She is slim, agreeable, profane, nice-looking, and middle-aged. She is not a successful horseplayer. She and her husband, a small-town businessman, have owned several horses, invariably old geldings that have worked their way to the bottom of the claiming ladder. She knows a number of trainers and cultivates the company of riders and their wives. She gathers in more information than she can successfully handle. During one meeting my friend Mike was going particularly well. She noted this and each day asked him what he liked best. He always told her. Late in the meeting she and her husband bought a ten-year-old gelding, once an allowance class horse, now running in $2,500 claimers. Before a race in which the horse was running, she took Mike and me aside. She looked about in all directions to make sure she was not overheard and then said: "I just want to tell you fellows. We've got a real shot today."

We both nodded wisely.

"Doug is riding him."

We nodded again. That fact was in the program.

Cleo looked around once more, then whispered from behind her hand: "Doug's going to use a buzzer on him."

We thanked her and she went on her way. Neither of us bet.

Cleo's horse left the gate with a dignity and restraint worthy of his years and former status. Down the backstretch he held himself aloof from the other runners, somewhat to their rear. He finished with no sign of distress and no interference from his rider, fifteen lengths behind the winner.

The facts in this case are worth reviewing. Cleo exists. So does her horse (or did, at the time). So does the jockey. So, for that matter, do buzzers. And there the facts cease. The horse did not have more than a slight chance in the race. I find it hard to believe that the rider—a man in his forties, serious, hard-working, an athlete in good condition, the sole support of a family, well established and earning, I should think, more than $50,000 a year—would risk suspension to use an illegal device in a hopeless cause. Yet what we heard was not a stray rumor passed along by a bartender, but a story told us as a special favor by the horse's owner. I do not think Cleo is a liar. I do not think she was trying to mislead us, which in any case she did not do. I think her story was an acting out of fantasy, the stuff which horseplayers' dreams are made of.

The buzzer, or battery, is a small electric shocking device.

Supposedly, it may shock a horse into running faster than he knows how, or it may jolt him out of lethargy when the stinging of an ordinary whip fails. I do not know if the device does a horse harm, but I do know that it is prohibited. Every week or two a jockey at one track or another around the country is set down for using the buzzer and being observed in the act. It is one of the most commonly rumored infractions. In my travels at least three people have taken me aside, sworn me to secrecy, and told me the identical story, of a first-rate stakes horse of a generation ago that only ran well for his favorite rider, and only ran for him because he used a buzzer. I talked about this story during a conversation with a very senior steward, generally called Whitey, in his shed on the grandstand roof of a Western track. Whitey is past eighty, massive, sharply dressed, with a snap-brimmed hat squarely set on his head and shading his eyes. He is too easily bored with evasion to give any but straight answers to questions. He has been a pricemaker, clocker, trainer, and adviser to owners. I believe in times long past he booked bets and had horses of his own. It seemed to me he might have watched more horses running than anyone else alive. He was openly scornful of clockers who needed to ask a trainer the name of a horse. He clocked works in the first pale light before dawn when a trainer was trying to sneak his horse onto the track unseen. He knows every connivance thought of by men to affect the outcome of a horse race. His large, brown-spotted hand, poised to press the single button which will lock all betting machines at the start of the race, still seems certain as fate.

About buzzers he said, "Anytime a boy seems likely to use one, we keep a camera on him from the moment he comes on the track till he leaves it. Most of the time it's a waste anyway. It won't make any difference to the horse. I don't think more than ten percent of horses respond to an electric shock any more than they would to the whip or a hand ride."

The buzzer is just one simple, outlawed device for encouraging a horse to win. Somewhat related is the problem of such drugs as bute, or butazolidin. Again, it is by no means clear that the drug does harm to a horse. It acts like a strong version of aspirin, reducing inflammation and pain. It does sometimes permit a horse to run better when sore. Use of bute, which is legal in California and an increasing number of other states, has made stakes winners of horses (Jungle Savage was one example) that otherwise were cripples.

Pitted against buzzers, abuse of bute, and other outlawed practices are stewards like Whitey and a long roster of other officials. The stewards in particular are most sensitive to how riders perform. One jockey may be penalized for interfering with another, or for abusing his horse, or even on occasion for seeming to ride in peculiar fashion.

Note that the most common violations cited by stewards are for trying too hard, and improperly, to win a race. But holders of winning tickets rarely complain. The uproar comes from those who think they have been done out of a winner. How do you prove a negative? Detecting people who may have caused a horse to lose is one of the trickiest of all problems.

Racing, like the airlines and public utilities, is a regulated industry. It is hard to think of another in which the regulating bodies keep so close a watch on the everyday conduct of business. The Interstate Commerce Commission, for example, does not have men riding shotgun on every train, nor does it screen every applicant for a switchman's job. The Federal Communications Commission does not have its people sitting in every broadcasting station.

Racing in all states comes under the jurisdiction of a state board or commission. The Jule Fink case of the 1950s (when one of the best handicappers of his time insisted on his right to an owner's license in New York, in the face of Jockey Club opposition) established not only the power of the state bodies, but their duty to exercise such powers without laying them off on private associations. As a result, a typical track today provides a special office for agents of the state board or commission, and these attend every racing day. The stewards have control of the races and officially determine winners; one steward represents the state agency. A typical lineup of officials, representing the state, the track, and racing associations may include veterinarians (two at California tracks), placing judges, patrol judges, paddock judges or horse identifiers, starters, clerks of scales, horseshoe inspectors, and state revenue agents who keep an eye on the flow of money and tickets through the mutuel apparatus, to make sure that, among other things, the state gets its cut. It should be added that the mutuel managers also watch for unusual betting patterns.

The California State Horse Racing Board, to take one major example, treats a prospective owner of a horse politely, but examines him as thoroughly as if he were a candidate for the judiciary. If a horseplayer is lucky enough to win a large bet at good odds, he can buy a Mercedes or Cadillac with no more effort than it takes to count out 150 hundred-dollar bills. Not so, should he wish to make himself eligible to claim a $15,000 Thoroughbred. He submits financial records and references, personal history, and fingerprints, and his records are checked with police agencies through Sacramento. Everyone working at the track, from mutuel clerks to stable hands, gets the same scrutiny, and men with past police records have been ruled off for no other reason.

Horses' financial records mainly concern handicappers, but the animals in other respects also are closely watched. Veterinarians observe them in the paddock and at the starting gate. If the horse seems unfit or appears to be behaving peculiarly, he may be scratched from the race literally seconds before post time, while the starting crew is loading the gate. Curiously, when this does happen, the crowd groans, only partly, it seems, because odds on the remaining horses go down. Scratching an unfit horse evidently promotes a fair race, but this, too, is viewed with suspicion.

After the race, the winner has to offer up a urine sample for laboratory testing. This task, often glibly referred to, is not always easy to carry out. While a hot walker leads the sweating horse in a circle, another man waits with a jug in one hand and a huge funnel mounted on a broomstick in the other. He must wait until the horse in the fullness of time decides to empty his bladder. Occasionally, a groom tries to help by tickling the horse's urethra with a straw. Usually, nothing helps but patience.

It can well be argued that the post-race tests have to be useful, if for no other reason than scaring off possible offenders. The positive findings, though, where tests are established, are few. According to testimony offered in 1972 by Charles Ginsberg, chairman of the Ohio State Racing Commission, tests of about 11,000 samples, taken after 5,582 races, revealed just ten cases of traces of depressants, stimulants, strong analgesics, or otherwise improper drugs. In New York during all of 1973, at Belmont, Aqueduct, and Saratoga, absolutely no positives at all turned up in 1,884 tests.

As for the findings of stewards, these too are relatively few and generally minor. At frequent intervals the *Daily Racing Form* carries a column briefly noting stewards' actions at tracks with meetings in progress. For example, the *Form* for May 30, 1978, reported twelve rulings handed down at Golden Gate Fields, Hollywood Park, La Mesa Park, Los Alamitos, and Santa Fe. Five trainers were cited for such offenses as lack of fiscal responsibility, parking in a restricted area, violating medication rules, and being abusive to security guards. A patron was barred from the grounds for getting into a fight in the stable area. An exercise rider had his license lifted for drunkenness. And several jockeys were given suspensions for failure to keep a straight course in the stretch, and, in one case, for hitting another rider with a whip in a stretch duel.

From the mass of such material it would appear that stewards are very much on the watch, that they take quick disciplinary actions, and that the violations they uncover are overwhelmingly minor.

Of course, the official rulings column in the *Racing Form* does not tell the whole story. From time to time far more serious allegations work their way into the general press. These are the stories of fixes and bribes and other offenses punishable by jail sentences.

In June 1973 six mutuel clerks were arrested in Los Angeles and charged with booking bets on the side and otherwise flaunting regulations. This case was more than a year in preparation. It was eventually thrown out.

In October 1974 the New York papers found some amusement in a fine levied against a trotting horse trainer-driver because the state testing lab found some caffeine in his horse's urine. It was later stated that the caffeine showed up because the horse had shared a cola drink with his groom, a twenty-five-year-old woman.

In November 1974 a much more serious account of conspiracy to fix races came out of a trial in Rochester, New York. This case resulted in convictions. The fixing took place at a track called Finger Lakes, sixteen miles from Rochester. The average purse per race at Finger Lakes in 1973 was a little over $1,700 (in contrast to an average of more than $12,000 per race across the state at Belmont, or across the country at Hollywood Park).

Even Belmont, however, had its troubles with investigations and unfavorable press notices in the fall of 1974. Traces of drugs were found in several horses at Belmont in September. An investigation dragged on for months. Then in May 1975 a trainer named J. L. Cotter charged jockey Angel Cordero with being part of a ring that fixed races. Cotter was a trainer whose horses during 1973 won 14 races out of 175 starts. Cordero was one of the country's leading riders. He rode 284 winners during 1973, for a grand total of more than $3 million in purses. Cotter, it turned out, had been under investigation for months in connection with the drugging cases of the preceding September. The state board failed to renew Cotter's license. He moved to get it back. He made his charges against Cordero, suddenly, at the end of his hearing. Cordero replied that he earned several hundred thousand dollars a year by winning races, not by pulling horses, and that he was indeed fairly often suspended by stewards—for trying too hard.

One more alleged fix broke into public print in May 1975, this time an account of a fixed exacta race at Bowie on February 14, 1975. Four jockeys and three others were indicted. In this case, incidentally, Bowie track officials started the investigation when they noted what they described as an "unusual wagering pattern" on the race. Convictions resulted in this case, too.

On September 23, 1977, a 57–1 shot, running under the name of Lebón, scored an easy win in the last race of the day at Belmont—and touched off the most resounding scandal in racing in many years. The investigations that were started at once uncovered a weird story, involving: (1) the strong possibility that Lebón, a cheap and essentially worthless plater, was in fact an excellent horse named Cinzano; (2) evidence that a veterinarian, Dr. Mark Gerard, may have had a part in importing both horses from Uruguay; (3) reports that Dr. Gerard had made, and won, a large bet on Lebón-Cinzano; and (4) an allegation that one of the horses had been killed, that the dead horse had falsely been said to be Cinzano, and that a $150,000 insurance policy on the horse had been paid off. Long before all the charges could be nailed down, at least one salient fact had emerged. As at Bowie, two years before, the public nature of racetrack betting, and the immediate spotting of a betting coup, led quickly to a highly publicized investigation. Almost exactly a year after the scandal broke, Dr. Gerard was brought to trial in Mineola, New York. In court, Dr. Gerard's estranged wife testified that she had engineered the Lebón-Cinzano switch. The defense also asserted that the death of one of the horses, presumably Lebón, had been an accident. A jury cleared Dr. Gerard of two felony charges growing out of the switch, but it convicted him on two misdemeanor counts involving the making of a false entry in a contest of speed.

One clear finding from all these stories is that an allegedly crooked horse race does command media attention. In passing, it might be noted that a fair number of fraud cases in one of the most respectable industries, banking, slip by without public comment. Christopher Elias, writing about banking in 1973, noted: "Bank fraud, in fact, is a growth industry, a view supported by John J. Slocum, chief of the [Federal Deposit Insurance Corporation's] Division of Liquidation. Slocum regards bank fraud as 'one of America's fastest growing enterprises!'" By way of evidence, Elias cited FDIC numbers: The number of bank frauds rose from 146 in 1968, to 180 in 1969, and to 245 in 1970. These several hundreds of frauds did not visibly shake confidence in the banking system, and perhaps one reason for that was the fact that they generally slipped by without significant publicity.

Still, smoke may not be a proof of fire, but it is cause to reach for a bucket of water. Only hustlers, touts, and fixers can gain from racing scandals. Horseplayers in particular stand to gain by serious examination of the charges of abuse of horses, fixed races, and generally shady operations, by shady characters, at racetracks.

In 1972 and 1973 a congressional committee, the House Select Committee on Crime, made a far-reaching probe of wrongdoing in horse racing. The committee's work needs the most careful examination. It began its hearings, in Washington, on May 9, 1972. The chairman, Congressman

Claude Pepper of Florida, said the committee would first look at parimutuel racing and then seek out connections between crime and other sports as well. The committee got well started on racing and never left it. The bulk of four volumes of hearings, covering more than 1,800 pages, deals with what the summary report calls "Organized Criminal Influence in Horseracing." The committee took evidence on twenty-four separate days, heard ninety-seven witnesses ranging from reputed gangsters to police officials to such entertainers as Sammy Davis and Frank Sinatra, and received dozens of supplementary documents for the record. If anything clearly lights up the dark side of racing, it should be the work of the Pepper Committee.

Mafia-watching has been a major industry in the United States, on a scale with Kremlinology, since the days of the Kefauver Committee in 1950. With the success of the two *Godfather* films, Mafia-watching may truly be regarded as a certified growth industry.

The Pepper Committee staff arranged for appearances of a representative scattering of reputed mobsters. Probably the highest-ranking witness, according to the special literature of the field, was Carlos Marcello of New Orleans.

If half of what has been written about Marcello is true, the committee could have had little hope of obtaining useful information from him. About horse racing he said nothing at all. For purposes of such a hearing, Marcello may be described as a sort of political totem, or symbolic figure. From some lesser figures, though, the committee did obtain a great flow of freely offered testimony. Typical of such witnesses was Joseph Barboza, New England mobster, who said he was part of Raymond Patriarca's Cosa Nostra family. At the time of his appearance Barboza was serving a jail term after having pled guilty to second-degree murder.

Barboza gave a graphic picture of beatings, but his testimony about racing was vaguer. Most of it centered around a place called the Ebb Tide and a man named Henry Tamello, reputedly an associate of Raymond Patriarca. "During the course of that time, a lot of jockeys from the race-track, Suffolk Downs, used to go inside the Ebb Tide," Barboza said. "They were wined and dined, given the best girls in the place, and so forth, and they didn't have to pay in advance. They had a tab there. They spent freely."

Later Barboza described making usurious loans to jockeys, and then, to render them further obligated, at the orders of Henry Tamello, forgiving them some of their debt. What favors did the jockeys have to return? That was never made clear, although the committee counsel led Barboza, at length, through the bloody trail that ended in a number of murder convictions in court.

Congressman Jerome R. Waldie of California broke in, after Barboza had elaborated on beatings, murders, and shakedowns, from Boston to Cleveland, to say:

"Mr. Chairman, let me interrupt. I am either losing the thread of this witness, or I misunderstand what the witness is talking about. Is this involving organized crime's influence on sports? Do you have anything to do with the sports or athletic field?"

The dialogue continued:

"Barboza: No, not really. Where jockeys are concerned—

"Waldie: Did you have any contact with jockeys?

"Barboza: I shook a couple of them up there for Henry Tamello.

"Waldie: What ones did you shake up?

"Barboza: I told him earlier, I don't know."

Waldie later asked, "Was that your sole and total connection with sports?" And Barboza said, once more: "Yes, sir. Really."

The Congressman's impatience with blood and guts is understandable. It is perfectly possible that jockeys did come to the Ebb Tide. It is not only possible, but likely, that Henry Tamello may have tried to do favors for them. As unthreatening a person as my friend Cleo cultivates the company of riders and their wives and does small personal favors for them. The question remains: What is returned for these favors? What could be returned?

Curiously, the Barboza testimony does shed some light on these questions. Congressman Frank J. Brasco of New York was conducting the witness through the matter of jockeys again:

"Brasco: And was Mr. Tamello, from your own knowledge, a heavy bettor on horseracing?"

And here Barboza tapped into a new vein in his recollections. He said:

"At one time [in] Mr. Patriarca's office, he said Henry Tamello lost at least one million dollars in his life gambling."

Lost a million dollars? Why did he lose anything if he could arrange the services of a number of jockeys? Unfortunately, that vein was not pursued.

Much testimony before the committee went to demonstrate that the directors of Hazel Park, in Detroit, had mob connections. The president of Hazel Park at the time of the hearings was Anthony Zerilli of Detroit. Anthony Zerilli is the son of Joseph Zerilli. Joseph, the elder Zerilli, has been named in many Mafia stories. Vincent Piersante, chief of the Organized Crime Division of the Michigan Attorney General's Office, told the committee: "In 1963 we named Joseph Zerilli, Angelo Meli, Peter Licavoli, Bill Tocco, and John Priziola as top members of that criminal organization in Michigan. All of them, as I said, had some interest in the Hazel Park Racing Association." Actually, the first charges against the younger Zerilli, Anthony, had been made as early as 1953, when he was in his twenties, but no state agency had found the evidence strong enough to force him out of the directorship of Hazel Park. Since the Pepper Committee hearings, he has divested himself of his racetrack holdings.

Another large section of the hearings brought forward evidence that Raymond Patriarca, Thomas Lucchese, and others frequently named as Cosa Nostra leaders had attempted to take over Berkshire Downs in western Massachusetts. The effort failed. In fact, Berkshire Downs was refused racing dates by state authorities.

Some 200 pages of the record of the Pepper Committee were devoted to the complicated story of the ownership of one horse, Jim French—an important stakes horse, second in both the Kentucky Derby and the Belmont Stakes of 1971, eventually bought for stud service by Daniel Wildenstein. The key figures in a highly complicated series of transactions were Ralph Wilson of Buffalo, New York, and Robert Presti of New Jersey. Wilson was described as a wealthy businessman and sports promoter. Presti was a sometime horse broker. Presti, according to the committee record, used fronts, or "nominees," to mask ownership of horses. Presumably, this was done because of mob connections in the background. These connections were never demonstrated.

Finally, Emprise Corp. of Buffalo was singled out for the major burden of the committee's investigations. References to the Emprise matter crop up throughout all the four volumes of hearings. Emprise owns pieces of racetracks and other sports enterprises, is the concessionaire for food and other services at a large number of tracks and stadiums all over the country, and, according to the Pepper Committee's final report, "has done business with individuals designated by public authority or authorities as organized crime figures."

In April 1972, two weeks before the House Select Committee on Crime began its hearings, Emprise was convicted in California, under federal anti-racketeering laws, of improperly attempting to buy into the Frontier Hotel and Gambling Casino in Las Vegas, Nevada. Since then, Emprise has undoubtedly suffered business setbacks. It has been forced to give up some of its food concessions, at Golden Gate Fields, among other places.

Several members of the Pepper Committee wrote separate views for the final report, expressing some doubts about the alleged links between organized crime and racing and in particular about the handling of the Emprise matter.

Congressman Morgan F. Murphy said, "There was not, in my opinion, any final committee determination that Emprise had links with organized crime, that they conducted business like organized crime, or that they consorted knowingly with organized crime figures."

In connection with the Hazel Park connection, Murphy said, "No credible evidence of illegal business transactions by Emprise or their associates was found. Committee reliance on 'guilt by association' is certainly questionable."

Congressman Charles E. Wiggins of California expressed broader doubts. He said, "A major portion of the committee's energies was directed toward condemning individuals who, so far as our record discloses, engaged in some aspect of the racing business in a manner which was entirely within the law and consistent with the public's interest in racing. We apparently found justification for this vilification because we were satisfied that the individuals were members of, connected with, did business with, or did business like, organized crime. The question which troubles me is the propriety of a congressional committee condemning those who may, during the course of a lawful business enterprise, have maintained a lawful business relationship with 'organized crime.' "

Wiggins is a Republican. His fellow Californian, Waldie, is a liberal Democrat. Nevertheless, Waldie in a briefer dissent said, "I concur in the essence of Congressman Wiggins' remarks although I support the committee's final recommendations." The recommendations called for (1) more interstate cooperation among regulatory bodies, (2) better data banks, (3) tighter rules on testing, exotic betting, conflicts of interest, and long-term racing dates, and (4) new federal laws aimed against dodges for fixing races or for concealing ownership.

In some degree the Select Committee may have fallen into a familiar trap in regard to organized crime and its alleged links with lawful businesses, including racing. Part of the appeal of the mob, in books and movies, is a mix of violence and mystery, a sort of perverse romanticism, based on sketchy knowledge. If a generation of Mafia-watching has demonstrated anything, it is that illegal money lusts not for further violence but for respectability. It seeks to follow the same paths as legal money.

Since the mass arrest of mob leaders in 1957 at Apalachin in upstate New York, Mafia chiefs have often been identified as respectable businessmen, with automobile dealerships, soft-drink distributorships, garment businesses, import operations in olive oil and other commodities. The fact is that money accumulated—by whatever means, whether by government contract, by sharp dealing, by ordinary trade, by stealing, or by brutal, bloody, murderous extortion—seeks the same investment channels. The steady, glacierlike movement of gang-tainted money into political campaigns during the 1950s was such common knowledge that it was referred to as "the unseen force," though Congress did not rush to investigate itself. Among knowledgeable racing people I have talked with, most knew, or thought they knew, of cases in which mob money might be glimpsed, floating gently, dimly seen, in the background of one or another racing operation. I do not know what can be deduced from this other than a similarity between racing and most other forms of business.

On one score at least, the House Select Committee took its stand with horseplayers. It was much concerned with jockeys. Jockeys are athletes with unusual skills, strength, and daring who can generally weigh in, stripped, at about 110 pounds. Necessarily, they spend much time in each other's company. Though the committee was unfortunately misinformed on this point, they have, among other things, legitimate labor organizations of their own.

By the original Jockey Club rules, carried forward by state commissions or boards, they may bet only on the horses they ride, and then through the trainers or owners of those horses. They do bet. They do not always bet exclusively on their own horses. Given these ingredients, the notion arises that conspiracies to arrange the outcome of races must take shape in a jockeys' room as naturally as a bird builds its nest.

The inevitable conspiracy theory overlooks a number of additional facts. It is very hard to arrange the order of finish of a race. Guaranteeing one winner means guaranteeing a large number of losers. One experienced rider may be able to escape notice when he runs his horse into difficulties. If half a dozen jockeys do the same thing, the resulting odor will most likely carry to the stewards' box. The number of people who have to be in on a fix expands rapidly.

Some years ago, at one track west of the Mississippi, a friend pointed out to me someone known simply as "the old man." He was indeed old (he is now dead), and grizzled, and he habitually wore a dingy mackinaw. It was his task, at that track, to carry bets out of the jockeys' room. Through my friend I learned the bets the old man carried. Two curious facts emerged. If the old man carried out five bets, they were usually on five different horses; the riders, in his experience, never agreed. And, secondly, they were terrible handicappers.

By far the most important argument against the conspiracy theory is a matter of economics. From thirty-five to forty riders can handle all the mounts at a single track. Among these, about ten leaders will account for roughly 60 percent of the winners.

These successful riders are placed on a large majority of the live horses, the ones likely to win. At major tracks, where the average purse size per race is $5,000 or more (and major tracks account for nearly two-thirds of the parimutuel action in America), the leading riders earn substantial pay—in the range of $50,000 a year and up. (The leaders at the New York and Los Angeles tracks earn far more.) I have just looked at the past records of the ten leading riders at a recent northern California meeting. In a preceding year all of them, except the youngest apprentices, accounted for a total of between $300,000 and $2 million each in purses. They (and their agents) receive 10 percent of purse money, plus a fee for each finish out of the money, and other fees as well. The rewards are substantial, and a jockey could scarcely duplicate them in another field. The unsuccessful riders may have little to lose if caught in a fix, but these are not the ones needed to set up a boat race. It seems to me that the successful rider, at a track with fair purse distribution, has too much to lose to engage in complicated conspiracies—unless he is extraordinarily stupid, or already deeply in trouble (and I have been told of a few such cases).

I realize that the economic incentives may be different at the minor Thoroughbred tracks, and the tracks for other kinds of racing, at all of which purse distribution may average no more than two or three thousand dollars per race. I am sure there are honest racing people, and diligent officials, in all these places. But I could understand it if temptation were more persuasive at a half-mile track, where a journeyman rider, approaching forty, accepts more than 500 races in a year, wins 10 percent of those, but brings in a total of only $80,000 in purse money.

In regard to conspiracies among jockeys overall, I believe it must be said the committee hearings made no case.

The Pepper Committee's star witness, in regard to races fixed in other ways, was a man introduced as "Bobby Byrne, horse-racing specialist and fixer of races." Byrne claimed to be able to enter the backstretch of any track at will, to fix any race he wished with no more than ten days' notice, and to do this with or without help on the inside. He aimed, he said, at exacta or perfecta races, where the bettor must pick, in correct order, the first two horses to finish. In a ten-horse race, he said, he aimed at knocking out the six most likely horses. Among the remaining four, all held at long prices on the tote board, two would straggle home first and second in the race. He and confederates, Byrne said, would have bet on all the combinations of the four supposedly live horses, thus being assured a winning combination, at long odds. The key to the operation was administering drugs to the six horses to be held back in the race. The drug of choice, he said, was acepromazine.

The number of defects in Byrne's story is almost as great as the number of his charges and allegations against racing. Quite in passing, he volunteered, without being asked: "I have an extensive police record. I have done three terms in jail, and I think my last time in jail was in 1966. Since that time I have been arrested probably about four or five times for burglar tools and opening safes and B and E and I haven't done a day in jail." Byrne did, in fact, attempt to fix a race, in exactly the way he described, on at least one occasion, a year before his committee appearance, at Suffolk Downs.

The evidence for this went into the record, unobtrusively, in a prepared statement by Spencer Drayton, president of the Thoroughbred Racing Protective Bureau. Drayton was not called as a witness. Drayton said that his organization, the TRPB, began investigating attempts to fix exacta races as early as May 1970. In the course of this investigation, he said, "The TRPB apprehended Robert Byrne on April 23, 1971, when he attempted to enter the stable area at Suffolk Downs. He was searched after his arrest and he was found to be in possession of two hypodermic syringes filled with a tranquilizing agent." Indictments were brought in 1972, one in Massachusetts charging fifteen individuals and one in Rhode Island charging twenty-two individuals. One case had already gone to trial, Drayton said, and four convictions had been brought in at the time of his statement.

Regrettably, no one on the committee asked Byrne what races he had fixed, or tried to fix, since April 1971. Neither was he asked pertinent details, which could be checked against published charts, about races he might have succeeded in fixing earlier. Above all, no one led him through what might have been an illuminating discussion of the difficulties in his mode of operation. Some of these are:

1. Acepromazine does tranquilize a horse, and might, if injected, keep one from running well, without otherwise harming him. But too small a dose would have little or no effect, while too large a dose would have visible effects. The horse's eyes would redden and sometimes they would be covered by a membrane, the third lid. Those signs would be visible all day long, to dozens of people, including grooms, trainers, and veterinarians. In answer to a question that scratched at the surface of this problem, Byrne said, as to the dosage, "We did it by experiment." Experiments, assuming they took place at all, imply some failures. In such a case, one of the better horses was almost certainly underdosed, and if he then came in first or second, the plotters would have blown their whole roll on losing tickets.

2. Byrne at one point said he arranged as many as four races in a day. That implied doping as many as twenty to twenty-five horses. It is easy to find one barn in the stable area, even in the dark. But the location of a particular horse's stall is not easy. How many people did he have to bribe to draw up a detailed map that does not exist anywhere else on the grounds?

3. At one point, Byrne seemed to imply that he, a complete stranger, could approach a horse and dope him while people were watching. Elsewhere in his testimony he seemed to recognize the difficulties here, and alleged that he did his work in the dark, before daybreak. Did he, among other things, ever hit the wrong horse in the dark? Did no stable hand ever wake up? Was everyone on the grounds in his pay? The difficulties compound until they rival the complexities of a locked room puzzle in a detective novel. Byrne refused to acknowledge that the security arrangements at any track would have given him trouble.

The last and perhaps the most interesting bit of chicanery described in testimony before the House Select Committee concerned ringers—good horses running under the names and papers of lesser horses, in races the ringers seemed almost sure to win. Again, the story was developed, not by an adversary, but through the effort of the racing industry to police itself. The witness was a TRPB investigator, Paul Berube.

The ringer theme in racing is an old one. It figures in "The

Silver Blaze," one of the Sherlock Holmes stories, and again in the Lebón-Cinzano affair of 1977. I asked a trainer once if he, in roughly forty years around racetracks, knew of cases where a ringer had successfully been brought into a race. He replied:

"I can remember a case—though this was before the lip tattoos came in. A fellow had two horses, both bay, no markings of any kind, same size just about. They really did look alike. One run short, the other run long. He took the one that run short and entered him in a race to run long. He finished dead last. Next time he took the one that really run long and entered him at his right distance, at good odds. He lost anyway."

Berube said that TRPB investigation turned up cases of six superior horses that were given forged records and new identities so they could be entered in cheaper races, where presumably large bets could be won. One of the most curious features of the story was that, so far as the TRPB could determine, the ringers entered in a total of forty-one races—and won only fourteen of those. The forgers could have had as good a percentage of winners by betting favorites—at worse odds, to be sure, but with less cost and bother and without going to jail.

At the end of the 1,800-page record of the House Select Committee on Crime, one conclusion is reinforced: There is no end to the dreams of crookedness in racing. But it is even harder to fix a race than it is to handicap one.

The notion refuses to die, however. An article in *Sports Illustrated* (November 6, 1978) carried many of the old charges and some new ones. The accuser this time was a presumed "fixer," Tony Ciulla. The charges had a familiar ring. They brought in prominent names and shadow names, including that of Bobby Byrne. Some of the accusations were taken seriously by racing people, were sifted by police as well as racing's own investigators, and resulted in criminal prosecutions in New Jersey and Michigan. The article said the fixing went on between 1972 and 1975 and had been under investigation for several years.

By curious chance, during that same week, newspapers across the country told of a man named Rafkin who allegedly shook down the electronics system of Security Pacific Bank in Los Angeles for more than $10 million. Also during that week, the news told of an art swindler who had bilked collectors of $2 million for bogus paintings.

People still deposited money in banks, collectors hung paintings on their walls, and horseplayers continued to back their opinions with wagers at the track—all evidently (and properly) assuming that the rules are enforced in a great majority of cases.

*"No one ever bet enough on a
winning horse."*
—UNKNOWN HORSEPLAYER,
in a cashier's line

 **MINE OWN
WORST ENEMY**

Mike's friend the Barber is a pudgy
man in his sixties, sandy-haired,
with pale blue watery eyes. He walks little, and slowly. He
spends his day at the track around the paddock and the concrete apron near the finish line. He does not carry glasses.
Presumably, he does not own them; in any case, he has no need
for them. He never carries a *Racing Form*, and Mike assures me
he could not read one if he did.

But the Barber is a horseplayer, and a classic of his type. His
play follows two unalterable rules:

If there is a race he will bet on it, so long as he has two dollars
in his pocket. He is totally unable to pass a race.

And he will always place his bet on the favorite in the race, no
matter what he may have said, or heard, in advance.

The Barber vaguely understands that betting every race is a
vice. Among others, Mike, who also has a touch of do-good in
him, has told him so. As for opinions on horses other than the
favorite, the air is full of them. The Barber seeks advice, listens
to it, glances at the tote board, and winces with pain. In the end

he goes to the window, full of instructions, and bets—the favorite. I have sometimes wondered what would happen to the Barber if by some chance the board showed exactly the same amount of support for each horse in a short field. He might explode with frustration, rather like the scholar's ass that starved to death halfway between two bales of hay.

In one way or another, something of the Barber is in all of us who go to the races. His is the flawed and secret face of weakness, or lack of control, which we all must put down to survive.

Betting too many races is, I suppose, the commonest vice of the uncontrolled player, though it is only one of many flaws, or vices. Knowledge of one's own weaknesses is the indispensable step toward becoming even a competent player.

Two demurrers should be filed and noted at this point.

First, rules about betting, and control, and anything else for that matter, do not apply to people out to enjoy a day's racing once in a while. Why should they not bet any number of races, when and as they wish? To them I simply offer the advice that they should include a wager on each race as part of the budget for the outing. If they lose every bet, they may be disappointed but not shattered. If they win any, they can rejoice in having beaten the game. Having gone racing occasionally for fun, though, they may want to go again, and then again for a more serious sort of enjoyment, and then they must think about the gambler's problems of self-knowledge and control.

Second, and just as obvious, discipline and money management have nothing to do with skillful handicapping or selecting. Stay around the tracks only a little while and you are certain to meet an excellent handicapper who understands the subtlest factors in a race but is a terrible bettor. Even reasonably good bettors can have days when they select well—and go home losers. If this sounds dubious, I offer the following specimen day, and I believe any honest horseplayer will admit to similar experience.

The player arrives at the track full of hope and with an opinion on horses in the sixth, eighth, and ninth races. To give himself a good running start, he buys half a dozen tickets on the daily double, in the first two races, though he likes nothing particularly in either race. His horses finish off the board, and he tears up those tickets. Somewhat irritated, he passes the third and fourth races—and rightly, too. In the fifth race he sees a horse he had not thought of the night before. It stands at 3-1. He hears that the stable likes the horse. A good player must be able to adjust, he tells himself. He tries to repair the damage of the daily double. The horse runs an unenterprising fourth. Our player is now thoroughly depressed. In the sixth race he encounters the first horse he really liked before coming to the track. In a flurry of betting in the first ten minutes, the horse is bet down to even money. Our man, gun-shy now, stays off. The horse actually closes at 3-2, and wins, and was probably worth the price, the bettor concludes sadly, after the race. Thoroughly annoyed, he bets $50, a large bet for him, on the horse he liked in the eighth race. And this time he does finally have a winner. Everyone in the park, it seemed, liked the horse, too, and it went off at 4-5. He cashes his ticket and finds himself still a little behind for the day. The horse he liked in the ninth and final race is the morning-line favorite. He assumes it, too, will be bet down to even money or less. He has had enough and he goes home without betting, a slight loser for the day. His selection for the last race, which he passed, does go off a favorite but at a startlingly good price, 5-2, and wins by a length and a half.

Does the incident have any ring of truth? It should. It happened on a pleasant June day at Golden Gate Fields. The winning horses in the sixth, eighth, and ninth races were Oak Harbor, Stained Glass, and Our Land. And I was the unhappy bettor.

Of course, there will also be the good days: days when every horse you pass turns out to be a well-beaten favorite, the information you take seriously proves to be bonded, and your bets are fairly rewarded at reasonable odds.

What this suggests is that the player must learn to swim with the erratic tides of chance. And, to bear himself with equanimity, through good days and bad, he must as a first step learn his own style and how to live with it.

From much of the literature on handicapping, it would appear that there is but one way to handle oneself at the track— namely, that way set forth in each book. The truth, I think, is more complex. It seems to me there are a number of betting styles, and the player can hold his own, and sometimes prosper, in at least a couple of ways.

For convenience, three main styles of play can be singled out: (1) often playing favorites, (2) looking only for overlays, at a price, and (3) a catchall, including hunches, angles, and a multitude of systems.

Chalk players have something of a bad name around racetracks, and this is strange since there are so many of them. (The word "chalk" for a favorite is old betting parlor language.) My own preference is for another style of betting. But I think undiluted abuse of favorite players is ridiculous. It is possible to bet in much worse ways, and most people do. Some players point out, with a touch of scorn, that two-thirds of the favorites lose. I find it just as interesting that fully one-third of all favorites win.

Studies of tens of thousands of races done in the 1960s showed a loss of 8 or 9 percent from betting on all favorites. Since then, the takeout has continued to inch upward. By the late 1970s 10 percent had become a reasonable loss to expect from betting either all favorites or, what comes to the same thing, a random selection of them.

The number to compare with the 10 percent loss from favorite play is 17 percent. Seventeen percent of the mutuel pool will be cut from the top and will be the average loss from the total of all bets. Nothing can affect that number—be the day rainy or fair, the horses excellent or broken down, the players expert or dimwitted. A statistical inference of the greatest importance follows from these numbers. If some players (about 30 percent, actually) lose 10 percent by playing favorites indiscriminately, and if the average loss from the whole mutuel pool is 17 percent, then it follows that some very large percentage of losers, needed to balance out the pool, actually lose a good deal more than 17 percent—in fact, in the neighborhood of 25 percent and upward. (Some implications of these numbers, which so far as I know have not been written about before, were pursued in Chapter 5 of this book.)

Another kind of inference follows from the numbers. THEY, meaning in this case the people who backed the favorites, really do know something. They know enough to lose less than most of the rest of the crowd. And here lies the tantalizing kernel at the heart of favorite betting. Some kind of special knowledge is at work over the long haul—wise money, for whatever that is worth—in the creating of favorites. Favoritism is one more factor which the winning player has to consider.

Some of the money pouring through the windows is superstitious money, some of it is ignorant money, some of it is misinformed or misled money, and some of it is really smart money. Can you tell when a sizable amount of smart money has helped create a favorite? This is the problem facing the systematic favorite player.

Obviously, the intelligent chalk player—and yes, he does exist—cannot play favorites at random. He selects, and rigorously. Unlike the Barber, who only seeks comfort in numbers, the smart favorite player looks for the maximum possible certainty. To achieve it, he accepts a low payoff—since what he sees is bound to be seen by many others.

If the intelligent chalk player selects, he also must throw out. If he is to have any chance of finishing ahead, he throws out the overwhelming majority of favorites. He bets only on those that meet his own rigid rules.

A book called *Horse Sense*, by Burton Fabricand, sets forth a system for winning by playing only selected favorites. I have never met anyone who knew anyone who actually used Fabricand's system. The rules are complex; among other things, they sound as if written with a computer program in mind. But Fabricand's argument is interesting. He is looking, literally, for confusion.

Most favorites are overbet. Therefore, Fabricand argues, look for a confused situation in which the favorite may be a more nearly square price. The confusion comes, according to his method, from finding at least one other horse in the field that meets just about the same handicapping requirements as the favorite. Another way of reading the same signs might be: the two horses are so nearly the same on form that they ought to be held at the same price. If one is favored, maybe smart money made it so. Curiously, the lengthy workout included in Fabricand's book could be interpreted to bolster the suggestion that some of the money that goes to make a favorite really is smart money. (Specifically, his winners paid only average favorite prices; but he had more of them. Were these simply overlaid favorites? Or had he introduced a new handicapping factor, based on flow of informed money?)

Contrasted with chalk players are the second major group: the overlay hunters who seek the longest odds consistent with a winning chance.

Strictly speaking, a favorite, too, can be an overlay. Secretariat on the eve of the Belmont Stakes—his best race, against a small field of horses he had already thoroughly beaten—may have been an overlay at any price (though I still would not like the bet; Secretariat only looked that much a sure thing *after* the race).

Generally the overlay player is most interested in finding the race with a false favorite. In the tradition of the most successful gamblers through the centuries, he is constantly weighing probabilities. Naturally, he must like his horse's chances (else why bet at all?). But he is just as much impressed by the odds. For him, the potential reward must far outweigh the clear risk. He may put a horse on top of its field, giving it perhaps a 30 percent chance of winning. That is, should the same kind of situation present itself ten times, he predicts his choice will win perhaps three times. Therefore, if such a horse goes off at 2–1 or 5–2, he is not interested. (Note that ten $2 tickets cost $20. Three winners at 5–2, 5–2, and 2–1, or $7, $7, and $6, would exactly break even.) If the odds rise to 3–1 or 4–1, the overlay player begins to think seriously. If the odds go to 5–1 or 6–1, he bets with enthusiasm.

Thus the intelligent favorite player looks for the horse whose virtues are as clear as possible. The overlay player looks for the horse whose virtues are somewhat overlooked.

Does the crowd often overlook a horse that is clearly best in its field? It seems to me I can spot half a dozen such cases each week at a track I am following—see them after the race is run, in any case, and sometimes, when I am fortunate, see them before post time. I imagine I must miss as many cases as I see, before or after the race. So the overlay player has enough to work with. But he has to discipline himself doubly to succeed. He must have a firm opinion about a horse, and an equally firm opinion about the price below which he will not bet.

In my opinion, the overlay is the play most devoutly to be

sought. The arithmetic seems to me overwhelming. If you can produce winners just 25 to 30 percent of the time, but at odds ranging upward from 7–2, you will win, and far more handsomely over the year than the favorite player laboriously grinding out an amazing 45 percent winners at low odds.

Still, while I have expressed my own preference, I recognize the importance of a player's finding his own style. Not only does the overlay player have to discipline himself doubly: he must be able to endure tension and erosion of his ego when he falls into a losing streak.

Favorites, too, can run out of the money persistently and with callous disregard for their backers' hopes. Just because a third of all races may be won by favorites does not mean that every day three out of nine races will go to the favored horse. Look at the charts for a whole meeting and you may find a few days on which favorites won six of the nine races. Correspondingly you will also find several days when not a single favorite won. I myself have seen more than twenty races in succession without a winning favorite, covering two full racing days and part of a third. I assume longer streaks could be found.

The overlay player must be prepared for even harder times. His losing streaks may last longer. He does not have the comfort of company. He must, no matter how case-hardened his ego, no matter how secure his opinions, begin at some point to wonder: What's wrong? Have I lost it? A racing official I know told me, in this connection, of a handicapper so well known that he bears the title "Genius" as a nickname. The Genius, while resident at an Eastern track where the official then worked, had a losing streak of more than thirty races going. He finally hit—with an odds-on horse that paid $3.60 to win. The Genius thereupon turned to a companion and said, "See? I am a genius after all."

The third style of betting must be described briefly. It includes all the rest: name freaks, jockey watchers, numbers mystics. Their variety is endless. And sometimes they may trample the more serious player in their rush.

The jockey Ted Atkinson, in his autobiography, *All the Way*, tells of a horse named Saint Dunstan entered on a day when everything favored him, but his form was well concealed. The morning-line odds were high. His owner, trainer, and rider all bet heavily on him. He did, in fact, win, but to the stable's dismay he had been bet down to even money. "The stands that afternoon had held hundreds of blacksmiths and foundrymen attending a convention in an adjacent city," Atkinson wrote, "and Saint Dunstan was the patron saint of blacksmiths!"

Just the same, it is worth examining the effects of some of the more common betting styles in the catchall category. Some players, for example, never know the name of the horse they are betting on, but they do know the name of the jockey. They follow jockeys because they like them, or jockeys on winning streaks, or jockeys in combination with certain trainers, or such combinations on favorites only or on long shots only. It is impossible to test the results of all these styles of play, but I have looked at the results of following each of half a dozen leading jockeys at a single track (that is, betting on all of that rider's mounts and on no other). I knew the method would lose, but I was curious to see by how much. I took six northern California riders, leading in the standings at that time and nearly always leading. Such exercises, if you have the patience, are valuable for demonstrating, among other things, the wide swings of chance. Rarely, one of the riders might have such a good streak that bets on all his mounts for a month showed a profit. Some had practically no winners for as much as a month. An average quickly asserted itself and reappeared over and over. Bets on leading jockeys, on the whole, lost a little more than 30 percent of the amount bet.

As another exercise of the same sort, I looked at the results of betting on the single longest shot in every race. Again, I assumed the method had to lose, but again I was surprised at how much. In this case, I carried the exercise (working backward, through books of charts) for two complete meetings at each of two different tracks. I thus looked at results of several hundred racing days and nearly 4,000 races. A couple of times, the freakish method showed a slight profit or broke even for as much as a month. It also went as much as two months in a row without showing a single win. Overall, the average percentage of loss on the amount bet was a little more than 35 percent.

Remember that random betting—sticking the program with a pin, betting the horse with the longest, or shortest, name in the field, betting numbers taken from license plates, badges, or birthdates—in the long run has to lose just 17 percent of the total bet. The systems of downright bad betting lose far more. And this is one more demonstration of the need to watch the action in the parimutuel pool. Not only does the crowd do a fair job of picking winners; it does even better at picking the worst horse in the field.

Thus only a few styles of betting offer the player hope of beating the crowd and actually finishing ahead, consistently. The one rule common to all styles must be repeated once more: No style applies to more than a few races a day, some to less. Unless the player has gone to the track for pure entertainment, he must school himself to pass races, and pass some more, and pass again.

I was sitting next to a man I had never seen before. As the horses reached the stretch, the favorite was fighting head and head with another horse for the lead. The man was on his feet, yelling encouragement to the favorite, "Go, Five!" He shouted at the rider of the Five, "Whip him! Whip him!" Neither the Five nor his rider paid attention. The other horse, the Three, pulled very gradually into the lead. At the finish it seemed to me the favorite had lost by a neck, though the photo sign had gone up. The man turned to me with a despairing look, saying, "Who won? Did the Five win it?" I said the angle was confusing. In due course the Three was posted as winner. The man slumped in his seat and momentarily he was silent. He waited while the prices went up on the board with the "Official" sign. Then he began to do arithmetic with his pencil on his program. The winner had been the second choice and paid a little over $8 for a $2 win ticket. "I bet thirty dollars," the man muttered to himself, and he glanced sidelong at me. "That's a profit of ninety-two dollars. That ought to be enough for the day." He rose and moved away, a picture of composure, firmly cast as a winner inside his own head.

Fantasy does indeed fill the racetrack air. It swirls in the racegoer's head in the morning as he showers and contemplates what kind of bet he will win on the fifth race exacta after having won the daily double on the first two races. Some players perhaps are immune. It may be they never savor the delights of a winning bet—before the race is run. Perhaps they never suffer delusions after losing. They must be rare birds indeed, and I compliment them on a cast-iron sense of realism. The rest of us have to learn to live with fantasy, and when necessary, by discipline to work against it.

The simplest possible control of fantasy is an exact record of bets made and their results. It amazed me to find out how few players ever do keep a record of their betting. It amazed me even more when I added up the number of years I had gone racing myself without keeping anything more than a few cryptic notes that presumably told me whether I was winning or losing. If put to it, I might have alleged that I didn't want to leave anything around for the Internal Revenue Service to find. Of course, the truth is that the notes I kept on scraps of paper could easily be fudged with a flick of the pen. A few years ago, when I did start to keep fairly good records, in the interests of science and literature, the experience sobered me.

From the outset I found myself doing battle with my own conscience. Did I really have to note the $6, or sometimes $12 or $24, I had frittered on daily double tickets? Those were not serious bets. My wife asked me to invest a couple of dollars for her on a certified long shot. Surely, I did not then have to record the $5 I had invested on a plausible 20-1 shot. I decided I did not. But then, in a bad race, on a slightly off track, I made a wager on a horse named Max Alert, because it seemed to have as much chance as anything else, and it rewarded me by winning at 35-1. Was I entitled to add those winnings to my record? That answer, at least, was easy, though unpleasant. I did not include the Max Alert winnings. (In Chapter 16 I will describe an even more stringent test of record keeping.)

The point, of course, is that the records must be accurate and complete, and consistent. The player must note the amount bet, the kind of bet (win, place, or show, daily double or exacta), the odds at which the horse went off, and the result. A few months of this sort of thing and he will make a number of useful discoveries. He will know, probably for the first time, how much he won or lost. And he can find out what kinds of bets did him the most good or harm.

Having done this much record keeping, the player can start his graduate course. He can make notes on what he sees on the track. And he can start the task of self-discipline in earnest.

The single most important edge the serious player can give himself is observing something not recorded in the official charts. Having made the observation, he must somehow record it, and store it for later use in handicapping. For myself, I make notes in my program on what I see on the track. When I get home, I throw the program onto a pile of others on the top shelf of a closet. One of these days— But no matter. Some of the best players I know really do put their notes on cards. And they do win bets, several times a week, on horses that may have been running especially strongly when blocked or bothered.

Along the way, discipline has taught the player to watch the whole race, to catch the pattern of the whole field in motion, not to keep his glasses fixed to the one horse that carries his bet. When he does enough hard, applied, disciplined looking, the player may finally enter the most advanced class. He may begin to catch sight of swellings and knobs on horses' legs. He may see meaningful hitches in gait. He may learn to evaluate—not just talk about—the importance of a horse's wetness or the state of his bloom. And then the player will hold in his hands an incomparable tool for handicapping: he can somewhat gauge fitness for today's race minutes before post time—a factor which cannot be carried in the *Racing Form* or anywhere else in writing.

Gauging fitness from appearance is written about in some books on handicapping as if it were a mechanical matter, to be readily described. In my opinion, this is at best delusion; at worst, fraud. I know good players who can recognize only the most obvious signs of a horse's fitness. Skilled practitioners of the art, in my opinion, learn it only by years of long, hard, applied looking.

Record keeping leads finally to what may be the most important part of self-management at the track. This is the matter of betting.

As for the scale of betting, that is obviously an entirely personal matter. A college classmate of mine is now the chairman of the board of a company in his hometown. He and his wife love to go racing. I imagine they handicap reasonably well. They make $5 and $10 bets. I know a warehouseman, not a good handicapper, who shops around for opinions, who says "I bet a couple of hundred on the Six," and I think he does in fact bet a hundred dollars at a time. My own observation, and I cannot dignify it by calling it a rule, is that I find myself becoming uncomfortable if I stand to lose, in a day, much more than I can earn in a couple of days.

A rule that does make sense is to operate with a special bankroll for the track. Bets then are based on the size of the roll.

There are as many bad ways to bet as there are to handicap. But I think there can be no doubt about the commonest form of bad betting: to raise the bet on a losing streak and to lower it after winning. You can regard yourself as an exceptional money manager if your first accurate records do not show you slipping into that trap. The psychology is self-evident. The loser wants to get back what he lost and a bit of profit besides. He increases his play, and a string of even three losses pushes him toward desperation. The winner wants to stay ahead. Ego begins to outweigh greed. For the sake of his own morale, he scales down his bets so that, come what may, he will walk away somewhat ahead.

The sound course is the exact opposite: to cut the basic wager when losing, to raise it when winning. One simple approach, often described, is to bet a fixed percent of the roll each time. That way, the bet automatically rises with winnings and drops with losses. Though the logic is flawless, I do not know anyone who follows this course consistently. Suppose you started with $500. You have fared well, and now you have $642. Have you ever seen anyone bet $64.20? Naturally, the player can round the bet to $65, but that amount is not convenient to bet, either. The method speedily erodes. It seems to me more practical to bet flat amounts throughout. You raise the bet when a predetermined sum has been won. You lower it correspondingly after a set amount of loss.

The best players I know bet only to win, and they tend to be scornful of place, show, and combination betting. On the other hand, I know some very good players who bet to win and place. Arithmetic favors straight win betting. Every workout I have ever seen demonstrates that if place betting wins, win bets on the same horses would have netted more. Unfortunately pure logic cannot govern betting. The losing player is sore afflicted in his soul. Suppose he figures to win one bet in three. Then once in five times his horse will not win, but it will come in second. The place bet would have been a hedge. The player can tell himself that in the long run he will profit more by loading the whole wager on the win end. But the pain of losing is immediate, not long run. The player has to decide for himself how well he withstands that pain and whether it affects his judgment. The place bet is most sensible, incidentally, when the horse is held at low odds to win. Also, the place bet is most nearly justified by handicapping if the horse is a steady sort that figures to be close at the finish, whether or not he wins.

Daily double betting arouses no strong feeling in me. Finding an overlay in the daily double pool is a complex matter. And I think the double encourages the player to make small bets on races he might otherwise pass. On the other hand, one rarely goes broke on the double, and I admit it is pleasant, when you win, to attack the rest of the card with found money.

I do like exacta betting (in which the player must pick the first two horses in the correct order). There is more irrational betting in the exacta pool than anywhere else. In any parimutuel pool, poor betting improves odds for the astute player. The handling of the exacta varies from track to track, depending on the skill of the players and the quality of the horses running. One special virtue of the exacta is that it often can be used profitably on a horse going off at low odds (because the place horse may be a long shot). For example, a wheel on the favorite in the exacta (that is, buying a number of tickets, with the favorite on top and each of the other horses in the place position) amounts to a win bet on the favorite. Over the course of a season, it pays more. In fact, it comes close to breaking even where straight betting on the favorite loses the usual 10 percent. I see two drawbacks: exacta betting speedily becomes expensive, and the player who lacks a firm opinion may start fishing for a winner by buying a variety of tickets with a number of horses in the win position. The player can thereby transform one of the best bets at the track into one of the worst.

Taken as a whole, betting calls for as much concentration as handicapping. Instead of analyzing a field of horses, the player has to understand himself, and his own reactions to stress, to say nothing of the currents of feeling reflected on the tote board. And, if he must guard against one blight more than any other, it is the deadly nonsense called "progression betting." Progression betting is an ancient device in all forms of gambling. It is the prime cause of people going broke in casinos or at the track. It takes the impulse to increase bets when losing—and exaggerates the impulse to the point of disaster. In effect, the progression system says: Keep on adding to the bet and eventually, when the losing streak comes to an end, you will get it all back. Unfortunately, no one can say how long a losing streak will last, and the player may be busted long before it ends. People who sell progression betting systems, it seems to me, have the same mixture of ignorance and fraud as salesmen of perpetual motion machines, and make about as much sense.

From the beginning of this book I have concentrated on principles, confident that the player who grasps principles in depth will work out procedures for himself. Nevertheless, the reader should see how some procedures work out, for purposes of illustration. I will therefore outline, step by step, two quite different approaches. One, based on careful selection among favorites, is so mechanical and straightforward that the entire procedure is given in the section that follows. For the other approach, the handicapper must use judgment at every point and will require the techniques set forth in the Appendix.

To summarize the advantages of working with favorites: (1) In the worst case, the player stands to lose only 10 percent of the total bet. (2) Losing streaks may be shorter. (3) If he looks only at the favorite, the player cuts the amount of work to a small fraction.

The basis of this approach, then, is favorable selection. The player throws out all favorites except those that meet fairly severe standards.

I am positive any serious player can work out his own standards. The steps that follow are simply those I worked out for myself, as an experiment, in 1970. I carried on the experiment for five years. Since the results were reasonably consistent, I saw no need to carry the study further, although, of course, conditions can vary from year to year. The only special material needed is a *Racing Form*. A notebook of charts and track variants is not needed. The work can be done at home or at the track. A beginner can use the method, as soon as he can read the past performances and understand the tote board.

Step 1: The player throws out, or disregards, any favorite that does not meet two standards of *consistency.* The horse must have been in the money in at least half his races this year, with at least three finishes in the money. He must have won at least one race in six, this year. During the first half of the year, if the horse does not have six starts, last year's figures may be combined with this year's. The horse cannot be selected if he has never won more than a maiden race. As with any mechanical approach, the numbers have to be applied exactly. If the horse has won, say, five races in thirty-one starts (not quite one in six), he must be thrown out. The point is that bending of rules introduces judgment. Use of judgment is a very different approach indeed. The second approach, to be outlined later, depends largely on judgment.

Step 2: The favorite is thrown out unless he shows enough *recent exercise.* For a horse running today in an allowance or stakes race, the standard is, simply, a race within the last month. For horses running in a claiming race today, the standards are a race within the last two weeks, or a race within the last month and a workout in the last week.

Step 3: The favorite must meet a standard for *recent good form.* One of his last two races must have been a good race. A good race, for this purpose, is a finish in the money, or within one length of the winner. The good race must have occurred in the last six weeks.

Step 4: The favorite is thrown out unless his past performances, in today's *Racing Form*, demonstrate that he *has no disadvantage* on any one of the eight standard handicapping factors. Applying these eight standards is not difficult. *Class:* The horse must show a good race in today's class (or within 20 percent of today's claiming price). *Weight:* If carrying more than 119 pounds today, the horse must show a good race carrying within a pound of today's weight. *Sex:* If a female running against males, the horse must show a good race against males. *Distance:* The horse must show a good race within a furlong of today's distance. *Age:* Here a double standard applies. The favorite may not be over eight, and, if three years old and competing against older, he must show a good race against older horses. *Shippers:* If coming from a lesser track, the horse must show a good race in a class higher than today's. *Footing:* The horse must show a good race on today's footing—on turf, or on an off track, if this race is on turf or on an off track. *Hard races:* Here again is a two-part standard. The favorite cannot be bet if he finished within a length of the winner in both of his last two starts, or if he won his last two.

Note that nothing is said about taking only a favorite with the highest class rating of one sort or another. It is enough that the horse show no disadvantage, either as to class or as to any of the other seven specified standards. With any experience, running through all these steps takes only a few minutes.

At this point, two observations will readily be made: The approach to handling favorites outlined here is not unique. And it makes no mention at all of speed. True on both counts. As to speed, I do not believe it can be rated properly without judgment and without a great amount of preliminary work.

What, then, comes of selecting favorites by this rather simple approach? I can only say that the results of my own observations have startled me.

The period observed extended from the beginning of 1970 to the end of 1974. It covered all or most of five meetings at Golden Gate Fields, all or most of five meetings at Bay Meadows, and parts of two meetings each at Hollywood Park, Santa Anita, and Del Mar.

I will insert one blanket disclaimer at the outset: Nothing that happened in a past year proves anything about what will happen next year. Nothing that happened at one track will necessarily be duplicated at another. Anyone who follows someone else's approach, at the track, with cash, before testing it on paper, needs to screw his head on tighter. With all that, I find these results worth thinking about.

For all five years, for all the tracks observed, the approach singled out 1,130 favorites that could be bet. Not much action, it might be said. No, not much action. From the total days observed, eligible favorites turned up at the rate of about seven per week. Some days there were none; some days, two or three.

But of the 1,130 bettable favorites, 466, or 41.2 percent, won. I believe any horseplayer will agree this is a high percentage of winners. More than that—and this will impress statisticians—the numbers show remarkable consistency. Out of roughly a dozen meetings covered, only one showed a percentage of winners as low as 34.8. The next lowest was 39 percent. For all the rest, the winning selections ranged from 40 to 45 percent.

The prices were low. There was no secret about any of these horses. Nevertheless, the selections over a five-year period showed a small profit. The cost of $2 win tickets on each of the 1,130 selections would have been $2,260. The 466 winners returned $2,447, for a profit on the total bet of 8.3 percent. Again the numbers are impressively consistent. Only one meeting (or racing season) showed a small loss: at Bay Meadows in 1973 the selections for sixty-four days observed showed a loss of just 1 percent. At another meeting the gain was just 2 percent. All the rest showed gains in the range of 4 to 20 percent.

Perhaps an average profit of 8.3 percent does not seem impressive. Actually, the total of all bets represents the bankroll turned over many times per year. If the typical bet represents 5 percent of the bankroll, and the selections total 250 in a year, then the return on the bankroll—the initial capital invested—comes to just about 100 percent. Still, the return might not seem princely. I have looked at literally hundreds of workouts, in magazines and books, claiming far greater returns for one system or another—usually tested for a month or two. I have taken a closer look at some of those systems and the results did not hold up—when I myself tried them on paper. But no one could catch up with all the systems in print. I will merely add that an approach or method carried on, with the same standards, for five years, is a notable rarity, and consistent results have to be impressive.

I do *not* claim that the results I have just cited prove that the races can be beaten. I do not even use this approach to betting myself. I have rarely been able to go to the track daily and when I do go, I want (a) more action and (b) the sense that I am master of my own fate. In short, I want to use my own judgment and do my own handicapping. I regard the numbers as a clear demonstration of several important facts: Control and careful selection are essential to survival at the track. An enriched selection of favorites is not to be sneered at. And sensible standards, judiciously applied, at the very least keep the player out of trouble with relatively little sweat.

One more warning: my five-year exercise with favorites was what scientists would call "retrospective." Each observed day—meaning each day I was in town and able to get a *Racing Form*—I looked at the favorites of the day before, tested them by the standards set forth, and noted whether or not the eligibles won, and if they did, at what price. Every exercise or "workout" I have ever seen, no matter who did it, was done retrospectively. The exercise to take most seriously will be one done "prospectively"—that is, with the selections filed before post time with an objective referee. The player who takes his bankroll to the track, makes a living with it, and ends the year with a bigger roll has carried out the most searching "prospective" test of all. But only he can say so, and who will believe him if he speaks?

My second approach differs in every respect from the first. It calls for independent judgment at every turn. It would only rarely put the player on a favorite. It is riskier and it yields more action. It demands hard work. I cannot claim that any of the best handicappers I know use it exactly as outlined. Yet it contains the stuff of real handicapping.

Step 1: Rate every horse in the field for class. Make no exceptions, take no shortcuts. In my opinion, every horse has to be looked at. What method for rating class? Examine the Appendix—and suit yourself. I use three, and I do not claim they are perfect. I use numbers like those in the Paul Renniks and Kelco systems (with some changes to account for California purse distribution). I look at the value of the purse a horse has most recently shared in. And I comb the past performances for clues to class: recent prices at which claimed, claiming prices at which a good race was run, and changes in tracks. It is hopeless to attempt this without having charts at hand for the preceding racing days. I mention all three methods of rating class because one or another may not apply to the field you are analyzing. In the end, one horse may seem clearly highest in class. Or several may seem to be the class of the field. Or the field may seem quite simply to be devoid of class, in which case you will have to make a selection, if any, without regard to class.

Step 2: Look at the speed numbers. Techniques for this purpose are given in the Appendix. Remember that they apply most clearly to sprints. Don't bother to start unless you have track variants at hand. Look at fractions. Given the distance and the post positions, what horses are likely to be in front after a quarter of a mile? After half a mile? If any of those horses are high in the class ratings, you may begin to feel a selection taking shape. But you are not ready.

Step 3: You may want to throw the whole race out, if nothing emerged from class or speed numbers. Or you may have a group of contenders at hand. These need to be winnowed, to the extent possible, for current form and fitness. Have they exhausted themselves in recent races? Is there sign of improvement—like a sharp burst of early speed in the last race after dull preceding races?

Step 4: Do you see any angles, or special factors, that you particularly fancy? Recent claim by a trainer you respect? Jockey switch to a rider you take seriously? Drop from middle distance to a sprint for a horse that has shown good early speed? One excellent but not winning race, recently, after a layup?

Step 5: Now you must decide whether the race can be played. Too many contenders? Pass the race. No contenders? Pass again. One or two, or sometimes three contenders? You have some more thinking to do.

Step 6: Of the contenders, which are hurt, which helped, by the distance, weight switches, post position?

Step 7: Assuming a selection has emerged, what are his chances of winning the race? What therefore are the minimum acceptable odds at which a bet can be made? It may be that one horse stood out already in Steps 1 and 2, on the basis of class and speed. Can you then assign him a 50 percent chance of winning? Assigning a percentage chance of winning is the last and most vital step; in my opinion, it is a matter of pure judgment.

Few horses rate a 50 percent chance of winning. Yet you need odds of 7–5 or better to make a sure profit on such horses. If you ever find yourself thinking about taking even money, remember that you are then saying in effect that your horse has at least a 60 percent chance of winning—a formidable edge.

But if the selection is one of two or three likely contenders, can you give him better than a 25 or 30 percent chance of winning? I think you cannot. In that case, you must not be tempted below the odds of 7–2.

Step 8: At the track, you look at the horses in the flesh, hoping to learn a little more about their condition. You make your final decision a few minutes before post time, when you see the odds on the board.

Does this approach seem complex? Is it loaded at every step with tricky judgments? Without doubt. Does it require experience and great knowledge? Yes. Does any handicapper go through exactly this process? I doubt it. The human mind outdoes a computer when it comes to the subtle blending of a dozen factors. No two blends will be the same. But these are the steps out of which the winning horseplayer's decision finally comes.

THE ODDS ARE

Assume that the player has done his handicapping well. Assume, too, that he knows he should only bet when the odds are right. He has been around long enough to know that the best of players have a highly developed sense of when the price on a horse is right. Yet at this crucial point he finds little if any help when it comes to pricemaking for himself.

I can say with assurance that I myself have found a few winning players at racetracks. I have only the vaguest notion of how they calculate odds. I suspect that most of them could not tell me.

Because the matter is of such importance, and so little help is to be had, I will venture to outline a procedure for setting one's own odds, based on general handicapping considerations and the arithmetic of parimutuel betting.

Step 1: Examine all the horses in a race and distribute percentage chances of winning among them. It is a 100 percent certainty (unless all the horses are swallowed up in a hole in the track, or lost in a backstretch fog) that one horse will win (or two, or even three, in a dead heat). How do the entrants share that 100 percent chance? This, by the way, is the first step in making a price line. But it is not necessary to make a complete price line. It seems to me that assigning a percentage chance to every horse in the field is largely a work of fiction. Most horses have no calculable chance. You have completed Step 1 if you look over the whole field, pick out the legitimate contention, and assign a percentage chance to each of several horses, or to only one horse if one stands out. Example: One horse stands out. You assign him a 40 percent chance of winning. Or one horse seems to overwhelm the rest of the field, like a Secretariat among a field of middling claimers. You assign him a 90 percent chance, on the assumption that 10 percent of the time some misadventure can happen to any horse in any race. Or it is an undistinguished ten-horse field and three horses seem to be somewhat better than the rest with little to choose among them and, you assume, about a 50 percent chance that one of the three will win. You give each of the three a 15 to 20 percent chance. Note that the numbers are approximate. In my opinion, anyone who thinks he can assign a precise number, like 17 percent, to a horse is kidding himself.

Step 2: Assume, as you must, that your handicapping is right. Then a horse that tops its field with a 30 percent chance of winning should win three of ten races, if exactly the same circumstances present themselves ten times. Ten $2 win tickets will cost $20. Three winners at odds of 3–1 will return 3 × $8, or $24—for an overall profit of 20 percent on the total amount bet. Considering the ebb and flow of luck, it seems to me a 20 percent profit rate is needed for any margin of safety at the track. Clearly, when you put a horse on top and give it no more than a 30 percent chance of winning, you cannot afford to bet on it at odds of less than 3–1.

Suppose the horse seems to you a much more solid bet. You give it a 40 percent chance of winning. That is, you would expect to win four of ten such bets. You still need odds of at least 2–1 (an expenditure of $20 for tickets, a return of 4 × $6, for the same total of $24). The same kind of arithmetic quickly tells you that if you are willing to bet on a horse when the tote board tells you the odds will be 8–5, you are assuming the horse has at least a 45 percent chance of winning. If you take a price as low as 7–5, you are giving the horse a 50 percent chance: you assume you will win at least half the bets you make under such circumstances, which is no small assumption. To take even money on the horse, you have to be able to persuade yourself that the horse has fully a 60 percent chance of winning the race. Incidentally, I think the player can only rarely assign more than 60 to 65 percent of the winning chance in the race. About a third of the total chance will usually remain in doubt, obscured by questions of racing luck or the prospect of an outsider suddenly jumping up and running back to better form of months ago.

It might appear that by the time you have assigned percentage chances, and figured minimum odds for the horse you favor, the job is done and you have only to see if the right price shows on the board late in the betting.

I do not think the job is done. If the player has done only this much, he will have concentrated too much on the one horse he favors. He will not have examined the field as a whole.

Step 3: I suggest that the player now place each race in one of four categories, based on study of the whole field. Of the four, the first and fourth are so much the simplest, that I will take them up first, if only to get them out of the way.

The handicapper should place in Category I only those races in which one horse clearly stands out. He must be able to assign at least a 40 percent chance to the horse, and no other horse in the field can have more than a 30 percent chance. Such horses will almost always be favorites. It would be nonsense to pretend—as some system peddlers do—that concealed form will often reveal so solid a horse. But overlays are still possible. The horse with a 50 percent chance is a fair bet at 7–5, a distinct overlay at 8–5. How often can you find such opportunities? A couple of times some days, no times at all other days, on the average perhaps five or six times a week.

Category IV, the other relatively simple case, is the race the handicapper decides he must pass, without bothering about odds. To take an obvious example, the race may bring together twelve two-year-old maidens, five of which have run nothing but bad races while the other seven are first-time starters showing poor works and dubious bloodlines. Or the race may be for older horses, cheap claimers whose past performances demonstrate nothing but problems. You cannot give any one of them more than a 15 percent chance. Get involved in such races and the state's 17 percent takeout from the mutuel pool will quickly grind you down.

Category II is what I conceive to be a meat-and-potatoes race for many good players. It deals with the field in which not one but two horses stand out—a two-horse race within a race. The crowd makes one of these two its favorite. Obviously, you will sometimes think the crowd is right. But in a fair number of cases you think the other horse should be on top—for reasons of trouble in the preceding race, or speed numbers properly corrected for a track variant, or evidence that the favorite is past the peak in form. The two horses together account for at least a 60 percent chance of winning. Your horse, you are convinced, has somewhat the better of it, though in such a case not necessarily a 10 percent margin. If you can hold your own against the crowd, you automatically have a favorable betting situation. More often than not, you will get odds of 3–1 and better on a horse that ought to go off the favorite.

Category III is for the postgraduate handicapper and calls for subtle appreciation of every nuance and angle in the race. No single horse stands out. You cannot persuade yourself that it is a meat-and-potatoes situation with two horses standing out. Yet it is not a Category IV race, with nothing resembling form. Rather, some horses do stand out, but there may be as many as four of them. With proper respect for the uncertainties of life and horse racing, you hesitate to put any one of the four horses much above the others. Each of the four, in other words, seems to have a 15 to 20 percent chance of winning. This is the situation made to order for the searcher after plausible long shots, at prices of 10–1 and better. And, if the race truly falls into Category III, you will fairly often find two of the four legitimate contenders at long odds. In such a case, you can afford to scale down your bet and take both of the two horses held at high odds. If your handicapping is right, and the two long shots together have a 30 percent chance, the payoff if one wins, with both, for example, exactly at 10–1, will be 9–2—a more than fair return.

How can such a circumstance arise? Any number of ways, but one good example is this: the two most heavily backed horses ran fairly well in a race at a higher claiming price; the two long shots come out of an apparently cheaper race, which the track variant and pace numbers reveal to have been a better race. Another case can arise out of a distance switch: the race is at a mile and a sixteenth. One of the four horses you regard as the contention is held at a long price, presumably because his past performances show nothing but fairly good six-furlong races. The record shows him to be a steady sort of goer, your own notes say he finished full of run last time, and the fractions suggest strongly that he should be several lengths in front coming out of the clubhouse turn. You conclude he certainly has at least a one in five (20 percent) chance of stretching out and staying in front all the way. No other horse seems to you to have a better chance, and so the odds of better than 10–1 are highly attractive. I believe Jule Fink to be an artist at digging out such situations. My friend Harry, one of the two people I know who actually went racing with Al Winderman, specializes in spotting gross overlays in connection with dropdowns. The horse is running for a substantially lower claiming price. The crowd, instead of backing him, dismisses him as a cripple because his recent form is bad, and the odds rise correspondingly. Harry bets in such cases, sometimes with spectacular results in exacta races, if he can find slight signs of improvement in the most recent race, plus clear evidence that the horse once was better, coupled with a significant switch today—like an important jockey change.

One highly important point applies to all three bettable categories: do not bet against the horse you like best.

It is obvious in Category I that you can only bet on the outstanding horse, and you must pass the race if the price is not right. The same reasoning, while less obvious, applies equally to Categories II and III. The player, in my opinion, has no business betting on any horse except the one to which he gives either his highest number or a number at least as high as any other. Otherwise, he can too easily fudge slightly and raise his estimate of a horse's chances because the odds look so attractive.

Step 4 concerns a checkup on your own results.

I have seen a few purely mechanical systems that use handicapping data to calculate a price line, or an individual horse's percentage chance of winning. Such systems seem to me to be largely misleading if used to pinpoint a specific percentage chance. In the end, the estimate of a horse's chances of winning must rest on the handicapper's judgment. If he is a good handicapper, he will prosper at the track to the extent that he improves his reckoning of odds by remembering failures as well as successes.

The three bettable categories of races suggested here can be used as a convenient check on your own handicapping and pricemaking. As a starting point, of course, you must keep a record of what categories you attached to each race and what the results were.

In Category I races, the check is simple. The horses you singled out should win at least 40 percent of the time. For comparison, note that favorites as a whole win just one-third of the time.

In Category II races, one or the other of the two horses your handicapping coupled at the top of the field should win 60 percent of the time. Again, for comparison, note that overall either the favorite or the crowd's second choice wins about 50 percent of the time. The second control question for Category II races is: Where one of your top two horses does win, and where you had an opinion contrary to the crowd, did you win at least half the time? In other words, did your Category II choices win at least half of 60 percent, or 30 percent of the time?

The check on Category III races, understandably, is the most complicated. Settle for a test of your overall handicapping. Some one of the several contenders you selected in a Category III race should win 65 percent of the time.

In all three bettable categories the two ultimate questions are: Were your bets profitable? and, In which categories were the bets most and least profitable? For the serious player, willing to keep records and analyze them, the answers to these questions can take years off the time needed to approach the level of judgment achieved by the best handicappers.

SOME WINNERS—
AND ONE CLOSER LOOK

In the end, to prove that all horse-players don't die broke, I needed only one certified winner. Actually, before I was done I found many excellent players. I was able to satisfy myself that at least five of them had been consistent winners for years. And, in learning what I could about the qualities of the winners, I stumbled into an adventure of my own, which I will relate in due course.

Naturally, one thousand cases would be more satisfactory than five. I cannot produce one thousand cases, nor can anyone else. My approach is what a scientist might call "anecdotal." But the word "anecdotal" does not put me off. For example, if someone asserted that a nuclear weapon is violently destructive, I hope that no sane person would demand one thousand tests, or even ten.

My first certified winner is my friend Mike the Baker. I am sure he has won a good deal less than the others, but his case is the simplest for me to make. For the last six or seven years, whenever we have met at the track, I have known exactly what horses he bet on, and the outcome of the bets. Of Mike I can say simply that I know, to a certainty, that he finishes ahead, on the average, at three out of four meetings. Incidentally, Mike's ability as a handicapper is not my secret. He takes pride in his work. Many people at the track know him and ask for his opinion, and he offers it generously. Curiously, the people who ask do not thereupon become winners. Long before they reach a seller's window, they get caught in the switches.

My friend Edward bets more, at longer prices, wins less often, but comes out farther ahead in the course of a year. At his own tracks Edward is something of a celebrity, too; people hover about hoping to catch a piece of his action. I do not see Edward at the windows as often as I see Mike. What I do see impresses me. Also, I have other evidence about Edward. He and I have a mutual friend who was part of his household, through a difficult period some years ago. Without question, my other friend says, Edward supported the household. While some of his winnings came from poker, his principal occupation was betting at the track.

My third winner I will call Les Winter (because of the wishes of his widow). I saw Winter, late in his life, at Southern California tracks. He had spent all of a long, working lifetime at race courses between Vancouver and San Diego. He came to this country a penniless immigrant from England, in his teens, with a still younger brother to support. At his death, past eighty, he lived in a much more than comfortable house, in one of the most solidly prosperous communities in the West, San Marino. Aside from returns on savings, the track furnished his whole livelihood.

The fourth and fifth cases are the clearest of all. Both Jule Fink and the late Al Winderman have been public figures. Neither is my discovery. I have had the benefit of meeting Fink, at the track and away from it. Friends of mine, including Edward, knew Winderman well.

Fink told me he came from Cincinnati, started going to tracks near there when he was sixteen, and has been a handicapper ever since. He became equally known as a successful owner of horses. Both divisions of the Knickerbocker Handicap at Aqueduct's 1977 fall meeting were won by horses Fink judged promising and picked up from other stables.

Winderman, when very young, was a New York cabdriver. By

his early twenties he was already a full-time, winning player. So far as I know, he did not own horses. Both published and private accounts agree that he was one of the heaviest bettors of his time and probably the most successful. According to one account, he went bad at a New York meeting and died broke. Friends of mine will swear that story is false. They were with him at Los Angeles tracks in the last years of his life, and they say he was doing well again.

And what did these five have in common? On the surface, nothing. In some important respects, everything.

In appearance and manner they differ, or differed, widely. Mike is a shy man and could have practically nothing to say to the others. Both Edward and Fink are worldly and cosmopolitan figures; when Fink first tried to get an owner's license in New York, Herbert Bayard Swope and Bernard Baruch were among his sponsors. Les Winter, a heavy, rather solemn-looking man in a dark gray suit, sitting in a box at Santa Anita, looked like a retired banker out for a day's amusement. Winderman, I am told, was a man of fierce intensity, quick to dispute, who was likely to sound like a cabdriver arguing with another for a place on a stand.

But the qualities they share, as a group, are far more important than the differences.

To start with the most obvious: like sculptors, master toolmakers, poets, brain surgeons, train dispatchers, composers of music, and justices of the Supreme Court, they regard what they are doing, when they are doing it, as the most important thing in the world. To say they work hard is almost misleading. They work with concentration, as long as they need to, without measuring the effort.

Nearly as obvious: they are an able group. All started with one or another degree of disadvantage. For each (Edward is a special case), the track was an open door. Again it is almost misleading to say merely that they are intelligent men. More important are the special kinds of intelligence they share. They are all highly observant, quick to sense patterns (in a field of running horses, or in the past performances), with retentive memories.

I cannot think of a less sentimental group.

They all calculate well and have a strong sense of probabilities. I know some first-rate theoretical statisticians who I believe would feel comfortable, and interested, in their company.

Finally, and above all: they have an unshakable opinion, when they reach one. They will unhesitatingly stand alone, or in a minority. Even Mike, who looks for the most solid choice possible and therefore places most of his eight or ten bets a week on favorites, beams with delight when a horse he likes is somehow overlooked and goes off at a price.

These qualities would serve in a number of other fields. As Edward said about Winderman, the cabdriver turned handicapper, "He could have made a success anywhere."

Why, then, do they all remain in racing (including Edward, who has another, and very distinguished, career)? I daresay the simplest answer is they like it.

I said they have a sense of odds. That implies a sense of the likelihood of something happening. It also demands acceptance of the possibility that it might not happen. And that suggests a special reward in being part of an ebb and flow of chance.

Of course, what I am describing applies not only to winning horseplayers but equally to their first cousins, speculators on the grand scale.

Bernard Baruch admired James R. Keene above all others in Wall Street (both, incidentally, loved racing). Baruch said that Keene was asked once why, since he had made his fortune, he continued to speculate in stocks. He quoted Keene as replying: "Why does a dog chase his thousandth rabbit? All life is a speculation. The spirit of speculation is born with men."

Keene's "spirit of speculation" also implies a special kind of resilience. Horseplayers, in particular, are bound to have many bad days. They must be able to go home, sleep it off, and return to the track the next day with every expectation of winning.

And it was while contemplating this last quality of the horseplayer that I undertook an adventure of my own.

I have never made a living at a racetrack. I have gone racing solely for pleasure.

I do not wish to play mock humble, but in truth I have no reason to put myself among the best horseplayers I have known. Still—when I thought about it—I realized I did share at least one of their qualities. I have had my full quota of losing days. I dislike them. I have sometimes broken off a remark at dinner, later, to wonder how I could have been so stupid as to bet on one of so-and-so's dropdowns, when the horse had to be a cripple. And yet the next morning I awoke cheerful enough and fully prepared to tackle that day's card.

And having thought of this, I took another step and reached a conclusion. It seemed to me that having written this much about racing, and about winning horseplayers and their methods, I was obligated—in fact, I was honor-bound—to test what I had written on my own person.

I started my experiment at Bay Meadows, on September 13, 1977, having first set a number of rules for myself.

The most obvious rule was that I must record every dollar bet, and the value of every ticket cashed, to see which total was larger at the end. This I did, without fail, more precisely than I had ever managed to do before, for every bet from first to last.

How much to bet? This question was more complicated than it might have seemed. I was aware of at least half a dozen handicapping books that ended with alleged excursions to the track during which large sums were wagered and much larger ones won. At least a couple of these books seemed to me to be frauds or, at best, paper "workouts" put together after the races were run. I wanted to describe a series of bets, on the spot, as they actually happened—with no pretense of testing my nerves under the stress of large wagers. I settled on a basic $20 bet because that seemed to me a fair average for most of the part-time players I knew. Curiously, in spite of myself, I sometimes varied the bet, and when I did I generally suffered for it. All bets were to win.

What to consider as a bet? Even that was not a simple question. Since I often make several small bets on long shots in a single race, I decided to continue my normal practice. I set aside one regular bet per day, to be broken up into small bets, scattered as I wished, including bets on the $2 daily double.

Finally, I determined that I would run the experiment for 100 consecutive bets, taking them exactly as they came, skipping none on any grounds. I estimated I would need six or seven weeks. Actually I finished the series near the end of the seventh week—averaging four days a week at the track.

After several hours of study of the *Racing Form* for September 13, I had concluded that three races were bettable.

In the third race (for three-year-old colts going six furlongs) I thought Swaby and Flying Amazon stood out. (The crowd agreed with me; the two went off nearly co-favorites in an eleven-horse field. Neither speed nor class numbers separated the horses; life's problems are not always tidy.) I bet $20 on Flying Amazon because his fractions suggested he ought to be five or six lengths ahead of his rival after half a mile.

Flying Amazon broke from the gate as well as I had hoped. But Swaby broke far better than I expected, and with them was a horse I had not considered, Never's Martini. They ran the length of the backstretch together. I tried (futilely) to make myself sweep the whole field with my glasses, wondering all the while if my horse would be the one to quit. He did not. Rounding the far turn, he smoothly opened a two-length lead, and he was two and a half lengths clear at the wire. He paid $7.60 for a $2 win ticket. In my contest with myself, I had jumped off to a $56 lead.

In the sixth race it seemed to me another three-year-old, Lieutenants Image, which had been running at Del Mar and Hollywood Park that summer, was clearly the class of the field. So, too, did a majority of the Bay Meadows crowd. They bet him down to 4–5. I passed. Lieutenants Image showed speed briefly, then faded to third. I shook my head and wondered if I should give more credit to my luck, or to my wisdom and virtue.

My last choice, Mr. Machine in the seventh race, was bet down to even money, and I passed the opportunity again. In this I was joined by all the trainers with stables at Bay Meadows. Mr. Machine was taking a huge, and therefore suspicious, drop in class, from about a $30,000 to a $5,000 claiming price. No one entered a claim for him. The horse won as if out for pleasant exercise, by six lengths, and was eligible for starter's allowances (safe from claim) through much of the rest of the fall. It was generally agreed that Mr. Machine's trainer, Art Hirsch, by a daring gamble had earned a license to steal. As for my own, lesser progress, I had made one bet that day and had won it.

The next day I met Mike the Baker at the paddock. I asked

him how he liked Proese in the first, a race for maiden fillies at 1¹/₁₆ miles. Much as I value Mike, I wish I had not listened to him. He said, with gusto, "My best of the day." The horse opened at 5–2 in the morning line, was speedily bet down. I bet, too. I somehow hoodwinked myself into thinking the price might come back up. It closed, in fact, at 4–5. Proese went to the front, but first one horse, and then another, came up to challenge her, head to head. All the way around the turn, and the whole length of the homestretch, I kept asking myself, Why? Why? Why take such a price? Proese struggled desperately, down to the wire, and won, in very poor time, by a short neck—and paid only $3.80. I made a long, slow tour of the stands to clear my head, ineffectively. I liked Cobeau's Colleen in the third race. For no reason except uncertainty about my own judgment, I cut my bet in half. Cobeau's Colleen, at odds of 2–1, drew clear turning for home and won by three lengths. I had made two bets and won both, but counting, as I had to, several wasted tickets in the double, I had netted only $29. I left the track early.

On Thursday, the fifteenth, I walked briskly from the parking lot to the grandstand, thinking at least I had won three for three, even if I had profited little. I quickly set matters straight by losing bets on Papela and Cash in Hand. I recovered with a bet on Windsor Grey, which had excellent speed numbers but seemed to be moving up in class and therefore went off at 4–1. I then managed to lose my profits with bets on two more races and finished the day exactly even.

I began Friday with a win, then successively lost on four horses which finished third, second, third, and second. I told myself that I seemed to have picked live horses, but in cold fact I had had my first losing day. At the end of the week I had collected on six of fourteen bets (better than I had expected) but was only $53 ahead.

Over the weekend a drought in California suddenly, if temporarily, broke. The track on Tuesday, the twentieth, was muddy. Through the first five races I tried unsuccessfully to deduce, from skimpy evidence, which horses might like a gooey track. In truth, the horses, like all other living creatures in the state for the preceding two years, had been strangers to rain. I might well have called off operations for the day, except for a horse I liked in the sixth race. This was a race for three-year-olds at a claiming price of $16,000. Marsalon, my choice, had last run for $10,000. But it seemed to me the jump in class was largely imaginary. His speed numbers were the best in the field. And the year before, as a two-year-old at Del Mar, he had shown speed against far better horses—on an off track. He went to the post at nearly 13–1. I bet the last $10 I had left in my quota for that day. Marsalon ran close to the pace down the backstretch, moved into the lead halfway round the turn, and increased his lead all the way to the finish. I accepted Mike's congratulations modestly.

On Friday, the twenty-third, I won my first bet, then lost three in a row. Not particularly disturbed, I returned on Saturday with two firm selections, Asian Admiral in the fifth and Getaway Terresto in the sixth. Moved solely by impulse (perhaps because I had won a bet on him at the Pleasanton Fair), I suddenly found myself betting $30 on Getaway Terresto. In any case, both horses showed speed for a quarter of a mile, both quit badly. I still do not know what was wrong with the handicapping.

The losing streak continued on Tuesday of the next week, and by the fourth race on Wednesday, the twenty-eighth, I had lost ten bets in a row. Though I did not realize it, my net profit at the moment was down to $4. I recall that it was a cloudy, mild day, with some promise of an end to the drought. I paced the concrete apron between grandstand and track and contemplated my condition. I kicked at an inoffensive paper cup and could find no reason to change my opinion about the fifth race. I was deeply suspicious of the favorite, which was dropping in class for a fourth time. I liked the second favorite, for several reasons including good numbers and a recent, strong closing effort. I bet on Happy Idea, at 7–2, and he won by seven lengths, handily. My personal drought was over.

I showed at least some profit on each of the next six racing days.

Around the middle of October, on a day when I could not go to the track, I reviewed my daily records and found that I had already made seventy-one bets and had won twenty-four of them. I then had three more or less break-even racing days and thus arrived at October 21, a day of unusual importance in my journey.

I began undramatically by piddling away a handful of small bets on the first two races. I recovered the loss, with interest, by betting on Bildonna in the third. That left just one more race that interested me—the fifth.

My colleague Mike passed the fifth race without a second thought. Nothing in it seemed to him at all solid. I could not let it go that easily. A full field of twelve fillies and mares, entered at claiming prices of $7,500 to $6,500, were racing six furlongs. The obvious favorite was Catch Marie, who had run just eight days before in a 1 1/16-mile race at Santa Anita's fall Oak Tree meeting. She showed no Bay Meadows works. She had run in August at Del Mar for still higher claiming prices. Why the dropdowns? If she was good enough to win at Santa Anita, why did they bother to ship her? I mistrusted her enough to look elsewhere.

My eye was caught by Fleet to Win. She had won her last race easily and had been claimed for only $5,000, but she had earned a high speed number. I was preparing to settle for a bet on Fleet to Win, but I kept thinking about still another filly— 20–1 in the morning line, 27–1 on the board—Right Arrow. The reasons for the long odds were clear enough. She had finished last, beaten twenty-one lengths, on September 21; she had been seventh, beaten eight lengths, on October 4. But I had a visual recollection of an excellent race she had won on opening day, before I began my series of 100 bets. She had drawn the outside post that day, was on the outside again today. She could find her stride without jostling. I liked a jockey switch, to Roberto Gonzalez. Both of her bad races were against better horses. The very bad September race came during the few days of off tracks. In the more recent race she showed good early speed—a possible sign of returning form.

In the end, I decided to bet on both Fleet to Win and Right Arrow. I would like to say I had such faith in my own conviction that I split the $20 bet down the middle and bet half on each horse. I did not. I went to the $5 window and bought three tickets on Fleet to Win (9–2) and one ticket on Right Arrow (27–1).

I was right about the favorite, Catch Marie. She broke poorly, showed nothing, and finished seventh. I was wrong about Fleet to Win. She managed to stay behind Catch Marie at every call.

As for Right Arrow, Gonzalez rushed her from the gate, had her clearly in front passing the clockers' shed on the backstretch, and had opened a three-length lead in the middle of the turn. But the filly was no candidate for a cup race, at a distance. Through the stretch she began to labor. The leaders of the pack closed on her at every stride. The horseplayer's plea stuck in my throat, not quite spoken—stay there, stay there, please. At the finish she was still ahead by the length of her body. She paid $57.80. And I agreed again with the unknown man, standing behind me in a cashier's line, who had once said: No one ever bet enough on a winning horse.

The next day I won a $79.60 daily double (one of only a handful of doubles I won during the series). With thirty-one winners out of eighty-eight bets, and only twelve bets to go, my margin was great enough so that I could no longer show an overall loss.

Sometime during the week that followed—the last week of my trial—I wrote some critical notes on my own betting. I noted that I had passed the ninth race every day. True; I had to leave early, indicating I was not really devoting full time to the task. I bet almost no exactas, though my win percentage on exacta races was good. The answer there is that my stakes were set too low. Playing an exacta as I think it should be done (three or four $5 exacta tickets with a single horse on top, and a similar amount on that horse to win) costs at least $30 or $40 per race. The implication is that I would have won more if I had played exactas, which, of course, is not proved (because I cannot assume I would have picked the right place horses). The notes criticize my handling of daily doubles; actually, I broke even on them, but that did represent a loss of time and effort and lowered the percentage of profit. I tended to bet too low on my best high odds bets (several others besides Right Arrow). True enough, Mr. Self-Critic—but how could you know it was a "best high odds bet" until after the race was run?

Finally, a cryptic note about "Great Wall" suggests a certain timidity toward the end. I looked back at my *Racing Form* for the day in question and the note is, I fear, just. My handicapping marks and figures on the *Form* clearly put a horse called Great Wall on top in his race, on every score. I somehow convinced myself that his odds were dropping too low, and I went home. In fact, he won his race and paid a more than satisfactory $11.20. I suspect that on that afternoon I had simply lost my appetite for the struggle.

All through the last four days, while I made the final dozen bets to round out the series, I felt my tension growing. I had to fight off a constant tendency to reduce the bets, to protect my lead. And I must have bet poorly. I won five more bets but reduced the margin by a few dollars.

Overall, I won thirty-six bets (representing 36 percent, of course; favorites at that meeting were winning less than 30 percent of the time). And the payoffs were substantially higher than the prices paid by favorites. The total of all bets came to $1,804 (the composite long-shot bets reduced the average wager from $20 to $18). I collected $2,115 on winning tickets, for a profit margin of $311, or a little more than 17 percent.

I have received scores, perhaps hundreds, of promotions for can't-lose systems of betting. Without exception, they promise far greater rates of return. Fair enough. Hope should spring eternally from the hard rock of the human condition. But my own modest figures offer some interesting projections. Remember that 17 percent is a return not on the starting bankroll but on total, turnover capital, the sum of every bet made, or the grand total at risk. My series of 100 bets took seven weeks. The player with a sound constitution can easily find forty weeks of racing in a year, for a series of 600 bets. At a track with a medium-sized daily handle (say, a million dollars), the average wager—assuming the player's nerves are strong enough and his discipline flawless—could be raised twenty-five-fold to $500 a bet, without jostling the parimutuel system noticeably. At the New York and Los Angeles tracks, with some care, the wager could be raised fifty-fold. I leave it to the reader with a curiosity about other people's earnings to multiply 6 (600 bets instead of 100) by either 25 or 50 (for the increase in wager), by 300 (for the size of my own small earnings). The smallest projection, not to be furtive about it, is $45,000. The scale, as I say, could be greatly increased at the major tracks. Finally, while I can offer no proof of this, I believe the most gifted handicappers and bettors, fully dedicated to their task year round, could double my rate of return (though I would want convincing of consistent returns beyond that). The disposable amount of cash is, if not overwhelming, at least interesting.

At any rate, when I made my one hundredth bet, on October 28, I was too intent on the present to contemplate visions of wealth and glory. I finished the series as I began it, with a $20 win bet. My last win was in the seventh race, on Barbie Carol, and she paid $7.60.

I went home that day not very much richer, but happy enough and satisfied with my lot. And yes, on the way out I did buy the next day's *Racing Form*, though I had so much work piled up I could not get back to the track for a week.

During that week, in downtown San Francisco, I met a statistician friend. I told him of my experiment and its result, and I asked his opinion of my numbers.

"Winning is certainly better than losing," he said.

I pressed the point a little, and suggested that the sample seemed adequate.

He shrugged, and assented mildly.

Very well—but how to improve the experiment?

He grinned then, and said, "Do it again."

And that, of course, is the point of it all, and why horse racing remains an eternal sport, in all seasons, for anyone with a taste for a bet on the shape of the future, on the event not yet seen, on the outcome of the furious drive through the stretch where one horse, under the whip, eyes wild and nostrils flared, may lunge his neck forward to be the first across the line.

A Guide for Handicappers

FOR BEGINNERS ONLY

Lesson One
1. Learn how to read the *Daily Racing Form*.
2. Read the *Daily Racing Form*.

Lesson Two

1. For each race on a day's card, answer the following questions. Which horse recently ran today's distance in the fastest time? Which horse has won the greatest sum of money this year and last? How many horses won their last race, and if none, which finished closest to the winner?

2. From the charts of that day's results, answer the following concerning the horses named in answer to question one. At what odds did the horses go off? Where did the horses finish?

3. Proceed to the study of handicapping with some confidence. Many in the crowd at a racetrack never do anything more sensible than what you have already done.*

---

*Most editions of the *Daily Racing Form* contain instructions for deciphering the past performances and charts. The *Form*, on request, will mail an instructional pamphlet entitled "How to Read the New Expanded Past Performances."

CALCULATING ODDS

Table B–1 (p. 205) permits the most basic of a horseplayer's calculations. Called a "betting percentage table," it permits the handicapper to translate a horse's assumed percentage chance of winning a race into the form of odds. The starting assumption is that among all the horses in a race there exists a 100 percent chance that one of them (or in the case of a dead heat more than one) will win. That 100 percent chance is then apportioned among the entrants in the race. The specific percentages are translated into odds by Table B–1. Thus a horse has a 25 percent chance of winning the race. This amounts to a one-in-four chance of winning; in 100 runnings of the race under the same circumstances, the horse could be expected to win twenty-five times. The natural, or break-even, odds on such a horse would be 3–1.

By similar reasoning, a horse with a 16⅔ percent chance of winning would be held at odds of 5–1.

Table B–2 (p. 206) tells what a $2 win ticket will pay, if the horse wins, at various odds. The table adds nothing to the understanding of handicapping. It is included here simply to make clear the terms used. A horse that goes off at exactly 3–1 is said to pay, if it wins, $8. The $8 obviously consists of the bettor's own original $2 plus 3 times 2, or $6, for a total of $8.

Table B–3 (p. 206) illustrates how to make a price line. Suppose the handicapper has accurately estimated the chances of each horse in a race and has assigned a proper percent to each. Suppose then that the crowd, in the interval of betting before that race, on the average agrees with the handicapper. Nevertheless, the odds shown on the totalizator board before the race will not agree with the odds derived directly from the percents by Table B–1. The odds will in reality be lower. If the natural odds are 5–2, the board will show 2–1. Thus, if that horse wins, a $2 win ticket on him will pay only $6, not $7. The explanation, simply, lies in the fact that the parimutuel pool has been cut by a predetermined amount—generally around 17 percent—to pay government and management and provide purse money for the horsemen. In the days before parimutuel betting the bookmakers so constructed their odds, or price lines, that they, too, cut the bettors' pool, by an amount known as the "vigorish."

One easy procedure for making a realistic price line is: (1) assign percents (winning chances) to each horse in the race; (2) multiply those percents by 118 (100 percent plus 18 percent to give a safe margin for the takeout, or official vigorish); (3) translate the inflated percentages into odds, using Table B–1. The larger percentages will give lower odds, to provide realistic comparison with tote board odds.

Now, if he has done his work completely and if the tote board shows lower odds than does his price line, the handicapper is looking at an underlay; if the tote board shows higher odds than his price line predicted, he has encountered an overlay. If a horse he picks to win is sufficiently overlaid, the player has an appropriate bet. The winning player is always consciously seeking overlays and bets only when in his opinion he has found one.

Table B–4 (p. 207) demonstrates yet another aspect of the use of odds. Clearly, the percentage of winners needed to show a profit varies with the average odds at which bets are made. Thus, if a player, on the average, laid his bets on horses going off at even money (1–1, paying $4 for a $2 win ticket), he would have to win a good deal more than half his bets. In fact, to show a 20 percent profit on the total volume of his bets, he would have to win 60 percent of the time (a very considerable accomplishment): that is, if the player, in succession, bought 100 $2 tickets at even money, he would have to collect on sixty of them to get back 60 times $4, or $240, for a 20 percent profit. If the 100 bets were made at odds averaging 4–1 (with an average payout of $10 for a $2 win ticket), the winning of only twenty-four bets would yield a profit of 20 percent. Realism compels the reminder that while winning bets at 4–1 is far more rewarding than even money, finding the winning 4–1 is far more difficult. Incidentally, the profit margin of 20 percent certainly does not represent a minimum, but aiming for such a margin does reinforce the notion that the successful player must look forward to doing generally well enough to carry himself over the inevitable desert stretches where the likeliest horses run out and his few remaining winners are disqualified. Table B–4 shows the percentages of winners needed, at average odds ranging from 4–5 up to 5–1, for profit margins of 20 percent and 33 percent.

Occasionally, the player may look for an overlay in the place pool. To calculate possible place prices, he goes through the following procedure. Start with the number shown on the tote board as the total bet to place (the place and show pools, as well as daily double and exacta pools, are calculated separately in the parimutuel system). Subtract (for convenience) one-sixth for the takeout. The remainder will be distributed to holders of place tickets on the two horses that finish first and second. Add to the amount bet to place on your horse (or the horse that interests you), the largest amount bet on another horse. Subtract that sum from the amount available for distribution. Thus, if the whole place pool shows $120,000, five-sixths leaves $100,000 for distribution. Suppose $20,000 to have been bet (at the moment you are analyzing the board) to place on your horse. Suppose the largest amount on any other horse is $32,000. The sum of $20,000 and $32,000 is $52,000. This subtracted from $100,000 leaves a profit of $48,000, which, assuming both place, will be split evenly among the ticket holders on the two horses. The profit of $24,000 added to the $20,000 bet on your horse will make a total of $44,000. This, divided by 10,000 (the equivalent number of $2 place tickets represented by $20,000 in the place pool), gives a place price of $4.40. If some other horse, at longer odds, placed with your horse, the place prices would be higher. The place price on the other horse, by the same kind of calculation, would theoretically work out to $3.50 but the track rounds such sums downward to an even dime, or $3.40. The difference is known as "breakage"; it adds to the takeout more or less invisibly and causes horseplayers added suffering. The calculation of show prices, incidentally, proceeds in the same fashion, using the first three finishers, with the profit (after subtraction of takeout and cost of show tickets on the three horses) distributed in three even parts.

TABLE B-1: BETTING PERCENTAGE TABLE

Odds	Pct.	Odds	Pct.	Odds	Pct.	Odds	Pct.
1-1	50.00	18-1	5.26	12-5	29.41	45-100	68.97
2-1	33.33	19-1	5.00	13-5	27.78	11-20	
2½-1		20-1	4.76	14-5	26.31	55-100	64.52
5-2	28.57	25-1	3.85	16-5	23.81	13-20	
3-1	25.00	30-1	3.23	17-5	22.72	65-100	60.60
3½-1		40-1	2.44	18-5	21.73	15-20	
7-2	22.23	50-1	1.96	19-5	20.83	75-100	57.14
4-1	20.00	60-1	1.64	21-5	19.23	17-20	
4½-1		75-1	1.32	22-5	18.53	85-100	54.06
9-2	18.19	80-1	1.24	1-10	90.91	19-20	
5-1	16.67	100-1	.99	3-10	76.92	95-100	51.28
5½-1		150-1	.66	7-10	58.84	2-3	60.00
11-2	15.39	200-1	.50	9-10	52.63	2-7	77.80
6-1	14.29	250-1	.38	11-10	47.62	2-9	81.90
7-1	12.50	300-1	.33	13-10	43.47	3-4	57.14
8-1	11.11	500-1	.20	15-10		8-15	65.20
9-1	10.00	1-5	83.33	3-2	40.00	17-15	46.95
10-1	9.09	2-5	71.42	17-10	37.04	1-2	66.67
11-1	8.33	3-5	62.50	19-10	34.47	1-3	75.00
12-1	7.69	4-5	55.55	1-20	95.20	1-4	80.00
13-1	7.14	6-5	45.45	3-20		1-6	85.68
14-1	6.66	7-5	41.67	15-100	86.95	1-7	87.50
15-1	6.25	8-5	38.46	7-20		1-8	88.89
16-1	5.88	9-5	35.71	35-100	74.07	1-9	90.00
17-1	5.55	11-5	31.25	9-20	68.97	1-10	90.91

*American Racing Manual (1977), p. 465. Copyright © 1977 by Triangle Publications, Inc. Reprinted with permission of copyright owner.

TABLE B-2: APPROXIMATE PAY TO WIN (for $2.00)

If the odds are—

Odds	Pays	Odds	Pays	Odds	Pays
1-5	$2.40	5-2	$ 7.00	15	$ 32.00
2-5	2.80	3	8.00	18	38.00
1-2	3.00	7-2	9.00	20	42.00
3-5	3.20	4	10.00	25	52.00
4-5	3.60	9-2	11.00	30	62.00
1	4.00	5	12.00	40	82.00
6-5	4.40	6	14.00	50	102.00
7-5	4.80	7	16.00	60	122.00
3-2	5.00	8	18.00	70	142.00
8-5	5.20	9	20.00	80	162.00
9-5	5.60	10	22.00	90	182.00
2	6.00	12	26.00	99	200.00

TABLE B-3: PRICE LINE TABLE

Horse number	Natural odds*	Odds expressed as percentages	Percents × 118	Price line*
1	12-1	7.69	9.07	10-1
2	5-2	28.57	33.71	2-1
3	8-1	11.11	13.11	6-1
4	7-2	22.23	26.23	3-1
5	6-1	14.29	16.86	5-1
6	5-1	16.67	19.67	4-1
		100.56 (%)	118.65	

*"Natural odds" of 13-1 and price line odds of 11-1 would bring the total percentages almost exactly to 100 and 118; however, price line odds are generally rounded.

TABLE B–4: PERCENTAGES OF WINNERS NEEDED FOR PROFIT

Average odds over series of bets	Percentage of winners needed to yield:	
	20 percent profit	33 percent profit
4–5	67(%)	74(%)
1–1	60	67
6–5	55	60
7–5	50	55
3–2	48	53
8–5	46	51
9–5	43	48
2–1	40	44
5–2	34	38
3–1	30	33
7–2	27	30
4–1	24	27
9–2	22	24
5–1	20	22

EXAMPLES:

Average odds 1–1 (payoff $4); 100 tickets cost $200; 60 winners return $240, 67 winners return $268.

Average odds 3–1 (payoff $8); 100 tickets cost $200; 30 winners return $240, 33 winners return $264.

CLASS

The following are specific methods for rating horses according to class.

Total winnings: The first and simplest, and not necessarily worst, measure comes, without calculation, straight from the earnings box in the upper right-hand section of a horse's past performances. This is the total amount earned this year and last. (Occasionally, the record skips a year, when the horse has been laid up for a year; watch for this.) In the last half of the year, this year's earnings alone are usually all that need be considered. Early in the year, the earnings for the two years can be combined.

The defects of this very simple measure are obvious. One horse may have been out twenty times this year, the other only five, yet both show earnings of $5,000. Evidently, one's average earning per race is far higher than the other's. Also, a horse may have run up its earnings half a year ago, while running well, but may have done nothing since. It may, in fact, be in bad condition.

The warnings are clear. The fact that a horse shows higher earnings than any other in the race does not warrant a bet. *But,* it is always worth taking a second look at the horse with highest earnings.

Average dollars won per start: Again, this measure is worth a quick look and some rapid estimating; it also can be misleading. The average is presumably more meaningful than the gross amount earned. But the average, too, can be skewed by large earnings in one or two races run many months ago. The average makes no distinction among the parts of purses won by a horse for second-, third-, and fourth-place finishes. A far more sophisticated method for deriving a weighted average of purse money won—the main tool for several classification and handicapping systems—is set forth on p. 213.

Claiming price: This is the most obvious and clear-cut measure of class, but still sometimes perplexing. It is an obvious measure because a specific dollar price has been placed on the horse by its trainer in entering it. It may be perplexing because the past performances for a horse often show no decent races at today's claiming price. The handicapper therefore must protect himself by asking a number of key questions. At what claiming price did the horse most recently finish close up or in the money? A reasonably good performance at, say, a claiming price of $5,000 suggests that the horse actually may be worth $5,000. At what price has the horse recently been claimed? A claim is a clear statement of supposed value by the trainer and owner who entered the claim.

Suppose, as sometimes happens, one horse appears to show a higher genuine claiming value than any other in the field. Suppose, too, the horse has shown reasonably good recent form. Such a horse *may* be an obvious bet. The problem lies in the word "obvious." The apparent class advantage is obvious to everyone in the park. The horse is very likely to be bet down. Here handicapping is relatively straightforward; betting is crucial. The player must assign a realistic percentage to the horse's chance of winning. Then he must watch the tote board equally realistically, to see if the odds are justified by the horse's chances. If the odds seem right, the player has a bet. If the odds are too low, the player has encountered one of the commonest sorts of races that should **be** passed (equally common is the opposite case, in which **the** whole field seems devoid of class).

To be probed for is the horse with concealed class superiority. A friend of mine, an excellent handicapper, looks for the horse that is dropping in class after several dull races which at first glance might seem bad enough to rule the horse out. My friend sets up several rules. The horse must have run within the last few weeks. He must have won at least two races in the last two years. His last race must show at least a slight sign of an improving effort—and the trainer must have revealed his hopes by a jockey switch (unless he retains a jockey who has won on the horse). Other signs of concealed class may be revealed by the earnings box in the past performances (see particularly the weighted average method on p. 213), or by purse values, or by race conditions (see p. 212).

And what if the horse is dropping down substantially (30 to

50 percent in claiming price, say) after two or more genuinely bad races? The handicapper must warn himself that the dropdown may only be a signal of despair by the handlers of an ailing horse. If he convinces himself of this, he may look elsewhere in the field for a bet—at a fair price.

What if several horses seem to share the class advantage? The player looks to other techniques—including the study of speed and fractions, to be discussed in the next section—to separate the contenders.

And, for still another problem in the handling of class, what of the horse that is moving up the price ladder? If he has shown nothing special recently, the player may conclude (1) that he has been entered, safe from claim, to prepare for future races, and (2) that he will warrant another look if his name crops up in the entries in a week or two, at a lower price. But, more interesting today, what if the horse is moving up off a very strong recent race? Here, particularly with three-year-olds, the handicapper looks twice for signs of a genuinely improving horse (for example, unusually good times and fractions). Such a horse may be held at long odds today if the crowd believes him to be running against better.

The problems can be illustrated at least several times a day on any racing card. For example, in the fifth race at Aqueduct on May 5, 1978, eight three-year-old fillies going a mile were entered at claiming prices of $20,000 to $18,000. One of the eight was dropping down. But the dropdown was imaginary; the filly ran badly at the higher price and in fact had never won anything but a middling maiden race the year before. Four of the fillies had last run for today's claiming price, and three of these had recently been in the money at that class; they seemed to be properly placed. The remaining three were moving up. And it was one of these, French Lass, which won—and won easily, by six lengths. French Lass had last run for $16,000, but she had won the most money thus far in 1978—more than $21,000, compared with a second highest earning of about $13,500. Her earnings per start were also substantially higher than any of the others'. And, finally, her consistency record was much the best of the field: she had won more than a third of her starts in 1978 (three out of eight) and had finished in the money six of the eight times. Her record as a two-year-old had been nearly as consistent. In this case, as in many others, the winner's class was to be sought from a number of signs besides claiming price, and far from the least of these signs was consistency.

Can claiming prices be compared among different tracks? The problem is knotty. One approach is to do a quick tabulation, from charts, of the prices at which claims are actually made, for the two or three tracks which most concern you. At the best tracks the lower claiming prices may be inflated because, among other reasons, stall space will be available only to horses running for a fairly high minimum claiming price. At a lesser track the highest claiming prices may be nearly meaningless—because habitually no one claims at those prices at that track. The dollar standard applies best, and therefore most nearly uniformly, for the price levels at which claims are actually made.

Consistency measures: Robert S. Dowst was the principal writer on handicapping to appear in the 1930s following relegalization in many states and the rapid spread of American racing. Consistency was the cornerstone of Dowst's method. In a six-month exercise in 1936, Dowst said he found about one bet a day, selecting horses only on the basis of those that had won at least a third of their starts this year, or this year and last, and had been in the money at least half the time. He reported that 44 percent of his selections won and that they paid somewhat more than all favorites would have done. Nearly twenty years later, in 1954, he was still writing and still pushing consistency. He said then, "If you find some one horse which seems to have a material edge in point of consistency, is not overweighted, can probably set or stay with pace, and is not stepped up against better horses than he has met in the past, then you probably have a winner and can back him with money if the price is not too short, say close to even money or less." After the passage of still another generation, Dowst's consistent horses are harder to find, but consistency is still a significant measure of a horse's capacity to cope with a class in which he fits. A useful rule of thumb for measuring consistency, post-Dowst, is that the horse must show 50 percent of its starts in the money (based on at least six starts, using this year's and last year's records, if necessary); the horse must have won at least one race in six (to avoid chronic second-place finishers); and the horse must not otherwise be disadvantaged as to class, distance, or footing.

Measuring class in allowance races: In the absence of claiming price, the handicapper first looks at purse value as a measure of class in allowance races. Purse value does not appear in the past performance lines. It does appear in the full text of the daily result charts for each race, in the first line of the text which sets forth the conditions of the race. The class handicapper, until some other evidence changes his mind, assumes a horse that has won part of the purse money in an allowance race with a $15,000 purse has accomplished more than the horse that has been in close contention in an allowance race with a $9,000 purse. To reach any conclusion at all, the handicapper must save and consult the daily charts.

To compare purse values in allowance races is standard handicapping advice. But the handicapper can also sometimes classify allowances by looking more closely at the actual conditions of the race. Example: a three-year-old, in the fall, ran last time in a race for three-year-olds and up. Today he is entered in an otherwise similar allowance race, at the same distance, for threes only. He may have an easier time. Similar is the filly that ran last in an allowance race open to males, but today runs in a similar-looking race restricted to females; her chances correspondingly go up. Sometimes the conditions of the race are more obscure and call for some knowledge of the horses stabled on the grounds: At Del Mar, a summer meeting, a horse was entered in an allowance for four-year-olds and up, open to "non-winners of $5,500" since the preceding summer. He entered next an allowance at the same distance and for about the same purse but open simply to "non-winners of two" races. The previous race actually was open to some good horses; the race today drew an easier field.

Much handicapping instruction calls on the player to enter into the minds of trainers. Just as important, as shown by the conditions of allowance races cited above, is the thinking of the track's racing secretary, the author of the condition book which at intervals of ten racing days offers the horsemen stabled at that track a choice of races. The racing secretary has ninety races to dispose of for the ten-day interval—not a very large number. At most tracks perhaps fifty races will have to be set up for the many claiming horses, male or female, of various ages and classes, then in training. Another twenty or so may be set aside for maidens. That leaves only about twenty races, or two a day, for allowance and other better-class horses. And the allowance races too must provide for males and females, for older and younger horses, and for at least two and possibly three categories by ability. Yet each of these eight to a dozen separate groups of allowance horses should have a chance to run every couple of weeks. The truth is, and this is a clear warning against too great reliance on classification by conditions and purse value of an allowance, the trainer's choice may be greatly restricted and he may enter a horse in a particular allowance race because he has nowhere else to enter him.

One last warning concerning classification of the contending horses in allowance races: all of the above refers to comparison of races at a single track. It is difficult to save charts for more than one track. And in any case comparisons may be misleading. Allowance horses competing for a $15,000 purse at Hollywood Park in July may enter races with an $11,000 purse at Del Mar in August. Similar horses may run for $10,000 purses at Golden Gate in June and for $8,000 at Longacres in July. At the least, the handicapper in such cases must ask himself: Did the horse ship to another track because he had nowhere better to go, or was a different level of competition being sought?

Weighted average purse value: With a little extra labor, the handicapper can, by giving appropriate weights to the number of a horse's wins, seconds, and thirds in the earnings box (and at least those fourths shown in the past performance lines), greatly improve his figure for average purse value. The weighted average value is one of the more useful devices for classifying horses. The principle involved is used as the basis of several sold-by-mail handicapping systems and has been given such names as the "established class principle" and "purse effectiveness." The idea appears in an article by Paul Renniks entitled "High Caliber Plays," apparently from *American Turf Monthly* in the early 1950s. The Renniks article is included (at page 56) in a compilation by Henry Bomze, *A Treasury of American Turf* (Amerpub, New York, 1967).

In all cases, whether calculating mentally, or using paper and pencil, or working a plastic adding device sold by direct mail, the handicapper multiplies the number of wins for a given horse by one weight, the number of seconds by another weight, and the thirds and fourths by still others. The products are added together. Their sum is divided into the horse's total earnings. The result is the classifying number.

The weights most commonly used are 6 for each win, 2 for each second, 1 for each third, and ½ for each fourth (the fourths are obtainable only from the past performance lines and some may therefore be excluded—a minor inaccuracy). It can be seen that in fact these weights approximate the proportions for division of purse money at many tracks, including Aqueduct and Belmont. (The actual division of purse money for most races at the New York tracks is 60 percent to first, 22 percent to second, 12 percent to third, and 6 percent to fourth.)

For simplicity's sake, at tracks where 60 percent of the purse goes to the winner, fourth place can be skipped and the weights 6, 2, and 1 used for first, second, and third. However, these weights give poor results at California tracks. And the reason can quickly be seen in race charts. In California the winner gets 55 percent of the pot, second gets 20 percent, third gets 15 percent, fourth gets 7½ percent, and fifth gets 2½ percent. The weights to be used for first, second, third, and fourth at Santa Anita, Hollywood, Del Mar, Bay Meadows, and Golden Gate are 11, 4, 3, and 2 (forgetting about the fragment going to fifth). The sum of the products based on these weights must be divided by two. That number is then divided into total earnings. Dividing with the simplest of cheap slide rules makes the calculation easy, and the class number can be written directly on the horse's past performances. Otherwise, paper and pencil will usually be needed.

A California example: The horse ran ten times during 1978 and won twice, came in second once, third twice, and fourth once (with the fourth recorded only in the past performance lines). He won a total of $14,520. Multiply 11 (for first) by 2. Multiply 4 (for second) by 1. Multiply 3 (for third) by 2. Multiply 2 (for fourth) by 1. Add the products 22, 4, 6, and 2—for a sum of 34. Divide by 2, giving 17. Divide the earnings, $14,520, by 17. The result is $854. For convenience in calculating, a decimal point has been moved one space. The answer actually is about $8,500, representing a weighted average of the size of purse the horse has been able to share in after six of its ten starts. Again for convenience, the classification number to be used is 85.

Who beat whom? Or, the company they kept: Possibly the most positive aid in classifying horses is either a strong memory or a system of records that shows which horses ran well with what other horses. As a matter of record keeping, this is sure to be laborious since it requires going back and forth between past performances and charts. But it also pays off in rewards for effort and good works.

Example: The past performances show that Horse A is stepping up in class today off an unusually good last race. The record keeper makes a note of the name. Horse A wins today's race. The chart, of course, cannot show the class in which he previously ran. But the record keeper has his notation from the past performances. He therefore looks back at the chart of Horse A's previous race. If he simply left the rest of his field far behind in that previous race, nothing significant may be indicated. But suppose Horse B ran a good second to A. The record keeper makes a note of Horse B and waits eagerly for his name to turn up in the entries soon.

Another example: The record keeper notes in the day's charts that Horse C won a race in time that was excellent for the class of horses running. Horse D ran a good second, finishing within a length, losing no ground in the stretch after being carried wide on the turn, and leaving the third-place horse four lengths behind. Horse D's name also goes into the records, to be watched for his next appearance.

Yet another example: The handicapper is looking at back charts as he analyzes the record of Horse E, entered in a race today. He finds that E has run respectably with horses clearly better than those he encounters today. Again the handicapper gives Horse E a boost in his class rating.

Also valuable is a careful noting of trouble a horse in today's race may have met in his last race. The trouble (in the gate, or in close quarters along the way, or being blocked and having to take back, or being carried wide at the far turn) may have been noted in the caller's footnotes to the chart. Best of all, the handicapper may have seen trouble not recorded elsewhere, in which case he has an advantage over most of the rest of the crowd. Some handicappers claim to have made a steady profit by waiting for the return of beaten favorites that encountered trouble in the races in which they were favored.

Stakes: In a stakes race the track adds money (thus the term "added money race") to the nominating and entry fees (the stakes) submitted by the owners of horses, to make up the total purse. These are the feature races in any racing program, occurring from only once to several times a week. Handicappers are sometimes advised to pass these races: because the contention may run too deep; because visitors (or raiders, if you wish) from other parts of the country ship in to take the locals' money away with them. This is often sound advice. However, a few simple devices aid the handicapper in these races, too (in addition to normal, sound handicapping approaches).

It is sometimes necessary to evaluate the importance of a stakes entry in a horse's past performances. Stakes races may be offered at a county fair or at Belmont at the climax of a season. Since 1973 the Thoroughbred Owners and Breeders Association has graded the best of the stakes races in this country into Categories I, II, and III. These, and a number in addition, are called "black-type" stakes because they are entered thus in sales catalogs by the Jockey Club Statistical Bureau. The list of stakes as graded by the TOBA appear in the annual American Racing Manual, published by Triangle Publications, Inc.

In some stakes the weights are established by the conditions of the race. In others, called specifically "handicaps," the weights are assigned by the track's racing secretary. The secretary's assigned weights can be a useful device for horseplayers. Lists of weights can be kept for future classifications and comparisons. And they sometimes directly suggest a bet. A friend of mine, a biostatistician who is also an excellent handicapper, watches for the following simple play (which I use with permission and the hope that I will not cause him to suffer further reduced odds). He bets on the high weight in a handicap stakes if the second high weight carries five or more pounds less. I have pointed out to him that for the rule to work, the racing secretary (a) must have good judgment and (b) must not be downright punitive to the high weight. My friend agrees. He bets at California tracks, and the racing secretaries who concern him are Lou Eilken and Harry Krovitz. How the rule might work in other parts of the country with less able and conscientious secretaries, I do not know. But I do know that my friend has spotted strings of as many as ten and eleven successive winners—a number of winners which more than makes up for the obviously low odds on the high-weighted horses.

SPEED

Speed, based on the electronically timed running of a race, is clearly one of the two most important factors in handicapping. (Class is the other.) Some experts regard speed as the most important of all. What follows are methods which can be used for putting the raw, unadjusted times for a race into comparable forms. To get the most benefit from these methods, the player should understand how they are constructed, and preferably he should reconstruct them for himself, from data collected at his own track.

Some handicappers either do not believe in speed tables and speed handicapping, or do not choose to do the sometimes laborious arithmetic. They can concentrate on other handicapping factors. Or they can buy ready-made tables, several sources for which will be given below.

Use of raw times: Horseplayers use the raw data, the unadjusted times for races, every time they look at past performances. They do so, as is said about mountains, because they are there. At least such times raise questions. Horse A ran six furlongs in 1:11 flat. Horse B went in 1:11 3/5. Horse A seems 3/5 of a second faster, a time advantage which convention holds to equal three lengths (actually, more nearly three and a half lengths). The handicapper's question is whether A is really faster. The speed handicapper does answer the question, but first he must cope with shifts from track to track (if the times were made in fact on different tracks), shifts from day to day at the same track, and possible changes involving pace, riders, and weights, to say nothing of post positions and the tactics of the race. In summary: raw times raise questions; they do not answer them.

Daily Racing Form *speed ratings:* A standard item in each past performance line is a speed rating, appearing between claiming price (or type of race) and the names of the first three finishers. The speed rating applies to the horse himself, whether or not he won the race. The calculation of the *DRF* speed rating begins by assigning a value of 100 to the track record for that distance. Then, for every fifth of a second which the horse ran slower than the record for the distance, one point is subtracted from 100. The horse won a six-furlong race in 1:11. The track record is 1:08. The difference is three seconds, or 15 fifths. The speed rating is 100 minus 15, or 85. Another case: The six-furlong race was won in 1:11⁴/₅, but the horse in question was beaten three lengths. For purposes of the speed rating, it is assumed that every beaten length equals a fifth of a second. The horse is therefore presumed to have finished in 1:12²/₅. The track record is the same 1:08. This time the horse finished 22 fifths off the record for a speed rating of 78. The same kind of rating is calculated by the *Form*, for the convenience of handicappers, for all distances and all tracks, where records have been established. Note that the numbers are not percents, though they start with a base of 100; they simply represent the number of lengths the horse is presumed to have finished off the record.

It is common among handicapping writers to bad-mouth the *DRF* speed ratings. And this is easy enough to do. Suppose two horses run six-furlong races in 1:10³/₅ on different tracks. Suppose the two racing strips are intrinsically of the same speed, and the two days were equally fast. But at one track the record was set by a world class sprinter in 1:07⁴/₅. At the other, the record is held by a good allowance horse in 1:09. One horse finished 14 fifths off the record, for a speed rating of 86. The other horse, running a race that was no better, finishes only 8 fifths off his track's record for a more splendid-sounding 92.

The second great difficulty with the *Form*'s speed ratings is seen in distance shifts. The two horses being compared in the same race today ran on the same track last out but at different distances: six furlongs and a mile and a sixteenth. If both horses tied track records, both had speed ratings of 100. But a player might go racing all his life without encountering such a case. In all other cases, the greater the distance, the faster the speed rating drops. To take some typical figures: with a track record of 1:08 at six furlongs, the median time for mature horses might be 1:11, for a speed rating of 85. But at the same track the record for 1¹⁄₁₆ might well be 1:40 and the median time 1:45, for a speed rating of 75. Realistically, the 75 at the longer distance would be about as good an effort as the 85 in the sprint. (Nomenclature here applies to standard tracks, usually a mile around, sometimes — in the case of eight specific tracks — larger. A sprint is any race below a mile. A route is a race of a mile or more. Occasionally, a mile, and 1¹⁄₁₆ miles, are spoken of as middle distances.)

So the difficulties with the *Form*'s speed ratings are clear. But this does not mean they should be ignored. To the contrary, they are very valuable, if used properly. Among other things, someone else has done for the player the work of incorporating beaten lengths into the ratings. The way to use the speed ratings effectively is: consider them only in races where the contending horses have been running today's distance, on today's track, and where the numbers have been adjusted for a good daily track variant (or, occasionally, where no daily track variant is needed). Up to 30 or 40 percent of all races at a track may be thus ratable.

Daily track variants: The speed of the running surface of a track may vary from day to day. The speed obviously varies during and after a rainfall. Less obviously, it varies depending on work done to the strip by maintenance crews: the blading, the harrowing and rolling or dragging, and the dumping on and working in of sand.

The simplest way to calculate a passable daily track variant is to pick a par time (any par time will do, because what you are interested in is changes, upward or down, but it is handiest if the par equals or approaches a median time for the most commonly run distance, almost always six furlongs at one-mile tracks). Look only at the times registered by mature winners (that is, not maidens, not two-year-olds and not three-year-olds

in the first half of the year before the threes run with older).
Look only at their time in races in the middle range of claiming
prices at your track. Suppose that range is $5,000 to $6,000.
You are dealing with the commonest category of races at the
track and you will find enough races to strike a simple average
of differences each day. Suppose three such races (in fact, the
median races on the track's program for mature horses) occur
in one day. Your par time is 1:11. The three times are 1:11²/₅,
1:11⁴/₅, and 1:11³/₅. The average variation is ³/₅ of a second,
slow. On my own small card with daily entries I simply enter the
number –3, meaning that in the future sprint speed ratings
for that day will have to be increased by 3 for comparability with
other days similarly adjusted. This method truly requires only
five minutes in a day, but it must be done daily. For races at a
mile, increase the sprint variant by a third. For longer races,
increase the sprint variant by a half (or 50 percent).

The more comprehensive way of calculating a variant is to
use a comparative speed chart, described below. In the construction of the chart, the player will have arrived at par times
for several *values* of horse and several *distances*. From these a
variance can be calculated for each race on the card for mature
winners. These variances can then be converted into rating
numbers (see Table D–1) and averaged to give an accurate daily
track variant.

Two warnings: The speed of the track may change during a
day (depending on weather); wind may influence the speed of
races differently at different distances. The handicapper who
seeks the greatest accuracy will have to keep special notes. He
may also want to calculate variance similarly in half-mile fractions as another clue to how the track was running on a given
day. Turf variants must also be calculated separately and then
only if enough turf races are run to afford comparability.

Mechanical devices or tabulations that give worthwhile variants can be bought. Amerpub Co., 505 8th Avenue, New York,
sells a pace calculator the back of which contains a standardized table which permits calculation of daily track variants. Millwood Publications, Millwood, New York, sells a booklet by William L. Quirin called "Par Times"; the booklet gives par
times for various classes and distances at forty-six American
tracks. Good daily variants can be calculated from these par

times. Eastern editions of the *Daily Racing Form* show a daily variant besides the speed rating. However, these amount to a daily average difference between winning time and track record for all races on the card; therefore, they reflect not only the condition of the track, but the quality of the horses running that day, as well as the mix of distances run. They should be used with caution.

A special warning about tracks in particularly bad condition: When a track is, for example, running unusually slow after a siege of rains, the variant may be very large—and thoroughly unreliable. Some horses simply cannot run at all on such tracks; adding the large variant to their times still gives no indication of their true ability on fast tracks. At the opposite extreme, some horses do their best on off tracks and eat up the goo like chocolate pudding; the large variant added to their times on off tracks would make it appear that they will break records when the going is fast—which they will not. Unusually large variants, therefore, should simply be regarded as a warning of dubious times.

Comparative speed charts: The characteristic tool of speed handicapping is a speed chart, sometimes called a parallel time chart, called here for purposes of accuracy a "comparative speed chart." The purpose is development of rating numbers which can measure and equate the worth of a horse's performance at different distances (at the same track, under the same track conditions). Such charts begin with an arbitrary number which is assigned to track record, or "maximum," or simply "best likely" times, at each distance. Then progressively lower rating numbers are matched with progressively slower times at the various distances. Charts of this kind were being used at least as far back as the turn of the century. Most if not all of the old charts made one elementary blunder: the intervals were the same in every column, no matter what the distance. Example: 500 might be the highest number, based on theoretical top speeds of 1:08 for six furlongs, 1:40 for a mile and a sixteenth. Then 350 might be the rating for a 1:11 six furlongs (three seconds slower), and under the erroneous system the same 350 would be the rating for a 1¹/₁₆ time of 1:43, also three seconds slower. Now, the whole point of the rating number is to point out *comparable* numbers, but these two numbers are not at all comparable. For six furlongs, 1:11 on a standard one-mile track, particularly in the West, is a very average sort of time for middling claimers. For 1¹⁄₁₆, 1:43 on the same track is reasonable time for pretty good allowance horses. The glaring arithmetic defect can be seen by looking at the percentage drop which three seconds produces in the times for the two distances. Three seconds off the six-furlong time of 1:08 is a 4½ percent drop (68 seconds decreased by 3), whereas three seconds off the 1¹⁄₁₆ time of 1:40 is a 3 percent drop (100 seconds decreased by 3). The so-called "best" time for the longer distances can be artificially lowered, to bring the median ratings more in line, but this is equally unsatisfactory. So, first warning: Beware of alleged speed charts that show the times dropping by the same amount, in the column for each distance, for each rating unit.

The earliest true comparative time chart, having properly graduated times, that I have seen was published by Pat Cabell in *American Turf Monthly* sometime before 1967 and appears in Henry Bomze's compilation, *A Treasury of American Turf* (Amerpub, New York, 1967). Of course, there may have been earlier versions that were sound. More recent books with properly graduated speed charts include *Picking Winners* by Andrew Beyer (Houghton Mifflin, Boston, 1975) and *Gordon Jones to Win!* by Gordon Jones (Karman Communications, Huntington Beach, California, 1976). Rather than a single chart, Beyer presents several series of matched columns for various distances. His numbers appear to apply to the 1¹⁄₂- and 1¹⁄₈-mile New York tracks, Belmont and Aqueduct. Cabell and Jones appear to have based their numbers on the one-mile Southern California tracks; their numbers therefore apply more nearly to the bulk of one-mile tracks around the country. William L. Quirin's "Par Times" provides most of the basic data for comparative time charts for forty-six principal tracks. Thus it is perfectly possible to do respectable speed handicapping using numbers published in several good sources.

However, a point made early in the text of this book can well be repeated here: good handicapping is not easy; the work of a master handicapper is done with much application and an independent mind, concentrating on live data from the track or tracks that he himself observes. To repeat: it is possible to make excellent use of bought numbers. But I would urge the handicapper—in this case, the speed handicapper—who wishes to go an important step or two further to make his own charts. Three benefits will accrue. He will better understand the numbers he uses. He will inevitably learn things about the racing program at his own tracks. He will be able to adjust his numbers, as the tracks themselves and the horse population stabled at them change somewhat from meeting to meeting.

Making a comparative time chart does not require even intermediate mathematics, but it does require some appetite and capacity for laborious arithmetic, and some of it must be learned in the doing. One set of guiding principles is outlined below (I do not pretend that there is a single best way of doing the job).

Start by picking an arbitrary top number. (Remember, this number may be exceeded when new records are set; no harm done.) In the specimen chart presented here (Table D–1, based on the Bay Meadows 1977 meeting and typical of American one-mile tracks), the top number is 144. I wanted a number that was clearly higher than speed ratings in the *Form*, but I did not want one so high that the large rating intervals between fifths of a second in running time would give a false impression of greater accuracy.

The next step is to pick top times for the principal distances run at your track. Merely in finding out what those distances are, the player will have learned something. At Bay Meadows in 1977, as anyone would have expected, six-furlong races made up 54 percent of the races, or about five out of nine per day. Races at a mile and a sixteenth exceeded races at a mile, but not as greatly as I had expected, and between them they accounted for another three races per day. The remaining ninth (one race per day) was widely scattered therefore among races mainly at 1⅛, 1³/₁₆, and 1¼ miles.

TABLE D–1: *COMPARATIVE TIME CHART Based on medians for median class, mature, winners, at BM, 1977*

	5f	6f	7f	1 mi	1 1/16	1 1/8	1 1/4
144	55³/₅	1:07⁴/₅	1:20¹/₅	1:33³/₅	1:39⁴/₅	1:46	1:58²/₅
143	—	—	—	—	—	—	—
142	—	—	—	1:33⁴/₅	1:40	1:46²/₅	1:58³/₅
141	—	—	1:20²/₅	—	—	—	—
140	55⁴/₅	1:08	—	1:34	—	1:46³/₅	1:58⁴/₅
139	—	—	—	—	1:40¹/₅	—	—
138	—	—	1:20³/₅	1:34¹/₅	—	1:46⁴/₅	1:59
137	—	—	—	—	1:40²/₅	—	—
136	56	1:08¹/₅	—	1:34²/₅	—	1:47	1:59¹/₅
135	—	—	1:20⁴/₅	—	1:40³/₅	—	—
134	—	—	—	1:34³/₅	—	1:47¹/₅	1:59²/₅
133	—	—	—	—	—	—	—
132	56¹/₅	1:08²/₅	1:21	—	1:40⁴/₅	1:47²/₅	1:59³/₅
131	—	—	—	1:34⁴/₅	—	—	—
130	—	—	—	—	1:41	1:47³/₅	1:59⁴/₅
129	—	—	1:21¹/₅	—	—	—	—
128	56²/₅	1:08³/₅	—	1:35	—	1:47⁴/₅	2:00
127	—	—	—	—	1:41¹/₅	—	—
126	—	—	1:21²/₅	—	—	1:48	2:00¹/₅
125	—	—	—	1:35¹/₅	1:41²/₅	—	—
124	56³/₅	1:08⁴/₅	—	—	—	1:48¹/₅	2:00²/₅
123	—	—	1:21³/₅	—	1:41³/₅	—	—
122	—	—	—	1:35²/₅	—	1:48²/₅	2:00³/₅
121	—	—	—	—	—	—	—
120	56⁴/₅	1:09	1:21⁴/₅	—	1:41⁴/₅	1:48³/₅	2:00⁴/₅
119	—	—	—	1:35³/₅	—	—	—
118	—	—	—	—	1:42	1:48⁴/₅	2:01
117	—	—	1:22	—	—	—	—
116	—	1:09¹/₅	—	1:35⁴/₅	—	—	2:01¹/₅
115	57	—	—	—	1:42¹/₅	1:49	—
114	—	—	1:22¹/₅	—	—	—	2:01²/₅
113	—	—	—	1:36	1:42²/₅	1:49²/₅	—
112	—	1:09²/₅	—	—	—	—	2:01³/₅
111	—	—	1:22²/₅	—	—	—	—
110	57¹/₅	—	—	1:36¹/₅	1:42³/₅	1:49²/₅	2:01⁴/₅
109	—	—	—	—	—	—	—

	5f	6f	7f	1 mi	1 1/16	1 1/8	1 1/4
108	—	1:09³/₅	1:22³/₅	—	1:42⁴/₅	1:49³/₅	2:02
107	—	—	—	1:36²/₅	—	—	—
106	—	—	—	—	1:43	1:49⁴/₅	2:02¹/₅
105	57²/₅	—	—	—	—	—	—
104	—	1:09⁴/₅	1:22⁴/₅	1:36³/₅	—	—	2:02²/₅
103	—	—	—	—	1:43¹/₅	1:50	—
102	—	—	—	—	—	—	2:02³/₅
101	—	—	—	1:36⁴/₅	1:43²/₅	1:50¹/₅	—
100	57³/₅	1:10	1:23	—	—	—	2:02⁴/₅
99	—	—	—	—	—	—	—
98	—	—	—	1:37	1:43³/₅	1:50²/₅	2:03
97	—	—	—	—	—	—	—
96	—	1:10¹/₅	1:23¹/₅	—	—	—	2:03¹/₅
95	57⁴/₅	—	—	1:37¹/₅	1:43⁴/₅	1:50³/₅	—
94	—	—	—	—	—	—	2:03²/₅
93	—	—	—	—	—	—	—
92	—	1:10²/₅	1:23²/₅	1:37²/₅	1:44	1:50⁴/₅	2:03³/₅
91	—	—	—	—	—	—	—
90	58	—	—	—	1:44¹/₅	1:51	2:03⁴/₅
89	—	—	1:23³/₅	1:37³/₅	—	—	—
88	—	1:10³/₅	—	—	1:44²/₅	1:51¹/₅	2:04
87	—	—	—	—	—	—	—
86	—	—	—	1:37⁴/₅	—	—	2:04¹/₅
85	58¹/₅	—	1:23⁴/₅	—	1:44³/₅	1:51²/₅	—
84	—	1:10⁴/₅	—	—	—	—	2:04²/₅
83	—	—	—	1:38	—	—	—
82	—	—	—	—	1:44⁴/₅	1:51³/₅	2:04³/₅
81	—	—	1:24	—	—	—	—
80	58²/₅	1:11	—	1:38¹/₅	1:45	1:51⁴/₅	2:04⁴/₅
79	—	—	—	—	—	—	—
78	—	—	1:24¹/₅	—	1:45¹/₅	1:52	2:05
77	—	—	—	1:38²/₅	—	—	—
76	—	1:11¹/₅	—	—	—	1:52¹/₅	2:05¹/₅
75	58³/₅	—	—	—	1:45²/₅	—	—
74	—	—	1:24²/₅	1:38³/₅	—	—	2:05²/₅
73	—	—	—	—	—	1:52²/₅	—

	5f	6f	7f	1 mi	1¹/₁₆	1¹/₈	1¹/₄
72	—	1:11²/₅	—	—	1:45³/₅	—	2:05³/₅
71	58⁴/₅	—	—	1:38⁴/₅	—	1:52³/₅	—
70	—	—	1:24³/₅	—	—	—	2:05⁴/₅
69	—	—	—	—	1:45⁴/₅	1:52⁴/₅	—
68	—	1:11³/₅	—	1:39	—	—	2:06
67	—	—	1:24⁴/₅	—	1:46	1:53	—
66	59	—	—	—	—	—	2:06¹/₅
65	—	—	—	1:39¹/₅	—	—	—
64	—	1:11⁴/₅	1:25	—	1:46¹/₅	1:53¹/₅	2:06²/₅

*Note that the table above can be extended as far as desired to include slower times. This would have to be done, as a matter of course, for tracks with slower median times. The times that are slower than the median, however, tend to be least reliable. Such times can reflect off tracks, which affect different distances in a variety of ways; or, they may simply record the efforts of erratic and unreliable horses. Note, too, that use of median times produces a table based on the running times of horses actually stabled at a particular track. At the New York and Los Angeles tracks, for example, the comparative times for 1⅛- and 1¼-mile races would probably be somewhat faster than those shown above.

Next step: By comparing records at all tracks in the region, pick times that can be accepted as the theoretical "best" (but not "unimaginable"). For example, in the chart above, the six-furlong time of 1:07⁴/₅ is the record at Golden Gate, while 1¹/₁₆ in 1:39⁴/₅ is a record at Bay Meadows. The times at the selected distances must make a smooth and reasonable progression; at several points in the making of a chart, a logically assumed number will make more sense than scattered and erratic live data. A special point to be noted: at the first distance to be run around *two* turns, a mile in this case, the times will make a slight extra jump upward before resuming a smooth upward trend.

The next step is perhaps the single most important: The handicapper must establish a valid median time for the commonest distance run at the track—six furlongs in this case. The median point is the exact midpoint of an array of all times for the distance, from fastest to slowest. It is likely to be very close to an average. Use only races for winners that are mature horses. With full knowledge that times for female horses, on the average, would be slightly slower than times for males, do not segregate the races as to sex. The ultimate difference will be slight, and at this stage you need to be assured of enough races to get a valid median. Use only races on fast tracks. (The specimen chart is based on 576 races, on 64 days, which yielded 313 six-furlong races, of which 121 were for mature winners.)

A good method of posting is to use sheets of lined paper with a fifth of a second on each line, counting down from fastest times to clearly slow times. A handy way to post is to enter, not a tally line, but the half-mile fraction for each successive six-furlong race. The half-mile fractions do not appear in the final chart, but something extra will be learned about the spread of fractional times. Do the tallying, by fifths of a second, and in four groups (vertically dividing broad sheets of tally paper: lowest-grade claimers, medium-low claimers, higher claimers, highest claimers plus allowance and better). Some experimentation will yield groups that have adequate numbers of races. In my opinion, it is a mistake to break the groups down into too fine divisions; you simply will not find enough cases for sensible results. Now, finally, from the spread of data, you will find the way times group among the broad classes of horses, and above all you will have a valid median six-furlong time which, in relation to the top line, for best times, is the cornerstone of the chart.

Repeat the process for all other distances for which enough data are at hand. For the chart presented here, the numbers for a mile and for a mile and a sixteenth were clearly valid. There were barely enough numbers for a median at 1⅛. All other numbers had to be estimated. (As a practical matter, it turned out that at that meeting a majority of races at 1¼ miles were on off tracks. It also turned out that the races at a mile, for the most part, were written for a group of horses different from the races at 1¹/₁₆; such discoveries make the labor rewarding.)

The median time for a six-furlong race for mature winners in this case was 1:11 flat, incidentally with a median half-mile fraction of :45⁴/₅. Four rating points were assigned to each fifth of a second. Since 1:11 is 16 fifths slower than the theoretical "best" of 1:07⁴/₅, the rating number for 1:11 was 80—that is, 4 × 16, or 64 points less than the top of 144. All the intermediate six-furlong times were arrayed at 4-point intervals, by fifths of a second.

The median times for a mile, a mile and a sixteenth, and a mile and an eighth were: 1:38¹/₅, 1:45, and 1:51⁴/₅; the estimated median for 1¼ was 2:05⁴/₅. These median times, when compared with the "best" times, made possible the following tabulation:

Distance*	Difference between "best" and median times (fifths of a second)	Rating units per fifth of a second**
6 furlongs	16	4.0
1 mile	23	2.8
1¹/₁₆	26	2.5
1⅛	28	2.3
1¼	32	2.0

*For all distances, "best" time has a rating of 144; median, a rating of 80.
** 64 divided by number in second column

It is immediately clear that the six-furlong times can be spaced, evenly, with four rating units per fifth of a second. It was, of course, planned that way, to make the ratings for the commonest distance the handiest. The four-unit gap between fifths makes 1 point equal a quarter-length, while 2 points equal a half-length, at six furlongs. Spacing the greater number of fifths between "best" and median times for the longer distances has to be uneven and somewhat arbitrary. But it should be remembered that no spacing, however ragged the chart appears, gives a rating more than 1 point off, or a quarter of a length. Any show of greater accuracy, on any chart, is imaginary.

Times slower than median times, and times for such distances as five and seven furlongs, have been estimated from the other data. In general, comparative times are least reliable as they drop below the medians.

Incidentally, if only the six-furlong median time seems reliable (because the data at other distances are too erratic, with the horses scattered among too many groups by age and class), percentages can be used. That is, the other medians can all be the same percentage greater than the "best" times, based on the actual percentage difference for six furlongs. But the medians, where it is possible to calculate them, are more realistic because they reflect the extra slowing down of a race run around two turns.

TABLE D–2: BEATEN LENGTHS ADJUSTMENT

(Rating points to be subtracted from winner's rating, by distance of race, and beaten lengths. Based on 4 points, per ⅕″, at 6f)

Lengths	6f	8f (1 mi)	10f (1¼)
¼	1		
½	2		
¾	3		
1	4	2	2
2	7	4	4
3	10	7	6
4	13	10	8
5	16	13	10
6	20	16	12

One final warning must be given on use of any comparative speed chart. One horse goes six furlongs in 1:10³⁄₅ and earns a rating of 88. Another goes 1¹⁄₁₆ miles in 1:44²⁄₅—for the same rating of 88. This does not mean that the sprinter can necessarily earn the same rating at the longer distance, or that the router can sprint successfully. The equal ratings suggest that the efforts represent the same quality—or class. It is the handicapper's task to estimate the chances of the horse's switching distances successfully.

Corrections for beaten lengths: The overwhelming majority of past performance lines do not show the horse in that line as a winner. Therefore, the rating for the winner's time, after it has been corrected for the daily track variant, must also be corrected for the number of lengths the horse was beaten. Example: The horse ran in a six-furlong race; the winner went in 1:10⁴⁄₅; the horse under study finished fifth, beaten 5½ lengths; his rating must be reduced—by 18 points, to 66 from 84, in accordance with Table D–2. This table of beaten length adjustments makes allowance for two variables: the horse really goes farther than a length (9 feet, by convention) in a fifth of a second; but he is going progressively less fast the greater the distance. Examples of reduced speed:

Time for a quarter-mile (seconds)	Number of feet per fifth of a second
22	12.0
23	11.5
24	11.0
25	10.6
26	10.2
27	9.8

A typical last quarter in a six-furlong race might be run in 25 seconds, with the beaten horses slowing down still more. In a route, the last quarter might be run in no better than 27 seconds; here the beaten horse might truly be going no faster than 9 feet in a fifth of a second.

Again a warning about beaten lengths: If the horse is beaten more than six lengths, the jockey had little reason to urge the horse to do his utmost. No matter how adjusted, the rating number may not represent the horse's true ability when pushed.

THE TRACK

The source of information concerning physical layout and basic statistics for American race courses is the annual American Racing Manual, published by Triangle Publications, Inc., 731 Plymouth Court, Chicago 60605.

In the Manual the handicapper can find individual track diagrams, records, locations, and specifications including composition of racing strips, width and length of stretch, and stable accommodations. All these factors enter into analysis of performances by horses on tracks otherwise unknown to the handicapper.

For tracks that can be observed directly, the handicapper must constantly check on (besides daily speed variants) records of horses breaking from different post positions at different distances. It will be seen that the effect of a post position depends greatly on the running style of an individual horse and the abilities of his rider. Thus a horse with early speed breaking from an inside post in a race at a mile, on a one-mile track, may be helped—particularly if his rider is known to be unusually alert in the gate. For a horse that habitually gets off slowly, the inside post may result in the loss of many lengths. At six furlongs—a race started from a chute along the backstretch on a one-mile track, and run around only one turn—the rail may be a trap for all but those horses speediest from the gate. An outside post, while it causes a slight extra distance, may favor the horse that habitually needs to find his stride without being bothered. The variations are many and the handicapper must look at each contending horse in terms of how he will be affected by the shape of the course, the post positions, and the probable tactics of the race.

Observations of the track may actually begin before the player arrives for a racing day. If the track is in a windy location, he may get an idea of the strength and direction of the wind by looking at whitecaps on nearby water or at flags whipping in the breeze. As a matter of course, he will use the times and fractions of the first two races to find out if the racing strip has changed since the day before. As soon as possible, he will try to answer a daily question: Is the speed standing up? When the answer is yes, the handicapper will be reluctant to bet, in a sprint, on any horse that does not show fast early fractions. And he will take a second look at sprinters attempting to stretch out to a mile or a mile and a sixteenth.

For tracks that the handicapper cannot observe directly, the problems compound, and it should be said outright that some of them cannot be solved. A horse ships in from another track; the player may have a reasonable idea of the general speed and character of that track, but he still needs daily variants to evaluate the shipper's past performances properly. And, in truth, a handicapper in New York can readily enough calculate variants for New Jersey tracks. Similarly, a handicapper in San Francisco, with zeal and time enough, can keep up with conditions at the Los Angeles tracks. But, with the best will in the world, the San Franciscan will most likely find it impractical to try to keep up with Portland Meadows, Longacres, and Exhibition Park, all of which ship horses into northern California.

Three general rules hold, concerning the problem of shifts in tracks:

1. Whatever the source of information about out-of-town tracks, the information must be constantly rechecked and kept up to date;

2. Where the handicapper confronts too many shippers of unknown quality, he has every reason to go for the escape hatch and pass the race;

3. All else being equal, the handicapper may be guided, not by the speed or physical layout, but by the intrinsic class of the out-of-town track.

The table below groups thirty-six principal American tracks in four class categories. Among them, these tracks account for more than 70 percent of the national total parimutuel handle and an equally overwhelming share in all other measures of racing activity. All the tracks listed here are a standard one mile around except for eight that are larger. Belmont is a one-and-a-half-mile track; Aqueduct, Arlington Park, Atlantic City, Hialeah, Laurel, and Saratoga measure one and one-eighth miles around; Keeneland, uniquely, is a one-and-one-sixteenth-mile track. All county fair tracks have been omitted (if for no other reason than their short meetings). All tracks of less than a mile have been left out as well, because they present too many unique problems in handicapping, though several—including Greenwood, Exhibition Park, Sportsman's Park, and Timonium—are clearly significant factors in racing.

The categories used in the tabulation that follows cannot be made absolute. Factors considered include average purse size per race, range of claiming prices, proximity to breeding and training centers, and, at the borderlines of categories, shipping relationships with clearly major tracks. The categories as they stand, arguable as they may be in some cases, will provide a rough guide to class for horses shipping from one area to another. Tracks not included in the table should be regarded as no higher than Category IV and probably lower.

    I. Aqueduct (Aqu)
      Belmont (Bel)
      Hollywood (Hol)

Santa Anita (SA)
Saratoga (Sar)

II Arlington Park (AP)
Atlantic City (Atl)
Del Mar (Dmr)
Garden State (GS)
Hawthorne (Haw)
Hialeah (Hia)
Meadowlands (Med)
Monmouth (Mth)

III. Ak-Sar-Ben (Aks)
Bay Meadows (BM)
Bowie (Bow)
Calder (Crc)
Churchill Downs (CD)
Delaware (Del)
Fair Grounds (FG)
Fort Erie (FE)
Golden Gate (GG)
Gulfstream Park (GP)
Keeneland (Kee)
Keystone (Key)
Laurel (Lrl)
Oaklawn Park (OP)
Pimlico (Pim)
Woodbine (Wo)

IV. Detroit (Det)
Longacres (Lga)
Louisiana Downs (LD)
Penn National (Pen)
Rockingham (Rkm)
Suffolk (Suf)
Thistledown (Tdn)

WEIGHTS AND RIDERS

Weight: Table F–1 (p. 236) is a modern American rendering of the work of Admiral Rous, the Jockey Club Scale of Weights for Age. Examination of the table leads to several conclusions:

Two-year-olds generally carry more than scale weight. This suggests that racing secretaries cannot afford to write conditions for races that cannot be fulfilled by available riders. To set a scale weight of 105 pounds for two-year-olds running six furlongs in September would simply be impractical because very nearly all the riders would be substantially overweight. This disparity highlights the feeling of some horsemen that two-year-olds should be raced very lightly, if at all.

On the other hand, three-year-olds from summer on, and older horses at all times, only very rarely carry scale weight. More often than not, they are about ten pounds under weights called for by the scale.

The scale, therefore, in current usage, applies mainly to the best horses on the grounds at any track. In handicap stakes the scale may bring out the racing secretary's true evaluation of a horse. For example, a three-year-old racing a mile against an older horse in August, under equal assigned weights, is actually, according to the scale, spotting the older horse seven pounds. Under the same circumstances and in the same month, a female horse carrying the same weight as a male of the same age, is—according to the scale—spotting the male five pounds.

The ancient saying that enough weight will stop any horse (or an elephant, or a train) is true enough, but it is rarely tried in practice.

Example: In 1975, 103 stakes races with a gross value of $100,000 or more were run. In 54 of those races, the highest weight carried by any horse was 122 pounds or less. In sixteen of those important stakes, the high weight was between 117 and 119 pounds. At the high end of the scale, where weight clearly counts, in only seven of the big stakes races did the high weight carry 128 pounds or more. In one of those cases, Ancient Title carried exactly 128 pounds and finished third. In all six remaining cases, the high weight was—Forego, carrying 129, 131, 132, 134 twice, and 135 pounds. In other words, of all the 50,000 or so Thoroughbreds in training in America that year, only one was considered capable of carrying weight in a major race, and he was the Horse of that Year.

For the handicapper, a practical conclusion follows from all this: Weight carried still figures large in the minds of horsemen and in their decisions to enter or not to enter a horse in a race. But as a practical matter the adjustments of ratings for weight carried should be used sparingly.

Many speed rating systems call for mechanical raising or lowering of a horse's number depending on any amount of weight on or off. It is suggested here that the handicapper look more closely at past performances before making such adjustments.

Adjustments of two or three pounds up or down appear to make little difference—below a weight of 120 pounds. A shift of as much as five pounds does warrant a closer look, but if the weight was picked up in a switch to an outstanding rider it is most likely worth it.

For any shift that brings the total weight to 120 pounds or more, the handicapper needs to look first to see if the horse has carried today's weight successfully (that is, in a good race) or, in fact, if he has run badly when asked to pick up more weight. In that case, if the horse is a poor risk, adjusting his rating will not be enough of a safeguard.

In borderline cases, where a shift of five or more pounds seems significant but not ruinous, or where the horse may be picking up pounds at the point where the weight begins to affect him, the following simple scale can be used:

One-length equivalents:

    At 6 furlongs—five pounds

    At 8 furlongs (1 mi.)—four pounds

    At 10 furlongs (1¼ mi.)—three pounds

In other words, where the weight shift needs to be considered at all, consider five pounds up or down as the equivalent of one

TABLE F-1: SCALE OF WEIGHTS FOR AGE*

Distance	Age	Jan.	Feb.	Mar.	April	May	June	July	Aug.	Sept.	Oct.	Nov.	Dec.
Half mile	Two years	—	—	—	—	—	—	—	105	108	111	114	114
	Three years	117	117	119	119	121	123	125	126	127	128	129	129
	Four years	130	130	130	130	130	130	130	130	130	130	130	130
	Five years and up	130	130	130	130	130	130	130	130	130	130	130	130
Six furlongs	Two years	—	—	—	—	—	—	—	102	105	108	111	111
	Three years	114	114	117	117	119	121	123	125	126	127	128	128
	Four years	129	129	130	130	130	130	130	130	130	130	130	130
	Five years and up	130	130	130	130	130	130	130	130	130	130	130	130
One mile	Two years	—	—	—	—	—	—	—	—	96	99	102	102
	Three years	107	107	111	111	113	115	117	119	121	122	123	123
	Four years	127	127	128	128	127	126	126	126	126	126	126	126
	Five years and up	128	128	128	128	127	126	126	126	126	126	126	126
One and a quarter miles	Two years	—	—	—	—	—	—	—	—	—	—	—	—
	Three years	101	101	107	107	111	113	116	118	120	121	122	122
	Four years	125	125	127	127	127	126	126	126	126	126	126	126
	Five years and up	127	127	127	127	127	126	126	126	126	126	126	126

One and a half miles

Two years	—	—	—	—	—	—	—	—	—	—	—	—
Three years	98	98	104	104	108	111	114	117	119	121	122	122
Four years	124	124	126	126	126	126	126	126	126	126	126	126
Five years and up	126	126	126	126	126	126	126	126	126	126	126	126

Two Miles

Three years	96	96	102	102	106	109	112	114	117	119	120	120
Four years	124	124	126	126	126	126	126	126	125	125	124	124
Five years and up	126	126	126	126	126	126	126	126	125	125	124	124

*Full footnotes to this table, including penalties and allowances, appear in the annual American Racing Manual, p. 465.
Copyright © 1977 by Triangle Publications, Inc. Reprinted with permission of copyright owner.

length (or the corresponding number of rating points) at six furlongs, four pounds as the equivalent of a length at a mile, and three pounds as equaling a length at a mile and a quarter.

It is only fair to say that more comprehensive and complicated weight adjustment scales have been advocated. The case for their usefulness is not proved. The serious handicapper should recognize that this is a question which he must decide for himself.

Riders: It is commonly said that the horse represents at least 90 percent, the jockey 10 percent or less, of a winning combination. For all that, the handicapper only reluctantly bets on a horse whose rider he regards as a big question mark.

On a typical day's program, about thirty-five jockeys may have one or more mounts. But of these, no more than six to eight will constitute the leaders at a meeting. Among them, six riders are likely to account for more than 40 percent, eight riders may account for fully half, of all winners at that track.

Look for the list of leading riders in the daily program. Note particularly those who not only have a large number of winners, but have won with 14 or 15 percent or more of their mounts. They will clearly be able jockeys. But, more important, their agents will be able to put them on "live," or contending, horses. In other words, trainers who believe their horses have a good chance are likely to make an extra effort to obtain a jockey with one of the better records.

A handicapper friend of mine makes a note of the jockey-trainer combination for each winner on the program. And he makes a special note of the combinations that crop up frequently. The point is not that the jockey makes a special effort only for certain trainers; he may, in fact, try with every mount. But if the trainer, for example, *switches* to a rider with whom he has had success in the past, the handicapper is alerted to the trainer's opinion of his horse's good chances in the race. Jockey switches are among the first points to be considered in a quick review of the day's races.

Apprentice jockeys, whose weight allowance may get them mounts from trainers looking to get weight off their horses, sometimes figure among the leaders at a meeting. But, unless they are clearly talented, they may be least successful in races at a route, where tactics and sense of pace count most.

 EXTRA INFORMATION

The *Daily Racing Form* conveys so much information, it may seem that no more can be absorbed. The fact is, some players seek an extra edge. They do compile more information for themselves. The only limits to how much they compile are time and energy. Not recommended but a matter of history: some players have been known to take photographs of the tote board at intervals during betting and at the start of every race. Other items of information include the following.

The most basic bit of extra information, taken from the *Form* itself, is a collection of charts. These give information which cannot be squeezed into the past performance lines, including detailed conditions of the race, purse values, the whole field in any race under study, and a better idea of the running of the race.

Of vital importance is a record of what the player sees on the track and writes in his own notes. Most helpful is any note on trouble encountered by a horse; the charts cannot catch everything that happens. How the player stores this kind of information is a matter of taste, as well as space and time.

If the player has a card file with a card for each horse being followed, he can add to it from the official files themselves. Example: The horse finishes a good second, well ahead of the rest of the field, in a race run in one of the fastest times of the day. All of this is in the charts, not in past performances.

Some players preserve in their daily programs information about special equipment (for example, bandages on or off) and a horse's appearance.

Some handicappers make a specialty of watching the horses running out after the race. They look for those still running eagerly and looking as if they want to go on.

Some maintain files of the daily workout tab shown in the *Daily Racing Form.* They can thus follow a horse's workouts over a period of months, instead of looking only at the last three or four given in today's past performances. They can also see how any particular work compares with others on that day.

The public handicappers in some metropolitan daily papers briefly note horses' trouble last time out. The newspaper's man may have seen something that both you and the chart caller missed, or he may be using information from racing officials (for example, the "bump sheet," compiled by patrol judges, based on trouble they have seen horses encounter during a race).

At some tracks the handicapper may be able to look at the "vet's list" of horses ruled—temporarily, at least—unfit for racing.

FITNESS

Signs of a horse's condition are hardest of all to read. Yet even a little skill in reading such signs is worth working for. Some often-mentioned suggestions follow.

Conventional wisdom holds that soreness can be told from hitches and other peculiarities in a horse's gait, or the way he bobs his head or switches his tail. Beginners can hardly hope to profit from such advice. Some excellent horseplayers freely assert that they can tell very little about a horse's condition by inspection. The most sensible prescription is to look at horses, and keep on looking, and hope for a gradually increasing sense of when a horse looks right. This kind of prescription will not gull the innocent, but it is realistic.

Of the conventional signs, wetness (or washiness, or kidney sweat) is the clearest. If your selection appears on the track well lathered, he may possibly win your bet for you, but you have fair cause for alarm.

The handicapper also combs the *Racing Form* for signs of condition. A clearly bad sign in past performances is lack of work—no races or workouts—for three weeks or more. Exceptions will be found, but the danger signal is clear.

Also clearly a bad sign in the past performances is the finding that the horse's two most recent races (in a class similar to today's) were bad: he finished in the bottom third in both races, ran many lengths back at every call in both.

Exceptions can be found to anything, but probably the most important exception to the point above is the maiden who has been soundly beaten in much better maiden races at a higher-caliber track. Every other horse in today's race might have done as badly. If the maiden in question (a) has worked at least moderately well since shipping to your track and (b) is in the hands of an able trainer who has given the mount to one of the track's better riders—the horse may run surprisingly well.

Another clear danger signal in the past performances is a showing that the horse has been in desperate stretch battles for a piece of the purse in two or more recent races.

The past performances also yield some signs of impending good form. One should be called the Evergreen; it has been written about through the decades and it remains good. This is a sudden showing of speed—a forward position, preferably through the first two calls in the most recent past performance line—by a horse that had been running drab races (and suffers no class disadvantage today).

Also a good sign in past performances is an in-the-money or close-up though not winning performance, in the last race, by a horse coming back from six weeks or more away from racing.

Stay around tracks long enough and you will certainly hear what passes for stable information. It is heady stuff and by no means to be cast aside. You will still have to decide for yourself how reliable the source is. If the information is straight, it will more often than not keep you off a horse.

Owners are incurable optimists. If you happen to meet them, listen to them politely and wish them good luck, because they need it, but think of something else while they are talking.